D0251497

DARING DIPLOMACY

To Zhanna and Julia

Other books by the author

America: A Place Called Hope? (O'Brien Press, 1993)

Melting Snow: An Irishman in Moscow (Appletree Press, 1991)

Phrases Make History Here (O'Brien Press, 1986)

Daring Diplomacy

Clinton's Secret Search for Peace in Ireland

Conor O'Clery

ROBERTS RINEHART PUBLISHERS

Published in the United States and Canada
by Roberts Rinehart Publishers,
5455 Spine Road, Boulder, Colorado 80301
Tel. 303.530.4400

Distributed to the trade by Publishers Group West

ISBN 1-57098-130-2

Library of Congress card number 96-72307

Published in Ireland as *The Greening of the White House*
by Gill & Macmillan, Goldenbridge, Dublin 8, Ireland

Typesetting:
Red Barn Publishing, Skeagh, Skibbereen, Co. Cork, Ireland

Printed in the United States of America

CONTENTS

Glossary

DUP	Democratic Unionist Party, led by Rev. Ian Paisley
IRA	Irish Republican Army
PIRA	Provisional IRA
PUP	Progressive Unionist Party, led by David Ervine
RTE	Radio Telefís Éireann, Ireland's national broadcasting station
RUC	Royal Ulster Constabulary, Northern Ireland's police force
SAS	Special Air Services. The special operations force of the British Army
SDLP	Social Democratic and Labor Party, biggest nationalist party in Northern Ireland, led by John Hume
Taoiseach	Irish prime minister
UDA	Ulster Defence Association, loyalist paramilitary organization with links with the UDP
UDP	Ulster Democratic Party, led by Gary McMichael
UUP	Ulster Unionist Party, led by David Trimble, formerly led by James Molyneaux
UVF	Ulster Volunteer Force, loyalist paramilitary organization with links with the PUP

PREFACE

I was born in Belfast and brought up in Northern Ireland, where I saw the Troubles start in the 1960s. Most of my reporting life as an *Irish Times* correspondent, in Belfast, London or Dublin, has had to do with Northern Ireland. For five years I worked in Moscow, then went to Washington in 1991. I did not foresee then that for the first time an American President would bring the Northern Ireland story right to the doors of the White House. Much of the action in the Irish peace process happened in Washington in the following years. It involved several "visa wars," breakdowns in the "special relationship," unlikely encounters, and an extraordinary love affair between the administration and the Irish. I was privileged to be the only Irish correspondent accredited to the White House when it was all happening. Central to the book is how individuals make history, and the surprising way decisions are sometimes made at the highest level in the United States, a process to which I was given unparalleled access by those involved.

This book could not have been produced without the goodwill and kindness of numerous people who gave generously of their time and recollections.

I am indebted to those who agreed to on-the-record interviews, including former Taoiseach, Albert Reynolds; Deputy National Security Adviser, Nancy Soderberg; former House Speaker, Tom Foley; SDLP leader, John Hume; James Molyneaux of the Ulster Unionist Party; chairman of the Federal Housing Board, Bruce Morrison; Irish America and *Irish Voice* publisher, Niall O'Dowd; Bill Flynn of Mutual of America; Congressman Peter King from Long Island, and New York political strategists, John Connorton and Chris Hyland.

I also drew on material supplied to me in interviews in Washington with President Bill Clinton; US Ambassador to the Vatican, Raymond Flynn; Senator Christopher Dodd; Senator George Mitchell; National Security Adviser, Anthony Lake and Sinn Féin President, Gerry Adams.

Others to whom I spoke when gathering material for this book include Trina Vargo, Ciarán Staunton, Andrew Hunter, Jimmy Breslin, Elizabeth Shannon, Ray O'Hanlon, Mary McGrory, George Schwab, Fionnuala Flanagan, Edna O'Brien, Martin Fletcher, Bill Barry, Peter Hitchens, David Ervine, Gary McMichael, Paul Quinn, Ed Kenny and Jeff Biggs. Some gave me invaluable information on background or read sections for accuracy, and wish to remain anonymous. To them I express my gratitude.

I also received invaluable guidance and assistance from the Irish Ambassador to Washington, Dermot Gallagher and the US Ambassador to Ireland, Jean Kennedy Smith. In the White House press office, Mike McCurry, Anne Edwards, Mary Ellen Glynn, Kathy McKiernan and Marlene McDonald were invariably helpful during my time in Washington, as were Nancy Soderberg, David Johnson, Jim Fetig, Jane Holl, Mary Ann Peters and Cathy Stephens in the National Security Council. Peter Westmacott and Peter Bean in the British embassy in Washington, and in the Irish embassy, Brendan Scannell, Michael Collins, later appointed ambassadors to Israel and Saudi Arabia respectively, Noel Kilkenny, Eamonn McKee, Pat Hennessy and many others were always courteous and helpful.

I have the great good fortune to work for *The Irish Times,* whose editor Conor Brady asked me to go to Washington at such an interesting time. I am grateful to him and also to Dermot O'Shea, Mick Crowley, Rachel Burrowes and Shay Kenny of *The Irish Times* photographic department, and to all those who offered advice and suggestions. I alone bear responsibility for any errors that occur.

A very special word of thanks to Daniel Franklin of *The Economist,* who read the text and whose eloquent suggestions I incorporated almost verbatim, to David McKittrick, the grand master of Northern Irish correspondents, who advised me on the chapters dealing with Northern Ireland and offered nuggets of information, and Frank Millar, the acknowledged expert on the peace process in London, who gave me the benefit of his wisdom on vital points. I gained enormously too from the professional advice of Fergal Tobin of Gill & Macmillan in Ireland and of Jack Van Zandt of Roberts Rinehart in the United States.

Finally I must pay tribute to the good-natured tolerance of my teenage daughter Julia while I shut myself away with a computer. And the book would not have been written without the inspiration, judgment, editing skills, and long hours brought to the project by my wife Zhanna, who so often provided meals and refreshment for many of the varied characters who appear on the following pages and without whose encouragement and help this book would simply never have been written.

INTRODUCTION

On an unforgettable November day in 1995, in a building located on the Belfast peace line, the President of the United States stood before an audience which included politicians and paramilitaries and delivered a message to those who would use violence for political objectives—you are the past; your day is over.

Ten weeks later a massive IRA bomb exploded at Canary Wharf in London, killing two people, causing damage amounting to millions of pounds, and shattering a peace which had lasted seventy-five weeks.

These were the high and low points in the extraordinary story of a peace process aimed at ending a deadly conflict which has lasted a quarter of a century and bringing about a settlement; it is a story in which a number of individual Americans and Irish Americans played a crucial part.

Forty-four million Americans have Irish or Scots-Irish forebears. President Bill Clinton's Irish, Scots-Irish and English ancestry symbolizes the intertwined relationships of the people of the United States and the islands of Britain and Ireland.

Remarkably, until this historical episode Irish Americans had been unable to make a real difference in deciding the future of British–Irish relations or of the political evolution of their native land. It was not for the want of trying.

The idea of American involvement has deep roots in the past. For two centuries Irish Americans have sought to influence the politics of Ireland by providing assistance to political or underground organizations or by persuading the United States government to intervene. Irish-American money and militarism were always important elements in the equation. As far back as the early nineteenth century, Irish Americans were sending dollars to support Daniel O'Connell's agitation for Catholic emancipation in Ireland. In 1866, the Fenian Brotherhood invaded British Canada, hoping vainly to seize territory to exchange for concessions in Ireland. Over a century ago Irish-American money was supporting the

Home Rule campaign of Charles Stewart Parnell and Michael Davitt's agrarian movement, while Clan na Gael was helping finance a bombing campaign in England.

When Gerry Adams made a fundraising tour of the United States, he was merely following in the footsteps of countless Irish politicians and revolutionaries. Parnell raised money from coast to coast to promote Home Rule. Eamon de Valera came to the United States to launch an Irish bond drive to fund the Irish Republican Army in the War of Independence which resulted in the formation of the Irish Free State in 1921–22.

The main goal of Irish Americans, however, has always been to get the American government on the Irish side, to make up for the disadvantage of being the smaller nation. There have been moments of modest success. Parnell's successor John Redmond established the United Irish League of America which won the endorsement of President William Taft for Home Rule. But American presidents have always been reluctant to intervene because of the powerful "special relationship" with Britain, based on strategic, financial, linguistic and cultural ties, which has dominated world politics. President Taft supported Home Rule because it was also British government policy. But when the Friends of Irish Freedom campaigned for the recognition of Irish independence at the Versailles Peace Conference after the First World War, President Woodrow Wilson put the special relationship first, and refused to offend Britain by pressing the Irish case.

Irish Americans did succeed in 1940 in getting the United States to warn Britain not to seize Irish ports as part of its war with Germany. But the circumstances were unique. At the time both the Irish Free State and the United States were neutral. Sympathy in America for Irish nationalism evaporated after the US joined the Second World War in 1940 and the Free State stayed out. Ireland declared itself a republic after the war and, in protest at the British presence in Northern Ireland, did not join the NATO alliance which bound the United States and the United Kingdom even closer together as allies in the Cold War.

The crisis in Northern Ireland after 1969 divided Irish Americans, who were forced to choose between supporting what some saw as a renewal of the old struggle against the British and opposing what most others saw as an unacceptable use of violence to gain political ends.

The violence and loss of life prompted a fundamental rethink of attitudes in Ireland and stimulated a debate among nationalists—

in Belfast, Dublin and New York—about the future of nationalism itself.

This process was accelerated when the United Kingdom and Ireland joined the European Economic Community in 1973. After half a century of a mini-cold war, the two countries found themselves partners in a united Europe. Politicians and civil servants began to meet regularly and develop contacts. In 1985 the two countries signed the Anglo-Irish Agreement as a direct result of an attempt by London and Dublin to tackle jointly the violence in Northern Ireland. By giving the Irish Republic an advisory role in Northern Ireland affairs it was designed to show that there were alternatives to violence.

Protestants who form the majority in Northern Ireland were angered at what looked like the opening of the door to Irish unity. But on the Irish side, a new realism prevailed; a united Ireland would only come about by consent. Just as many unionists believe there can be no going back to the old ways where Catholics had no say in the running of Northern Ireland, so too do nationalists know that accommodation must be reached with unionists on the principle of consent.

Britain also has been rethinking its role in Ireland, and after further dialogue between London and Dublin it has come to the point where it claims to have no strategic or economic reason for staying in Northern Ireland, if the majority of the population there should vote otherwise. With the demographic balance in Northern Ireland tipping towards the Catholics, who now form 44 percent of the population, the case for violent nationalism has lost further ground.

These were the factors which prompted the "peace process." For this to succeed, the alienated nationalists and loyalists had to be fully brought into the political process. Enter the Irish Americans. Leaders of today's Irish America viewed what was happening in Ireland with growing interest. Irish America is, at the end of the twentieth century, experiencing its most successful period ever. Irish names are prominent in politics, entertainment, finance and in corporate America. The modern Irish American does not live in a romantic past, but has a sophisticated knowledge of what is going on in the home country. Irish Americans frequently travel back and forth across the Atlantic. They access Irish news reports on the Internet. They have many opportunities to meet or hear the views of visiting politicians from Britain, the Irish Republic and Northern Ireland.

They know better than ever how complex the situation in Northern Ireland is. Their frustration and shame at what was happening in the name of Irish people were matched by a new appreciation of the potential of the United States to act as an honest broker.

The new thinking among the Irish and the Irish Americans coincided with major changes in the world. The end of the Cold War and the decline of Britain as a world power diminished the role of the special relationship. An American President took office with Irish blood who belonged to a generation which had not shared a wartime experience with Britain and who himself felt some of the same frustration at the seemingly never-ending conflict. He was open to the argument brought to him by some innovative Irish and Irish Americans—that only the United States could form a bridge to bring the isolated republican leaders into the political mainstream and nudge the peace process along when it stalled.

The full impact of the American involvement in the peace process essentially was due to the unique interplay among a number of people who found themselves in key roles during this historical development. They include President Bill Clinton and his foreign policy advisers, Tony Lake and Nancy Soderberg, Taoiseach Albert Reynolds and British Prime Minister John Major, members of the United States Congress such as Senators Edward Kennedy and Christopher Dodd, a former US judge and Senator, George Mitchell, two uniquely gifted nationalist leaders, John Hume and Gerry Adams, loyalist leaders like David Ervine and Gary McMichael prepared to take risks for peace, a number of highly talented individuals among a new, pragmatic generation of public officials and civil servants in London and Dublin, and a group of amateur peace envoys with a sense of mission, Niall O'Dowd, Bruce Morrison, Charles "Chuck" Feeney and Bill Flynn.

Four years ago no one could have foreseen the dramatic events that lay ahead, the bitter crises in the UK–US relationship over Gerry Adams, the Kissinger-like use of informal diplomatic channels to shape major US policy decisions, the throwing open of the doors of the White House to the Irish and the emergence of a new, dual set of special relationships—between the United States and both Britain and Ireland, and between Irish Americans and both peoples on the island of Ireland.

This is the story of how it all came about.

1

A Nice Thought

"If these goddam Irish don't vote for him they don't deserve anything."
Jimmy Breslin

On a chilly Saturday afternoon in New York in April 1992, about six hundred people, a mixture of whites, Hispanics, African Americans and street characters, gathered in a colorful mass at the corner of West 72nd Street and Broadway. They cheered when the gaunt figure of Jerry Brown appeared from a building. The former California Governor began walking along West 72nd Street, shaking hands, asking for votes.

From about twenty-five yards away a tall, well-dressed Wall Street lawyer called out, "Hey! Jerry, I need to talk to you." Brown pushed his way through the crowd and went into a huddle with the man, whom he recognized as a veteran Democratic Party strategist, John Connorton.

"Jerry, there it is in a nutshell," said Connorton. "You must come tomorrow night."

"There'll be a lot of Catholics there, right?" asked Brown.

"Right."

"You think I should do it?"

"I think you should do it."

"OK."

Connorton heaved a sigh of relief as Brown disappeared back into the crowd. The lawyer had killed two birds with one stone. He had just got one of the two candidates fighting the New York Democratic primary election to agree to appear at a forum on Irish issues in the Sheraton Hotel in Manhattan. And having got Brown to agree, the other presidential hopeful, Bill Clinton, would have to come as well. And he was the one they really wanted.

The primary election was only three days away. Connorton's friend and fellow party activist, John Dearie, had organized the Irish forum for the next night to get the Democratic rivals to listen to the concerns of Irish Americans. But he had been unable to persuade Clinton's campaign staff even to agree in principle to produce their candidate.

To Connorton, the problem was all too familiar. He himself had organized Al Gore's presidential bid in New York four years earlier, and had balked at allowing his own candidate to go to a similar forum organized by Dearie. A top adviser told Gore he would be crazy to get involved in the "troubled, boiling waters of Irish-American politics." People telephoned the Tennessee Governor from Capitol Hill saying, "Don't do it, these people are all Noraid," Connorton recalled. Irish Northern Aid, known as Noraid, collected money for IRA prisoners and no presidential candidate wanted to be associated with terrorism. Even so, Gore decided at the last moment to go, having received an assurance he could simply state his position on issues of concern to Irish Americans and get out again. Connorton hoped this precedent would now entice Clinton.

Clinton's handlers however did not want him to go anywhere near Dearie's event. The campaign aide in charge of ethnic outreach, Chris Hyland, was finding it difficult to get anyone in the Clinton camp even remotely interested in the Irish issue. They were anxious to keep their candidate out of the standard round of labor, black and ethnic groups so he could contrast himself with Jerry Brown on the big issues.

In any event the Arkansas Governor was bone-tired and his vocal chords raw from non-stop speaking. He had been plagued by hecklers during a nasty primary campaign. He was making mistakes and getting bad press. A few days earlier he had blundered by playing golf in Little Rock, Arkansas, at a country club that excluded black players. That was just the latest in a series of controversies and scandals which ranged from an alleged affair with Gennifer Flowers and involvement in a dubious real estate venture called Whitewater to charges of draft dodging and experimenting with marijuana—though not inhaling. His chief strategist James Carville believed the campaign was "hemorrhaging." His media director Mandy Grunwald told her co-workers, "We're in crisis." New York manager Harold Ickes thought they were "in free fall." They had just lost the Connecticut primary election to Governor Moonbeam, as they called Jerry Brown. Clinton had almost enough delegates to win the nomination but if the underdog new-age candidate beat him in New York as well, he was finished.

In the end Clinton's people said the candidate would only turn up if Brown was appearing too. That was why Connorton had gone to confront the Californian at 72nd Street. He had tried to get him on the telephone but Brown was moving around so erratically it was impossible to get him on the line. "Maybe we should try a seance, and call him up that way," a friend of Connorton's had suggested, referring to Brown's inclinations towards transcendental meditation.

There seemed little spirit left in the Democratic hopeful from Arkansas when Clinton eventually made it the next evening to the Irish forum in a small function room in the Sheraton Hotel, and wearily took a seat facing about a hundred people. The deal was that the two rivals appeared separately, answered a few questions they had been told about in advance and left. No campaign reporters seemed to know about the event or to have been invited. There were no Irish diplomats in the room either, possibly because one of the media panel was Martin Galvin, editor of the *Irish People*, the weekly Noraid journal. The Dublin government at that time discouraged its officials from any contact with IRA-related organizations. The other panelists were Patrick Farrelly of the *Irish Voice*, Ray O'Hanlon of the *Irish Echo* and Mayor Raymond Flynn of Boston, who was anxious for a place in a future Clinton administration. Clinton had telephoned the Boston Mayor that morning to ask him what issues were troubling the Irish.

The Mayor was given the honor of putting the first question. Would Clinton appoint a peace envoy to Northern Ireland to bring all sides together and encourage United Nations involvement in Northern Ireland?

"I would," said Clinton. "I think sometimes we are too reluctant to engage ourselves in a positive way because of our long-standing special relationship with Great Britain and also because it seemed such a thorny problem. But I have a very strong feeling that in the aftermath of the Cold War, we need a governing rationale for our engagement in the world, not just in Northern Ireland."

The response drew loud applause. The candidate had said he would go beyond the special relationship between London and Washington, the strategic alliance disliked by Irish Americans because it encouraged the US to accept Britain's right to treat Northern Ireland as strictly an internal problem for the United Kingdom. Clinton went further. He told Patrick Farrelly that a special peace envoy would focus on the work of Amnesty International concerning breaches of human rights by the security forces "and other forces of violence, other violators of human rights and other purveyors of death in Northern Ireland."

Galvin put a loaded question. "If you were elected President," he asked Clinton, "would you direct the State Department to allow a visa to Gerry Adams and other prominent members of Sinn Féin to allow them to come to the United States, state their views and defend them before the American people?"

Adams, who lived in Belfast, was the President of Sinn Féin, the political wing of the IRA and a member of the British parliament for West Belfast. He had been barred along with other Sinn Féin leaders from entering the United States since the early 1970s because of his association with the IRA. He had applied seven times for a visa in twenty years and had been refused on each occasion.

"I would support a visa for Gerry Adams and I would support a visa for any other properly elected official that was part of a government [*sic*] recognized by the United States of America," replied Clinton. "I think it would be totally harmless to our national security interests and it might be enlightening to the political debate in this country about the issues involved." There was another burst of applause from the group in the room.

Clinton also said he would endorse the MacBride Principles on fair employment in Northern Ireland (more applause). These were a set of equal opportunity guidelines drawn up in 1984 for US firms operating in Northern Ireland where there was a legacy of Catholic allegations of job discrimination. Irish-American lobby groups had persuaded more than a dozen states and almost fifty cities to enact laws tying their investments to corporate agreement to adhere to the Principles, named after the Irish Nobel peace laureate Sean MacBride. But nationalists in Northern Ireland were divided on their merits. The moderate Catholic leader, John Hume, opposed them as a disincentive to investment and the Irish government gave only lukewarm support.

As he edged his way out of the room, Clinton posed for the obligatory pictures. I asked him at the door if he knew of Galvin's Noraid associations. "Come on, give me a break," he said. "I'm doing my best."

John Dearie was overjoyed about Clinton's promise of an envoy. He had been pushing the idea of a special envoy since 1983 after he saw how President Reagan's special envoy to the Middle East, Philip Habib, had put that part of the world on the map. The possibility of something similar for Ireland occurred to him as he watched the banners come down at the end of the New York Saint Patrick's Day parade at the corner of 86th Street and Third Avenue that year.

"I thought to myself that day, people talk about Ireland for three days in the year, then they put away their bagpipes for another year and forget about it," he told me. Dearie had got the New York State legislature to adopt a resolution in 1983 calling on the US government "to designate a special envoy for the effectuation of peace in Northern Ireland." Also in that year, Daniel Patrick Moynihan introduced a resolution in the US Senate, co-sponsored by Edward Kennedy and Chris Dodd, calling on President Reagan to appoint a special envoy "to investigate and report how best the US could actively assist the Governments of Ireland and Great Britain and the communities in Northern Ireland to arrive at an early, just and peaceful resolution of the present conflict in Northern Ireland." Since he started his Irish forums, Dearie and his colleagues had got the 1984 and 1988 Democratic candidates, Walter Mondale and Michael Dukakis, to promise to send an envoy, but they had both lost the presidential election.

Bill Clinton could be a loser too. He might win the Democratic nomination, but few really thought he could beat Republican President George Bush. He was even running behind the national scold, Ross Perot, in opinion polls.

And there were also doubts about whether a Democratic candidate would carry out any pre-election promises made to Irish Americans. The only Democrat to get to the White House since the beginning of the Troubles had made similar promises in Pittsburgh in 1976. Jimmy Carter had even marched in that year's New York Saint Patrick's Day parade, where someone stuck a badge on his lapel saying, "England, get out of Ireland." Pictures of the grinning Georgia Governor wearing the slogan appeared in the tabloid British press, which accused the future Nobel Peace Prize nominee of exploiting Northern Ireland's tragedy to win votes. Carter had of course been unable to do anything to get England out of Ireland. He did however make some critical comments about British behavior and in a much-publicized statement on Northern Ireland promised to give financial backing to a settlement there, if there ever was one.

Peter King, comptroller of the New York City Borough of Queens, listened closely to Clinton in the Sheraton and concluded that he was serious.

"I thought Clinton was different from candidates who went before," said King, a Republican who attended the Democratic event because he supported Sinn Féin and was a friend of Gerry Adams. "He didn't say anything wrong. He didn't say, 'Some of my friends are Irish and we wear green ties on Saint Patrick's Day.' He was on a more sophisticated level."

While waiting for Brown to show up, King went downstairs for coffee with veteran civil rights lawyer Paul O'Dwyer, the ageing patriarch of the Irish community who had emigrated from Bohola in County Mayo seventy years previously. O'Dwyer was a legendary figure who had defended black farm workers in Mississippi and other oppressed minorities, and his blessing was sought by every candidate for public office in New York who needed Irish support.

O'Dwyer said he was genuinely moved by Clinton's remarks, adding, "I never heard a candidate who knew more about Ireland."

They were joined by Jimmy Breslin, the outspoken New York columnist, who told them, "If these goddam Irish don't vote for him they don't deserve anything."

Jerry Brown had a reputation for turning up late. He was due at 9:30 p.m. An hour passed. Then another. To amuse themselves the people who waited staged an impromptu concert. The Irish entertainer Áine and New York Assemblyman Joe Crowley took turns to sing Irish songs and ballads. Mayor Raymond Flynn of Boston rendered *Four Green Fields,* the Irish freedom song favored by the IRA.

The Californian only arrived at 11 p.m. at La Guardia airport from an out-of-town event. Connorton travelled the ten miles to meet him at the airport and brief him on the questions to expect. But for forty-five minutes Brown and his advisers calmly discussed future campaign plans standing on the tarmac while the polite lawyer quietly fumed. He then butted in to remind the group of the Irish forum.

The candidate's French guru, Jacques Barzaghi, raised his arms in despair at the mention of the Irish event.

"Djeree, Djeree, why are we doing zis?" Barzaghi demanded of the candidate.

"Jerry, I have a lot of people waiting for you, and on a Sunday night," said Connorton. "I need to call the sponsor and say whether we're coming or not. If you are we have to do it now."

The candidate agreed. "It's your basic pander situation, I guess," said one of his aides as they set off in a van. Ten minutes later Connorton looked out the window as they entered some narrow streets. They were totally lost somewhere in Queens.

It was well after midnight before Brown arrived at the Sheraton, accompanied by Barzaghi whose black beret and leather gear looked out of place among the wrinkled suits of the Irish Americans. Brown made much the same promises as Clinton. He added that the next President should make an effort to go to Northern Ireland himself. Everyone applauded hard. It was a nice thought.

2

Heartbroken By It

"I was a young man living in England and just fascinated by it and heartbroken by it."
Bill Clinton

Like Jimmy Carter, Bill Clinton came from the American Deep South, where ethnic lines among whites are often blurred to extinction. But he differed from the Georgia peanut farmer in one respect. Though no one suspected it at the time, Clinton saw himself as an Irish American of sorts. He was born in Hope, a sleepy town on the Missouri Pacific railway line where it runs across the pecan and soya bean fields of southern Arkansas. This part of the south was settled by English, Irish, Scots-Irish and Germans, most losing contact with their roots along the way. Clinton's mother was Virginia Cassidy, a nurse whose forebears may have come originally from County Fermanagh in Northern Ireland where the name Cassidy is common. There is a village there, Ballycassidy, which means "Town of the Cassidys." She once described herself as descended from "poor Irish farmers." His father was William Jefferson Blythe. He was a farm boy who sold cars and was of English descent, though the Irish names Hayes and Ayers featured among his ancestors. Despite her Irish surname, Virginia Cassidy's family memory did not extend back further than Alabama from where her people came in the 1800s. She was not an Irish Catholic mother but a southern Baptist who liked to live a little bit on the wild side.

Clinton's father died in a car accident before he was born in 1946. Four years later his mother married Roger Clinton and they moved to Hot Springs, forty miles to the north. Hot Springs was a gambling and resort spa in the Ouachita mountains. It was run in the war years by a dictatorial Irish-American mayor called Leo McLaughlin, who liked to parade down Central Avenue in a buggy pulled by two horses named "Scotch" and "Soda." The town was a rare cosmopolitan oasis in red-neck country, and drew people from all over the world. Its casinos and hot baths also attracted gangsters like Lucky Luciano and Al Capone from Chicago, and from the east coast the notorious Owney Madden, an Irish American with whom few would want to associate.

The schoolboy Clinton likely came across his first real Irish people among the nuns at St. John's Catholic school in Hot Springs where his mother sent him when he was seven, and where he was so eager to please that one nun gave him a lowly D instead of an A to curb his enthusiasm.

The biggest event in his teenage life was a visit to Washington in 1963 as a delegate for Boys' Nation, a youth movement to encourage political development. On this trip, the wide-eyed young politicians visited the White House to meet the first Catholic Irish-American President, John F. Kennedy. The sixteen-year-old Clinton asked the leader of his bus contingent and director of National Americanism for the Legion, Daniel J. O'Connor from New York, if he could have his picture taken with the President. "Sure," said O'Connor, and when they arrived and Kennedy walked forward to greet the boys, an ecstatic Clinton stepped up to shake his hand. The moment was captured on film. The President told the boys he had read about their conference in Washington the previous evening and was impressed by their initiative in passing a motion which said that "racism is a cancerous disease."

Meeting JFK was like a benediction for the young Clinton and helped him abandon any thoughts he had at the time of becoming a Baptist minister and to consider politics instead. Like millions of Americans he was captivated by the Kennedy family mystique, which undoubtedly helped shape his warm relationships in later years with the President's brother and sister, Ted and Jean. The teenage son of Virginia Cassidy was so identified with Kennedy that when the President was assassinated in Dallas four months later, he was called upon to give talks around Hot Springs as one of the last people in town to see him alive.

In those days, Bill Clinton was also an idealistic civil rights supporter. He was one of three southern youths who argued the case for civil rights at the Boys' Nation conference and helped carry the resolution which President Kennedy praised. His mother recalled that at the age of eleven, he appeared frustrated as he watched the television news of Governor Faubus's attempt to stop the integration of

Little Rock High School using state troopers. Years afterwards, when Clinton was a student at Georgetown University's School of Foreign Service in Washington, he became the "house liberal" on civil rights, according to his biographer David Maraniss, and fellow students remembered Clinton reciting Martin Luther King's "I have a dream" speech. He supported a resolution by Georgetown students endorsing the civil rights march in Selma, Alabama, which had been attacked by police and white extremists. A friend also recalled how he quoted from King's speech with emotion as he drove her across Washington to bring supplies to people affected by the riots which followed the killing of the civil rights leader.

It was at the Jesuit-run Georgetown University that Clinton, the Baptist boy from the Deep South, found himself rubbing shoulders with Irish Americans. Many of the students were Catholics from New York and Boston. His first room mate and close friend was Tom Campbell, an Irish American from Long Island. Clinton became interested in Catholicism for a while and attended Catholic services at the campus chapel. Kitty Higgins, cabinet secretary in the Clinton White House, told me the story of how Otto Hennz, a Jesuit seminarian who took classes at Georgetown, was so impressed by the eighteen-year-old student's knowledge of theology he made the assumption that Clinton was a Catholic. Over dinner he said to the tall, garrulous, Arkansas teenager, "I think you should seriously consider becoming a Jesuit." Clinton laughed and replied, "Don't you think I ought to become a Catholic first?"

Clinton's first girlfriend at Georgetown was seventeen-year-old Denise Hyland, one of six children from a prosperous Irish Catholic family from Upper Montclair in northern New Jersey. She took him home once and he charmed the whole household. The next summer, when Denise was on holiday in France, she said to some Texans she met, "Remember the name—Bill Clinton—because some day he will be President."

Four years later Clinton went to Oxford as a Rhodes scholar. He made one trip to Ireland, a weekend excursion to Dublin with the only African-American Rhodes scholar at the university, Tom Williamson, who wanted to meet up with a woman he had been romancing on the passenger liner across the Atlantic. They spent their time exploring the pubs before heading back without, it seems, achieving their goal.

At Oxford he told his fellow undergraduates of his determination to do something about civil rights by getting elected to public office in Arkansas.

This was 1968 and the Northern Ireland troubles were exploding onto British television screens as a civil rights issue. The English media gave sympathetic accounts of Catholic civil rights marchers being beaten off the streets in Northern Ireland by police and by loyalist gangs. On television there were dramatic pictures of police batoning defenceless demonstrators and of student marchers being stoned by members of the Protestant reserve police force, the "B Specials."

These vivid images deeply affected the boy from Hope, where he had learned respect for people of a different kind from the courteous way his grandfather treated black customers in his shop. He was outraged by what he saw on television at Oxford.

"I was there when the Troubles began, you know," he told me years later in an interview in the Roosevelt Room in the White House. "I was living in Oxford. It occupied the attention of the country obviously. And as someone who was there who had Irish roots, also Scottish roots, and on my father's side, English roots, I was fascinated by it at the time." Reflecting on the violence which followed he remarked, "Well, of course, we went through the whole thing at home. I could see it coming, that religious differences were likely to lead to the same kind of problems that racial differences had in my childhood. And I lived in a place that had some pretty tough racial problems. And that had a lot to do with my going into public life." Having been a child living in a majority of whites in his state with a passionate sense of the need for integration and equal opportunity for people, he said he had always been curious about the nature of the conflict.

"It's not a strict analogy. There are lots of complexities here which are different. But I never dreamed when it all started and I was a young man living in England and just fascinated by it and heartbroken by it, that I'd ever have a chance to do anything to help it. I hope I have. I hope I'll have more. You know, I've been fascinated by it for twenty-five years . . . from the day the Troubles began."

Clinton had a coffee with Jimmy Breslin in the Stage Delicatessen in Manhattan the morning after the Irish forum and reminisced about his days in Oxford. "He remembered being in Oxford and following Bernadette Devlin around and reading everything about her," said Breslin, who said he was convinced that Clinton's perspective on Northern Ireland was colored by what he saw and read while in England. Devlin had been elected a member of the British parliament in April 1969 at the age of twenty-one and had been portrayed by the media as a romantic Irish rebel and civil rights heroine. Her maiden speech electrified the House of Commons.

Back in Arkansas, Clinton entered politics and in 1978 became Governor of the impoverished state in which he had been born. The Irish issue did not arise then. Taking up attitudes on Ireland was not important in southern politics, as it was in north-eastern cities like New York, Philadelphia and Boston with their big Irish-American communities. Politics among southern whites was not ethnic, though some districts were known for their preponderance of Irish or German voters. Clinton's partner in the ill-fated Whitewater real estate venture, James McDougal, ran for Congress in 1982 in a district where many Irish lived. In order to pander to the Irish, he downplayed his Scottish ancestry, claiming his family lived in Ireland a thousand years earlier. He decked out his campaign platforms in green bunting and shamrocks. But it didn't work and he lost.

As Governor of Arkansas, Clinton lived up to his civil rights talk and appointed more blacks to state boards and chairmanships than all the previous governors combined. He also made a small gesture which indicated where his sympathies on Northern Ireland lay. At the urging of Rita Mullen, a civil rights activist from north Belfast who was working in Little Rock as a public health lecturer, he signed a decree on Saint Patrick's Day, 1978, declaring that day to be "Human Rights for Ireland Day" in all of Arkansas.

But only when he became President did he really discover how Irish he was—just as later when in London he would emphasize his English bloodline, and in Belfast he would emphasize how aware he was of his Scots-Irish ancestry.

"I've always been conscious of being Irish," he told *Boston Globe* reporter Jack Farrell, excitedly, after making a decision as President which had infuriated the British but endeared him to Irish Americans. "I mean, I'm sort of—I look Irish; I am Irish," he said, "It means a lot to me."

3

Bill's Rap on Ireland

"Whoever sits in the White House affects all of us."
Bono of U2

Chris Hyland, a voluble, balding, New York garment merchant with a neat moustache, had doubts about the seriousness of Clinton's Irish promises from the start. The owner of a high-class clothing firm in Manhattan with twenty employees, Hyland had joined the Clinton campaign as a full-time unpaid volunteer and had been made deputy national political director with the job of reaching out to ethnic groups. Of particular concern to the Clinton people were the so-called Reagan Democrats, blue-collar workers mainly with Catholic ethnic backgrounds who traditionally voted Democratic but had defected to first Ronald Reagan and then George Bush because they liked a tough line on communism and family values. There were many Irish-American Catholics among them and it was one of Hyland's tasks to get them back. His job was to put Irish-American support for the Clinton campaign onto an organized basis.

To find out who was who in New York's melting pot, Hyland went shopping for community journals. "I went to East Village and got every ethnic paper I could find," he said. "I got the *Irish Voice* and the *Irish Echo.* I rang them up but the only response I got was from O'Dowd."

Niall O'Dowd was the publisher of the *Irish Voice,* the livelier of the two middle-of-the-road weekly tabloids which dominated the Irish-American media market in the United States. A bearded keep-fit enthusiast, he neither smoked nor drank and was noted for his business acumen and sense of humor. He was also in his own words a "political junkie." In making contact with O'Dowd, the

Clinton aide had stumbled upon the one person in the city who had been looking around for ways to get the Democratic candidate interested in the peace process which was developing in Northern Ireland, who had contacts among all the important people in the Irish-American community and in Ireland, and who had energy and commitment to get involved in the campaign.

Originally from Thurles, County Tipperary, O'Dowd was brought up in Drogheda, where he played for the Louth senior Gaelic football team. He came to the United States at the age of twenty-five and settled first in San Francisco where he started the *Irishman* newspaper. In 1985 he moved to New York and founded *Irish America* magazine and the *Irish Voice,* the first two major Irish publications in the United States for over half a century. He had seen how Irish Americans buried their differences and came together to agitate successfully in the late 1980s for visas for a new wave of Irish immigrants, many of them undocumented. The 39-year-old publisher also perceived how Irish Americans had grown frustrated at being defined in terms only of the violence in Ireland, and believed they were now ready for a new, more positive, role. Irish America could even help shape US policy on Ireland if it could find cohesion and if the circumstances were right, which meant having a well-disposed President in the White House.

"Most Irish Americans who care feel they have only two choices," O'Dowd told me one day back then. "If rich enough they can pay five hundred dollars to some respectable Irish charity for dinner in the Waldorf Astoria, or they can grab a placard and march with Noraid outside the British consulate."

Just before Hyland's call, O'Dowd and one of his closest friends, Brendan Scannell, a diplomat in the Irish embassy in Washington with many highly placed friends in the US Congress, had been having discussions about how to "plug into the Clinton campaign." They felt that if George Bush were re-elected there was no hope that he would get involved in Ireland, but that Clinton might actually do something.

Hyland, who had been a Georgetown University room mate of Bill Clinton, proposed setting up a committee to rally Irish Americans behind the candidate, with the name "Irish Americans for Clinton," in parallel with other groups like "Croatian Americans for Clinton" and "Lebanese Americans for Clinton." O'Dowd suggested inviting former Congressman Bruce Morrison, a Connecticut lawyer, to be its chairman. Morrison was enormously popular with Irish Americans. He had written the legislation for Congress in 1989–90 which had guaranteed 48,000 new Irish visas. In this he had been helped by a vigorous grassroots lobby which ensured the support of important legislators like Senator Edward Kennedy. It had not gone unnoticed in the Democratic Party that many wealthy Irish Americans had contributed to the success of the visa campaign with considerable political contributions.

Hyland telephoned Morrison at his Connecticut law office and got his agreement to become chairman of Irish Americans for Clinton. Morrison and O'Dowd then got together to plan strategy on the fifteenth-floor *Irish Voice* office on Park Avenue South. They organized a founding meeting and Boston Mayor Raymond Flynn agreed to sign on as co-chairman. Flynn was also popular with Irish Americans. He had been a supporter of Noraid in the early days of the Troubles when the pro-IRA organization had widespread sympathy among the Boston Irish, but had drifted away from Noraid as he grew in political stature and heard different views from Irish diplomats and politicians. More important, he was anti-abortion, and his endorsement of Clinton, who was pro-choice, would encourage Catholics to see the Democratic campaign as a big tent, with room for different views.

On 14 June 1992, O'Dowd and Morrison attended a fundraiser for Clinton in New York and invited several other leading Irish Americans to join them. They found that fewer were interested than they expected. Clinton had in the end won the Democratic primary election in New York, thanks partly to a mistake the Brown campaign made in antagonizing the city's Jewish vote. But he was trailing in national opinion polls behind George Bush and still looked to be a loser. "Why bother? That guy's finished," one leading community figure told them. They had to fill the places at their pre-paid table with staff from O'Dowd's newspaper.

Clinton's fortunes improved dramatically after a well-staged Democratic Party convention in New York in August and the political climate changed. He began to look like the "comeback kid." The Arkansas Governor came to New York again in October and this time met O'Dowd, Mayor Flynn and Paul O'Dwyer as the likely next President of the United States.

All three were delighted at how well-briefed Clinton was. "His knowledge of detail was remarkable," O'Dowd recalled. "Without any notes he went over visa denial, the special envoy concept and the MacBride Principles with ease. We were really impressed." The Arkansas Governor told them, "I want you to know that I am committed to Irish issues such as the special envoy and I intend to deliver on them." He startled the group by saying that Raymond Flynn would be the "perfect candidate" for special envoy. Anyone acquainted with Northern Ireland politics would know that someone as green as Flynn would never be acceptable to the unionists. The delighted Boston Mayor suggested that Clinton drop into an Irish pub in his home town the next day. "Let's do it," the candidate replied.

In Boston, Clinton got his first taste of the popular support he was beginning to attract from Irish Americans. He had to elbow his way through applauding customers in the Eire Bar in the Dorchester suburb of Boston to get inside. It was to this same pub that Ronald Reagan made a highly publicized campaign visit eight years earlier to get the Irish vote. At the time "the blue-collar, working Irish Democrats were in fact going for Reagan," Mayor Flynn told me. Many of the patrons, while voting Democrat locally, had not supported a Democratic presidential candidate since 1976 because of their conservative views on abortion, anti-communism and race. By this time Clinton's Irish promises were known in the Irish-American community and the Eire (pronounced "eerie") resounded to the whoops of the patrons as Clinton and the Mayor climbed over the counter and the Governor of Arkansas pulled a pint of Guinness.

The 53-year-old Boston Mayor, a former all-American basketball player, later accompanied Bill and Hillary Clinton to the Catholic Notre Dame University in South Bend, Indiana, to reassure the audience that the pro-choice candidate was worthy of their support.

"The first question there," Flynn recalled, "and Governor Clinton was very astute in anticipating it, was, 'What do you say to those people who want change but don't believe they are welcome in the Democratic Party because it's not a party for people who are pro-life?' Governor Clinton replied, 'Well I just have to disagree with that because the national co-chair of the Clinton for President Committee is standing right next to me. He just happens to be Ray Flynn, President of the United States Conference of Mayors, who just happens to be pro-life.'"

Ireland was now on Clinton's agenda, at least in his own mind, and it surfaced in different ways in the last weeks of the campaign. When the Irish rock group U2 were being interviewed live on the New York Rockline radio station, they were taken aback to receive a call from Clinton, who played the saxophone in college. "You can call me Bill," the Democratic candidate told U2 lead singer Bono in his familiar "Aw-shucks" voice. Bono replied that it was "kinda cool" to be talking to someone who might be President and asked Clinton for his "rap" on various topics.

"We're an Irish band, Bill," said Bono, "and we come from Ireland and we're not really up to the ins and outs of American internal politics. But whoever sits in the White House affects all of us . . . America in some quarters has a very bad rap at the moment. You're seen as meddling in other people's foreign affairs. How do you feel?"

Clinton gave his rap. "We can't withdraw from the world," he said. "And you're right, you know. You're from Ireland and one of the things I wish that the United States could do, not on its own but maybe through the UN, is finally play a constructive role in bringing an end to the historic tensions that still exist on that island: but it's something we can't impose our will on . . . We have to just keep working and talking and hoping that by working with good people in other countries we can make a difference."

Just two weeks before the election, on 23 October 1992, Clinton put his "rap" on Ireland into writing in a letter to Bruce Morrison, co-chairman of what had now become Irish Americans for Clinton/Gore, as Senator Al Gore of Tennessee had joined the campaign as Clinton's running mate. It was in effect a manifesto of his policy on Ireland. It was drafted on Clinton's instructions by Nancy Soderberg, a former aide to Senator Kennedy who was working on Clinton's foreign policy team in Little Rock and who had been given responsibility for several countries, including Ireland. She had some help from outside sources who knew something about Irish issues, like Trina Vargo, one of three foreign policy staffers in Kennedy's office in Washington.

"That was Nancy's letter," said Bruce Morrison later. "She didn't really want to do it, because she said—what have we got to gain, we did the promises. From their perspective the election was won." Soderberg had joined the Clinton campaign at the urging of the candidate's advisers George Stephanopoulos and Tony Lake, not thinking that the Arkansas Governor would actually win. She assumed when she signed on that she wouldn't have to leave the capital, otherwise she would have declined. "They tricked me by saying the campaign would be in Washington DC," she said. "I can still remember George Stephanopoulos calling me up. I was in the middle of remodelling my apartment. He said, 'Your conditions have been met, will you take the job?' I said, 'Yes.' He said, 'It's in Little Rock,' and the phone went 'click.' I was there for eight months."

In the letter, Clinton went further than any previous Democratic presidential candidate on some issues concerning Northern Ireland. Those few people in the campaign who saw it in draft form felt that Clinton had gone too far, and they were skeptical about the Arkansas Governor actually carrying out the promise of a peace envoy if he won the election.

"Senator Gore and I share the goal of all Irish Americans for peace in Northern Ireland. We believe that the United States must reflect this concern more effectively in its foreign policy. We condemn the violence and bloodshed which has scarred Northern Ireland and oppose all attempts to achieve political goals through terror and violence," the letter said. "A Clinton administration will take a more active role in working with the leaders in those nations to achieve a just and lasting settlement of the conflict."

"A permanent and peaceful solution to the crisis in Northern Ireland can only be achieved if the underlying cause of the strife and instability is dealt with vigorously, fairly and within a time frame that guarantees genuine, substantial and steady progress," it continued. "I believe the appointment of a special US envoy to Northern Ireland could be a catalyst in the effort to secure a lasting peace."

"We believe that the British Government must do more to oppose the job discrimination that has created unemployment rates two and a half times higher for Catholic workers than Protestant workers . . . the MacBride Principles set forth appropriate guidelines . . . We also believe that the British Government should establish more effective safeguards against the wanton use of lethal force and against further collusion between the security forces and Protestant paramilitary groups."

"I was frankly amazed at the idea of a President making the MacBride Principles official federal government policy," said a campaign insider. The guidelines were opposed as counterproductive not just by John Hume but by powerful Irish Americans in Congress, including Democratic House Speaker Tom Foley and Senator Edward Kennedy, though it alienated them from many grassroots Irish Americans who felt strongly about discrimination against Catholics in Northern Ireland.

The letter went through several versions, and the contents were discussed informally with Irish embassy officials in Washington, before it was signed by Clinton and released to the media. It caused a stir in the British press. "That letter made London crazy," said Morrison. The British were upset about criticisms of the "wanton use of lethal force" and allegations of collusion with loyalists, a reference to a number of controversial killings by members of the security forces in Northern Ireland. But they noted that there was no reference to a visa for Gerry Adams or to a British withdrawal from Northern Ireland.

Moreover, campaign promises did not amount to policy. It was inconceivable to many students of the presidency that any American President would really get involved in Northern Ireland over the wishes of the British government, unless the political climate between London and Washington cooled considerably.

But the British now played their part in ensuring that it did. As election day, 3 November, drew near and Clinton moved ahead in the polls, a panicking Bush campaign accepted an offer from the British Conservative (Tory) Party Central Office to supply two officials to advise them on how to turn the tide. The Tories instinctively disliked the younger, more liberal, Arkansas Governor with his woolly foreign policy notions and were much more comfortable with Bush as a partner in the special relationship the two countries enjoyed. They had just managed to get John Major restored to office in a United Kingdom election despite a stagnant economy and an electorate ready for change, a feat they achieved mainly through clever exploitation of Labor Party leader Neil Kinnock's character and policy weakness. The Bush campaign was already trying to discredit the Arkansas Governor on the character issue, depicting him as a liar, a womanizer and a draft dodger. Bush even suggested on television that Clinton was a Soviet sympathizer who had made a trip to Moscow while a student at Oxford in the late 1960s.

The two Tory officials came up with some ideas the Bush people thought were less than brilliant. One was to put up billboards in major cities with a picture of Gennifer Flowers and the slogan, "AND NOW HE WANTS TO SCREW THE WHOLE COUNTRY." Another was to circulate fake photographs of Clinton as a long-haired hippy with a Vietcong flag. The Tory strategists were not central figures in the Major campaign, and the Republicans declined to follow up these crude suggestions, though they had already adopted the strategy the Tory officials recommended of attacking Clinton day by day on the two issues of taxes and character. Some negative television commercials directed against Clinton were copied almost exactly from the Conservative Party advertisements effectively used against Kinnock.

British officials also checked passport files in London at the request of someone in the Bush administration. It was not hard to know what they were looking for: anything that would indicate Clinton had sought to change his nationality in order to avoid the Vietnam draft. This was leaked to the media. To make matters worse, reports also appeared in the newspapers of how British Tory ministers were cheering on the Republican incumbent. Just before polling day, British Foreign Secretary Douglas Hurd sent a good-luck message to James Baker, his long-time counterpart in the Bush administration who was now in charge of the President's re-election effort. Referring to a hunting expedition they had shared, Hurd expressed the wish that Baker might "shoot down all his ducks" on election day. Much to Hurd's embarrassment, the telegram too was leaked.

Resentment at British meddling, especially the opening of Clinton's passport files, grew and festered in the Clinton camp. The British Conservative Party had made a dangerous enemy in the Arkansas Governor, who, despite their efforts, was elected President of the United States on 3 November 1992. John Major announced from Downing Street that he would travel to Washington within the month to say goodbye to George Bush and to greet Bill Clinton. But shortly afterwards the idea was quietly dropped. The President-elect made it clear that he would see the British Prime Minister in his own time.

4

Nothing Personal

"Not keeping your campaign promises is the venial sin, keeping them sometimes is the mortal sin."
Thomas Foley

After his inauguration as President on 20 January 1993, Bill Clinton found ways of letting it be known that he had not forgotten how John Major's Tory Party conspired to keep him out of the White House. He made fun of the British Prime Minister to an after-dinner audience in Washington.

"When I met John Major the other night he slapped me on the shoulder and said, 'You know you don't look anything like your passport photographs,'" the President said to laughter and applause. "And I said, 'Well, I really appreciate that, John, and there's nothing personal in what you tried to do to me. Nothing. And next week I'll send you a note to that effect through Jimmy Breslin when I name him our envoy to Northern Ireland.'" Everyone knew of Breslin's reputation as an outspoken, pro-Irish columnist.

At a White House press conference, when struggling for an analogy to explain his support for Boris Yeltsin, Clinton again made a dig at Major.

"We just had the Prime Minister of Great Britain here, right?" he said. "And the United States and Great Britain have had historic ties and shared values; you expect me to work with him, even if he is of a party that was openly supportive of my opponent in the last election."

The New York Times reported that Clinton generally did not bear grudges but that he had a lasting one against Major. The London *Sunday Times* went so far as to say Clinton hated Major, which prompted the new President to protest to Mark Gearan, the White House communications director, "I don't hate anyone. I forget the people I'm supposed to hate."

But he didn't forget what they did. When RTE reporter Charlie Bird began a question to him during a visit to the White House by President Mary Robinson with the words, "Mr. Clinton, we know you visited Ireland while you were in Oxford . . ." Clinton interrupted, laughing, to say, "So you read my passport file too?"

"There's nothing like a person who's wounded when he is weak and remembers when he is strong," the then House Speaker Tom Foley told me in an interview for this book. "I think there was obviously some personal bitterness on the campaign about the role of John Major. The British meddling was outrageous and I think it went very deep with Clinton."

The British Ambassador to Washington Sir Robin Renwick discovered for himself how things had changed. On a wet evening in March, two months after the Clinton inauguration, he and British Defence Secretary Malcolm Rifkind could be found peering forlornly through the wet windscreen of the embassy Rolls Royce on Pennsylvania Avenue, after being refused admission to a reception in the White House to which they had been invited. There was a mix-up over invitation lists and they were turned away. It was the sort of thing which would never have happened when Bush or Reagan was in office.

The accumulation of evidence prompted Niall O'Dowd to write in a memo for the Irish-American lobby: "There is clearly enough animosity there on Clinton's side to give an edge to Irish-American proposals. One must consider it in the light of the previous close relations between Thatcher/Reagan and Bush/Major."

During the ten-week transition period, a delegation from Irish Americans for Clinton/Gore, now calling itself "Americans for a New Irish Agenda," travelled to Little Rock to put the case to the Clinton transition team for an envoy and other initiatives. It was the first time any grassroots Irish lobby in the United States engaged an incoming administration. It was not a great success. It was one of twelve low-level meetings, bringing together campaign officials and special-interest groups ranging from American Indians to inner-city dwellers. Nancy Soderberg could not find the time to attend. Morrison, the group's co-chairman and most articulate spokesman, was delayed by snow from leaving Hartford, Connecticut, and by the time he reached Memphis it was too late to catch the connecting flight to Little Rock. The former Congressman used the telephone in the American Airlines lounge to participate in the meeting along with O'Dowd, Mayor Flynn, Bob Linnon of the Irish American Unity Conference, Paul O'Dwyer, his son Brian O'Dwyer, businessman Chuck Feeney, John Dearie, trade union executive Joe Jamison, and an aide to Flynn, Mike Quinlan.

Chris Hyland told them that the White House would welcome their suggestions on policy on Northern Ireland and advised them to draw up their recommendations in written form. He still believed however that the new crowd around Clinton, foreign policy advisers like Tony Lake, Nancy Soderberg and Sandy Berger, all of whom would become important members of Clinton's National Security Council, were not really serious.

"I don't care what anyone says," Hyland told me, "none of these people, least of all Lake, Soderberg or Berger, were acting in any way on the Irish issue. Nobody—the President, Gore—nobody wanted to deal with it."

There was a feeling, he said, that those lobbying for change in Irish policy were hotheads and that serious people like Senator Edward Kennedy were much more cautious about Clinton getting involved. Hyland had insisted on setting up the Irish-issues conference in Little Rock, and the initiative was so unpopular, he said, it cost him a job in the administration. Morrison too was under no illusions about the fickleness of those who made political campaign promises. Some Clinton aides, he said, were very cynical about courting ethnic groups. It was a case of "use them, lose them."

The idea that Ireland as an issue was more trouble than it was worth, had been taken for granted for a long time in the upper reaches of the US government. It was reflected in the conclusion of a 1993 Research Service Report on Northern Ireland, one of dozens of semi-official tracts published on Capitol Hill to inform members of Congress of the situation in different countries of the world. The report echoed the prevailing pessimism that "political stalemate is likely to continue," because in the view of many observers, "the conflict in Northern Ireland is being managed reasonably well" and "the British, the Irish, the unionists and the nationalists in Northern Ireland all seem to have become accustomed to the present level of violence." The report, subsidized by the British government which provided accommodation and a programme for the researcher, was so pessimistic in tone—it concluded with the words, "real change must await a new generation"—that the Irish Ambassador to Washington complained and some amendments were made.

Americans for a New Irish Agenda consisted of little more than a handful of activists, and had no formal structure, but clearly had broad support from the Irish-American community in New York and Boston where their names were well known. O'Dowd used the columns of his newspaper, the *Irish Voice*, to promote the idea that engagement with the Clinton administration could bring the United States into the Northern Ireland peace process and become an outside catalyst which could help break the deadlock.

They gave the new President a month to settle in, then Mayor Flynn took a five-point plan to the White House signed by himself and Morrison on behalf of the group, the main demand of which was a peace envoy. It also contained a series of perceptive suggestions about how the State Department's grip on US policy on Northern Ireland might be lessened. It proposed "appointing a US ambassador to Ireland with greater authority to press for a number of political, economic and social initiatives which fundamentally address Northern Ireland; appointing a consul in Belfast mindful of the political policy objectives of the Clinton administration, with a mandate to work closely with the US embassies in both London and Dublin, and appointing a fact-finding mission to London, Dublin and Belfast composed of American leaders, political, business and academics, to survey and report to President Clinton on the status of key elements outlined in this document."

The British government was quite apprehensive about the President's promise to appoint a special envoy to Northern Ireland, though Prime Minister John Major told *USA Today* on 23 February 1993, "It is very rare to find any serious divergence between the instinctive views of the United Kingdom and the United States." Journalists at Westminster were told by a government official the day of Clinton's inauguration that the British government would make it a priority to get the initiative dropped by the new administration. This had happened before. The US State Department, the cornerstone of the special relationship, had as far back as 1985 first killed the special envoy notion with a stern communication to the Senate Foreign Relations Committee which had dared to consider it. "The naming of a special envoy," it said, "would serve no useful purpose. Neither the British nor the Irish Government believes that such a diplomatic approach at this time would help in any way to promote reconciliation between the two communities and an end to the violence."

British officials hoped the State Department would see them right again. "It would be intolerable to have an American coming over and treating a sovereign government on the same footing as the political representatives of terrorism," a British source told me.

They could however live with an American fact-finding mission to Northern Ireland. If the leader of a fact-finding mission was called an envoy, the exercise might even defuse the highly dangerous notion of a full-time emissary. Even better if he was a well-disposed Irish American like House Speaker Tom Foley, who had a unique asset for someone of his background: Foley was an Anglophile, he loved most things British and regularly spent his holidays in England.

An elegant, cerebral politician, the 64-year-old Speaker with two Irish-born grandfathers had a rare sense of detachment, and a reputation as being skeptical of grand schemes. He was the father figure of the Friends of Ireland, which he had co-founded in 1981 along with twenty-four members of Congress and governors as a counter to Irish republican lobbying in the United States. Foley was also a close friend of John Hume, who had encouraged the setting up of the Friends of Ireland, and he had already visited Northern Ireland in September 1991 as the head of a small fact-finding delegation.

During that trip, Foley refused to meet Gerry Adams or other Sinn Féin leaders. He did encounter Protestant firebrand Ian Paisley in the US consul's house in Belfast and later related how the Democratic Unionist Party leader told him bluntly, "You're not going to solve the problem with twenty minutes of polite conversation. And we don't want your help. You deserted the Vietnamese." The Speaker's delegation toured Derry with John Hume, ending up in a private room of a Donegal restaurant where the SDLP leader's musician friend, Phil Coulter, entertained them with a take-off of Jimmy Durante and a rendering of his popular song about Derry in the Troubles, *The Town I Love So Well.*

While he was a strong critic of Irish republicanism, Foley's upbringing in the United States was typical of many Irish Americans. "I remember when I was sixteen and I read *My Fight for Ireland's Freedom* by Dan Breen, it got me terribly excited," he told me. He recalled being mesmerized by the movie, *The Informer*, based on Liam O'Flaherty's novel, and he still remembered lines learned as a teenager: "What excuse could we offer, what excuse receive, for keeping Ireland in the pit when other nations are rising from the darkness to the light?" His grandmother, he said, "was the type that fed you oranges at her knee and told you what the terrible Black and Tans had done, the work of the bailiffs, and so on, things she didn't experience herself." Romantic Ireland faded for Foley as the Provisional IRA launched its violent campaign in the 1970s. In Congress, he identified with those who tried to discourage Americans from supporting violence, for which he said he had a deep abhorrence. Unlike Congressional districts in New York and Boston, the 5th District of Washington State which regularly returned Foley did not have any significant Irish-American lobby for him to worry about.

"It seemed to me from the beginning that there was never a possibility of bombing the British out of Northern Ireland, and it didn't seem to me that that would produce any kind of justice or opportunity for the nationalists in the North," said Foley, who quoted admiringly the words of a Democrat from Pennsylvania who once said of the IRA campaign: "This is not a war. If this were a war, these would be war criminals, not war heroes." He had only contempt for those non-Irish-American members of Congress who supported extreme Irish nationalist groups like New York Congressman Mario Biaggi, "who, God help us, told John Hume to his face that he wasn't doing enough for the cause of Irish freedom—which provoked a couple of us to say, 'Mario, the biggest risk you face every day is slipping on the Capitol steps.'" He knew his detractors depicted him "as a phoney Irishman and as a lackey of the British." One of those to do so in print he described as a "universal pacifist, turn-the-other-cheek, make-love-not-war, save-the-whales" type of person, except when it came to Ireland and then he wanted "to help blow up Irish people."

Foley's attitudes made him unpopular with the rival group to the Friends of Ireland in Congress, which called itself the Ad Hoc Committee on Irish Affairs and which was sharply critical of British rule in Northern Ireland. However he was avidly wooed by successive Irish governments, especially after he became Speaker in 1989, as he could always be relied upon to look after Dublin's interests where they did not conflict with Britain's. Every year he ushered through Congress the annual $20 million contribution to the International Fund for Ireland, which was jointly administered by London and Dublin. And he always hosted the Taoiseach then in office and John Hume at a Saint Patrick's Day Speaker's lunch on Capitol Hill.

When he saw a copy of the letter Clinton sent Bruce Morrison just before the election, "I found myself appalled," Foley said. "Over the years it always seemed to me that a lot of people in public life played fast and loose with the Irish issue." They were "shamelessly indulgent of violence and pandered to what they perceived was the Irish vote." This letter appeared to fall into the same category. Foley considered it his duty to warn the young President-elect of the dangers of keeping his Irish promises and to make sure that Clinton knew he profoundly differed from the Morrison group regarding a peace envoy for Northern Ireland and the MacBride Principles, both of which he believed were bad ideas.

The opportunity came when he went to Little Rock in November 1992, along with the other leading Congressional Democrats, Senator George Mitchell and Representative Dick Gephardt, for a private dinner with the President-elect to discuss the legislative agenda of the coming term. Foley mentioned to the transition staff in Little Rock his intention of bringing up Ireland.

"I was told, 'Oh! No! No! Don't do that. It's a big mistake. You're down here to talk about other things,'" he recalled. "But I remember being just appalled at the notion that the administration was committing itself to policies that I felt were going to produce nothing but trouble and were just wrong-headed. I used to say—a line I tortured from what Bernard Shaw once said—"There are two sins in American politics, not keeping your campaign promises is the venial sin, keeping them sometimes is the mortal sin.'"

He waited until the dinner was over and stopped Clinton on the way out. "I told him what I thought about the envoy idea," he said. "I said it would create all kinds of tensions and problems without any possibility of reconciliation. I could see people standing up at Westminster and saying, 'Well, what about sending one to the United States to help them with their problems in Los Angeles.'"

The President listened to the case made by the elder statesman, seventeen years his senior. He didn't say very much, Foley recalled, "just that they were going to examine everything."

With the new President in office, the British tested the waters on the envoy issue, using a leak to members of the Westminster press lobby. Parliamentary correspondents were informed on 16 February, less than a month after Clinton was sworn in as President, that the British government was not in fact rejecting out-of-hand suggestions that President Clinton might appoint a peace envoy. Downing Street sources told *The Irish Times* London editor, Frank Millar, that the government "had no great problems" with the idea in principle. It was described as a "possible item" for discussion at a meeting between Major and Clinton set for later in the month in Washington. US State Department and British Foreign Office officials had in fact agreed in their ongoing contacts that a fact-finding mission would be an appropriate compromise, according to London press reports. The American Ambassador to London, Raymond Seitz, suggested in a speech in Belfast the possibility of Washington appointing someone sensitive to the complexities of the situation who could gather facts and report to both Clinton and Congress. Seitz said that what the United States was offering was "assistance, rather than interference." A career diplomat, he too was an Anglophile who made England his home on retiring in 1994, and who clearly shared his host government's views on Clinton's Irish promises. Tom Foley was obviously the man he and the British had in mind for the job. A senior British official told Reuters approvingly, "Foley has been very strong in his condemnation of the IRA and terrorism."

In Dublin the Taoiseach, Albert Reynolds, watched what was going on with some detachment. "The British were possibly calculating if it had to happen, let it be Foley because we're happy with him," he told me when interviewed for this book. "It could have been a London-inspired idea. They never wanted the envoy at all. They saw it as interference. That's the way they were reading it, so Foley, I think, could well have been the answer to it. Foley was very acceptable in London and at the same time he had done a lot here in Ireland over the years." To some officials in Whitehall, who had seen an American President wriggle out of pro-Irish campaign positions before, it may even have seemed that they were helping get Clinton off the hook. Foley's credentials as an Irish American would give political cover to the new President for what would be little more than a face-saving exercise.

But when the Speaker's name appeared in the media as a possible fact-finder, the Irish Americans reacted angrily. They saw Foley as Britain's straw man. "A fact-finding mission would be fine, but that's not the envoy," Bruce Morrison said dismissively. Some unionist politicians who tended to demonize Irish Americans failed to see that the British were actually trying to kill the envoy idea. Peter Robinson, deputy leader of the Democratic Unionist Party, complained bitterly at the prospect of an Irish American friendly to John Hume passing judgment on Northern Ireland. Sending Speaker Foley would cause "gross offence to unionists," he said, adding that the British government was in "full retreat" and "trying to save face." Hume, who was conducting private talks with Gerry Adams and who believed that the time was not right for an outside arbiter, called for an economic rather than a political envoy.

Foley told me that while it might have been mentioned to him by some advocates, no one in the administration sounded him out about going to Northern Ireland. Nancy Soderberg, who had been appointed staff director of the National Security Council, the President's foreign policy unit in the White House, confirmed later however that the White House had considered the Speaker as an envoy.

"There was actually some discussion about Foley," she said. "He, I think, had an interest in going. The President had a natural instinct that America had a role to play here. It wasn't that specific."

Clinton said on 22 February that no decision had been made and the controversy fizzled out after only a week. A report in the conservative London *Sunday Times* concluded that a "carefully orchestrated compromise, designed to defuse tension between the British government and the American administration, was in tatters this weekend after the deal was made public." The Irish-American activists were relieved. They had not got anywhere yet, but neither had the British.

5

Shamrock Diplomacy

"Put it on the shelf. But I'll be back with something different later on."
Albert Reynolds

The Derry entertainer Phil Coulter wrote a special number for the first event of Saint Patrick's week that year in Washington. He performed it for an audience including all the big names from Congress at a glittering dinner organized by the American Ireland Fund, a charity founded by Dr. Tony O'Reilly to benefit "peace, culture and charity" in Ireland. After he and John Hume rendered *The Town I Love So Well,* with the Derry politician waving a fist in the air, he sang a parody—to the tune of *Big Bad John*—of unionist reaction to rumours that Foley was to be peace envoy:

When the word got out he was coming to town,
The barricades went up and the shutters came down.
They said we'd better be prepared.
The truth is they were running scared
From Big Tom, Big Tom, Big Bad Tom.

Speaker Tom Foley was among those who laughed uproariously. But the patrician Congressman had little reason to celebrate. Not only had his chances of going to Ireland as a fact-finder been dashed, he had just lost a bitter contest over who should be the American Ambassador in Ireland during the Clinton administration. William FitzGerald, the octogenarian Ambassador appointed by President Bush a year earlier, automatically resigned when the Democrats took over the White House, and the splendid official residence in Dublin's Phoenix Park was vacant. Whoever filled it would become a pivotal figure. Foley wanted the President to nominate former Congressman Brian Donnelly, a fellow House Democrat from Massachusetts, for reasons as much to do with Congress as with Irish-American politics: Donnelly had successfully masterminded Foley's campaign to become Speaker in 1989 and Foley felt a strong obligation to him. Representing the Boston Irish neighborhood of Dorchester, Donnelly was a streetwise, working-class Democrat who liked to promote Ireland in America; he often, for example, sent his colleagues gifts of Ballygowan Irish mineral water. Like Morrison, Donnelly was a hero to Irish Americans for sponsoring an immigration law which eased restrictions on Irish immigrants through what became known as the Donnelly visa program.

Senator Edward Kennedy, however, had decided that his older sister Jean should get the job. Jean, the eighth child of Joe Kennedy, who had been Ambassador to London before World War II, wanted the job. She had been on holiday in Ireland in 1992 and as she said to a friend she had been reminded how crazy the Irish people were about her brother Jack. How incredible, she thought, if thirty years later his sister returned as US Ambassador. Old Joe Kennedy had promoted the men in the family while the women stayed in the background. But Jean, having raised four children with her husband Stephen, who died in 1990, had carved out a career of her own. She had founded the Very Special Arts Program to foster art for the mentally disabled in 1974, and it had established branches in all fifty American states and fifty-five countries, including Ireland. She always resented being described as a dilettante.

"Some people dismissed her as someone who did charity work," said Kennedy family friend, Bill Barry. "But if Jean were a man they would say she was head of an international organization."

On arriving back in the United States from her Irish holiday, she suggested to Ted that maybe, one day, she would return there as Ambassador. She had no experience in diplomacy or international politics but this was hardly a disqualification for a post which had become a rest home for retired political fundraisers.

To some Irish Americans it looked risky for the Massachusetts Senator to cut across a popular figure like Donnelly to elevate his sister, especially as he was facing re-election in the New England state the following year. The *Irish Voice* publisher, Niall O'Dowd, and Mayor Raymond Flynn in Boston believed that Donnelly would in fact do a much better job than Jean Kennedy Smith, who had no record on Irish issues. But there was enormous emotional appeal to Irish Americans, and to the Irish, in the idea of a Kennedy in the Park.

For several days, rumors of the fight for Phoenix Park circulated in Washington. Friends of Donnelly said that when he rang Ted Kennedy seeking his support, the Senator replied something along the lines of "Oh, shit! My sister is interested . . . but you deserve it." Donnelly was so upset about reports of a feud between the Kennedys and himself over the Dublin posting that he told the *Patriot Ledger* in Massachusetts that he had nothing but the closest friendship with Ted Kennedy. "Bad blood? That is absurd," he protested. There was a third runner. In Boston, Elizabeth Shannon, widow of the Ambassador nominated by Jimmy Carter in 1976, William Shannon, was backed by retired House Speaker Thomas "Tip" O'Neill and the *Boston Globe.* She too sought Kennedy's approval. "I wrote to Ted," said Shannon. "He said he would like to support me but he was supporting someone else." When she realized it was his sister, she knew her chance had gone. Foley also told me that once it became known Senator Kennedy was promoting Jean Kennedy Smith, there was little doubt about the outcome.

The President planned to make the formal announcement on Saint Patrick's Day, when the Taoiseach would be visiting the White House, but a week earlier I was tipped off by an aide to Jean Kennedy Smith's nephew, Congressman Joe Kennedy, that President Clinton had decided already to nominate her as Ambassador to Ireland. The Kennedys evidently wanted the story out to make it difficult for the President to change his mind, though that would have been unlikely, given Clinton's admiration for the legendary Irish-American clan and his dependence on the Senator for support in Congress. When Kennedy reportedly asked him to "do this for me," when lobbying for his sister Jean's nomination, the President found it impossible to refuse such a personal request.

Having checked with other sources and written a story for the next day's *Irish Times,* I drove to Capitol Hill for a pre-arranged interview with Speaker Foley about the envoy rumors. I was greeted in an outer room by Jeff Biggs, the Speaker's press officer. "What have you been writing about today?" he asked casually. I told him. "Excuse me a moment," he said and disappeared into the Speaker's office. I was left waiting for an hour. Only later did I learn that Foley had not at that point been told that the President had decided to give the job to Jean Kennedy Smith rather than to Donnelly. As I waited outside, he was making his anger known. His former aide and ally, Werner Brandt, the Sergeant-at-Arms in Congress, rang the Irish embassy to ask an embarrassed diplomat why the Speaker had not been told of the President's choice, and why he had to learn it from a journalist. But the embassy also had not been informed.

When I was admitted to his elegantly furnished room, Speaker Foley's face was like thunder. He did not discuss the Ambassador appointment but vented his anger on Clinton's promise to appoint an envoy. "No promise should take precedence over doing the right thing," he said, heatedly. "It is stupid and wrong-headed and wrongful to do a bad thing, a wrong thing, against the interests of those values and purposes that the campaign promise was given for, merely in order to say I kept my campaign promise. A lot of good was done by candidates who were wise enough to revise their decision when they saw better information and not foolishly to follow their campaign promises to wrong-headed and bad results."

Afterwards I heard that Donnelly got the news from the *Boston Herald*, when a reporter rang and said, "You're dead, we hear." He was later made US Ambassador to Trinidad and Tobago.

On 16 March, the eve of Saint Patrick's Day, just after lunch, President Clinton telephoned Jean Kennedy Smith and formally asked her to accept his nomination as Ambassador to Dublin. She said, "Yes." At the same time he called Mayor Raymond Flynn in Boston and invited him to become America's Ambassador to the Vatican. He too accepted.

The British were appalled at both appointments. Flynn was sure to embarrass them in Rome with his outspoken criticisms of their role in Northern Ireland. But a Kennedy as Ambassador in Ireland didn't bear thinking about. There were still bad memories in London of the period when Jean's father was Ambassador to the Court of Saint James. Joe and Rose Kennedy with their nine children had arrived in the British capital in 1937 to an enthusiastic reception, but this had cooled considerably when the Boston Irishman repeatedly predicted that Germany would defeat Britain. He became even more unpopular when during the Nazi blitz he abandoned the grand American embassy residence at 14 Prince's Gate, in London, to seek sanctuary in the countryside. Joe Kennedy was withdrawn from Britain by an embarrassed President Roosevelt in 1940. For a long time the Kennedy name was anathema to some members of the Tory establishment. In the mid-1970s, when I asked Lord Hailsham, the then Lord Chancellor, what effect it had on

British government policy when Irish-American politicians like Ted Kennedy called for reforms in Northern Ireland, he angrily slapped his hand on the table and retorted, "Those Roman Catholic bastards! How dare they interfere!"

The President turned up at the American Ireland Fund event that evening and chatted with a shy and demure Jean Kennedy Smith, accompanied by Ted Kennedy sporting a bright green tie and a wide grin. Caught up in the gaiety of the moment, Clinton allowed himself to be persuaded to join in singing *When Irish Eyes Are Smiling* in a line-up with Speaker Foley, John Hume, Albert Reynolds, Irish Ambassador Dermot Gallagher, Tony O'Reilly, Congressman Dave Obey and Elizabeth Bagley, a wealthy patron of the SDLP leader who would soon be nominated US Ambassador to Portugal.

Next day Reynolds called to the White House for his first formal meeting with Clinton. Ireland is the only country in the world whose Prime Minister has a fixed, annual date, Saint Patrick's Day, 17 March, with the President of the United States. Jean Kennedy Smith was there for the formal announcement of her appointment. The Taoiseach shook her hand and said "Welcome home."

The chemistry was excellent from the start between the man from Arkansas who liked to play the saxophone and the rural Irish businessman/politician who gained a fortune in dance halls and pet food. Both leaders were country boys who had made it to the top in politics. Reynolds had a direct style with few pretensions and saw politics as "the art of the deal," and Clinton liked his brand of straight business talk.

The Americans had put the peace envoy promise at the top of the agenda, assuming that the Dublin government would welcome the prospect of a powerful intermediary with Britain. Reynolds, however, had come to bury the idea. Before leaving Dublin he gave an interview to *The New York Times* correspondent James Clarity who reported that the Taoiseach "wanted to discuss the sending of a fact-finding mission rather than an envoy." Irish Americans again reacted with alarm, and Clarity found himself being shot as the messenger. An Irish government spokesman protested that the Taoiseach had not intended to convey the impression that he preferred a fact-finding mission to a US envoy, which in fact he did.

Reynolds had a tactical reason for his preference. He had been working quietly with John Major on what, nine months later, would become the Downing Street Declaration, laying down principles for the future of Northern Ireland. His adviser Martin Mansergh had opened secret contact with Sinn Féin's Martin McGuinness six months earlier at the urging of an intermediary, Father Alex Reid, a Redemptorist from Clonard Monastery, Belfast. Reynolds had told Major privately that he was exploring unconventional ways of finding a formula to end the violence. He sketched this out to Clinton and told him that, as he and Major had something else going together, he should put the envoy promise on hold. He had seen how unhappy the British were about it, and sensed that it might not benefit the process in any event. The wily Reynolds instead wanted to turn the issue to his advantage. He had offered to do Major a favor and get the peace envoy off the American agenda, and Major would "owe him one."

Clinton was taken aback. He had been serious about sending a peace envoy to Ireland.

"Oh! He wanted to do it," Reynolds told me later. "He talked about his commitment to try to find peace in Ireland and how he felt an obligation to Irish America and he had an inclination to send an envoy. My reaction was, 'Look, I don't think it will work and the last thing you want or I want is failure, so I think you should put the idea on the shelf, not scrap it, just put it on the shelf, hold off, because I would hope to return to you with a different idea which will still fulfil your commitment. If you do it now nobody will talk to this guy.' We sat down and we talked it through. I told him about my relationship with Major going way back. I felt that if he sent an envoy then it wouldn't do anything for the relationship with the Irish in America because it would be seen as one-upmanship. He said his understanding of history was that it was always traditional to have hostility between an Irish Prime Minister and a British Prime Minister and I said, 'Well that may be in many cases but in this one it's not. We work together and we're going to work together.' It was an eye-opener for him. I said, 'I don't want to come over here and go back with a victory in my pocket. It would be short-lived.' He said to me, 'Well I do have a commitment to the leaders of Irish America and this will be seen as walking away from it. Will you speak to them? Will you explain that to them?' I said, 'Yes, sure I will.' I said, 'You can tell them that my advice, my request to you, is put it on the shelf. But I'll be back with something different later on.'"

It was an excellent meeting, Reynolds said, "with young fellows coming in and out with cards and bits of paper. We had a great chat about politics in general and about Ireland and if there was any movement forward, and what have you."

Nancy Soderberg confirmed later that the envoy "was actually seriously being considered, but both the British and the Irish felt that the timing wasn't right. We did actually keep it under consideration and never ruled it out."

Afterwards at a shamrock presentation ceremony in the Roosevelt Room, the President effectively shelved the envoy idea, saying, "We decided, after our consultations, that it is certainly an option I should leave open." He was "going to stay in touch closely with Prime Minister Reynolds, we're going to talk frequently, and I expect to have an Ambassador in Ireland pretty soon," he said. "The most significant thing I should be doing now is to encourage the resumption of dialogue between the Irish and British governments, which I think is a critical precondition to any establishment of a lasting peace." He added, "I'm going to continue to stay on top of the situation, involved in it."

The Taoiseach responded to these remarks with effusive praise for Clinton as an "Irish American," which no one ever called him before, and enthused about the fact that the White House was designed by an Irishman called Hoban, as every visiting Irish politician to the White House did on Saint Patrick's Day. It seemed to reporters crowded into the room, who knew little of what he had told Clinton and nothing about his contacts with Major, that Reynolds was failing to respond with appropriate seriousness to the first American President prepared to consider how the United States could help move the situation along. "Reynolds Engages in Shamrockry at White House" read the headline over my report in the next day's *Irish Times.* But what Reynolds had achieved with a conspiratorial nod to Clinton was a promise by the President to lend his support to the process when needed. "I couldn't have asked for a better assurance from an American President," he said after he emerged from Speaker Foley's Saint Patrick's Day lunch of corned beef and cabbage. Clinton had undertaken to encourage both governments to strive for a settlement. But the Irish needed no encouragement; the leader of the only superpower in the world was in effect promising to encourage the British to move forward.

Reynolds met John Hume in the Phoenix Park Hotel near Capitol Hill after the lunch and told him what had happened was "way beyond my wildest dreams." The Derry man was also elated after a lengthy talk with the President over lunch. He and Reynolds slapped hands in an Irish version of American high-fives.

For Hume, many years of lobbying Washington were paying dividends. The SDLP leader had been cultivating members of Congress since 1972 when he was telephoned one day by Senator Kennedy with a request to meet. "I was at home when he rang and said, 'This is Ted Kennedy,'" recalled Hume, "and I said, 'Pull the other leg.'" Through his friendship with Kennedy, Hume encouraged the setting up in 1977 of "the Four Horsemen"—Speaker Thomas "Tip" O'Neill, Senator Kennedy, Senator Daniel Patrick Moynihan and Governor Hugh Carey of New York—to help break down the traditional reluctance of some other Irish-American Democrats to condemn republican violence and to encourage constitutional nationalism as a viable alternative. Tip O'Neill started the tradition of Saint Patrick's Day lunches which gave Hume access to the top. "I have had lunch with every President since Carter," Hume told me. "The difference was, Reagan and Bush sat politely and listened, but Clinton questioned me very deeply. I was absolutely astounded by the depth and detail of his knowledge. I told him that sending a peace envoy would be politically difficult. I suggested an economic envoy. He thought that was a good idea."

Bruce Morrison was not so sure. The former Congressman went to the White House to tell Nancy Soderberg that Americans for a New Irish Agenda still wanted a US peace envoy among other things. They were unhappy with what the President had had to say. She told him the idea of a special envoy was not in fact off the table.

When he got back to Dublin, Albert Reynolds got a call from the British Prime Minister about the decision by Clinton to shelve the envoy promise.

"Major was delighted," he told me. "He phoned me after I came back over the envoy being turned down. And he was very grateful. He said, 'Fair play.' 'You know,' he said, 'you weren't playing games.' And I said, 'No, we're not playing games.'"

6

The Box Theory

"That was the first time I had been made to feel like a draft dodger."
Bill Flynn

This guy walked in and sat down," said Niall O'Dowd. "He never said anything. He just sat there. I talked for forty-five minutes. I drew diagrams on a napkin. I had no idea what he was thinking—maybe who is this crazy American? He just sat with his pint of Guinness. I put it to him—you have to get the Americans involved. How do you get them in? How do you bring them into play? You have no credibility. You have to do something for them. Give them something first. It's no use just going to the Americans and saying they'd better live up to their campaign promises. That's not the way it works. Show them that this is an incredible opportunity."

The bearded publisher from New York then put his pitch to the Sinn Féin contact he was meeting for the first time in a hotel in Dublin just after Clinton's election. He asked him to see if Sinn Féin could arrange for the IRA to call an informal ceasefire for a set period if he put a group together to come to Ireland to meet them.

Such a ceasefire would serve several purposes, O'Dowd believed. It would make it more acceptable for members of a delegation drawn from the world of business and politics in America to talk to Sinn Féin. It would signal that the IRA was serious about a longer ceasefire, and disciplined enough to impose it. It would establish the credibility of the Americans for a New Irish Agenda with the new Clinton administration.

"Then he left," said O'Dowd. "I wondered was I mad pushing this theory. I was coming in on a completely different tangent from Irish America. But it worked. It's a brilliant theory."

It was the first of several meetings he held with the same Sinn Féin contact, and in the following weeks O'Dowd set out to put together an ad hoc group of Irish Americans to make a pathfinding visit to Northern Ireland. He had a sense of personal mission. O'Dowd did not belong to any political party or organization but he was basically an Irish nationalist who believed that the republican movement was looking for ways to end its campaign of violence and adopt an unarmed strategy, and that American involvement was the key. But no one was talking openly to its political wing, Sinn Féin, which was ostracized by the British, Irish and American governments and by the other Northern Ireland parties because of its support for violence. Irish Americans, he believed, could form a bridge over which republicans could cross to take the political path towards a settlement. He talked to several political and business acquaintances about how this might be done. He was particularly taken with the theory that only an outside force could free up the situation, as all the parties in Northern Ireland were locked in position and whatever step one group made the other group countered it, and there was a continuing stalemate.

"I recall taking Jim Reilly of IBM to dinner in the Kinsale Pub in New York, and saying to him, Jim, how would you deal with Northern Ireland?" said O'Dowd. Reilly drew a diagram on a napkin. O'Dowd recalled that he said, "This is what America represents, the outside-the-box entity. For this to work you've got to change the dynamic in the box. If one of those parties changes its relationship fundamentally with an outside force, and the only outside force is the United States, then you change the dynamic within the box because then everyone else has to relate with the outside force as well." The theory was used in conflict resolution in business all the time, said the *Irish Voice* publisher.

O'Dowd talked about the "box" theory with Ciarán Staunton, an employee of Muldoon's pub in Manhattan who came originally from Louisburgh, County Mayo. Staunton had close ties with Sinn Féin in Ireland and had been the national US fundraiser for the IRA prisoner support group, Noraid. He and O'Dowd became friends three years earlier during the campaign for visas for undocumented Irish immigrants in which they were both involved.

"Ciarán had been under orders from Sinn Féin to try and broaden the base of the outreach of nationalists in Northern America, and get beyond the old Noraid base," O'Dowd said. "I knew from him that things were starting to change, though he was never specific." As Staunton was trusted by the Sinn Féin leadership, unlike some other prominent officials of Noraid which republicans feared was infiltrated by the Federal Bureau of Investigation, O'Dowd had asked him to put him in touch with someone at the top in the organization. This was no easy task, as the obsessively secretive republican leadership was wary of journalists. "He became my passport to the top," he said. It was Staunton who set up the meeting between O'Dowd and a top Sinn Féin official in a Dublin hotel.

O'Dowd also discussed the "box" idea with Brendan Scannell, the shrewd, no-nonsense Kerry man who kept a copy of the Easter 1916 Proclamation hanging in his office in the Irish embassy in Washington and who was also valued by members of the new administration for his advice and insider analysis. They talked about how it was becoming clear that a fundamental shift was happening in Irish America. After years of division, when one section sided with the Irish government and the other with the IRA, there was a growing weariness with faction fighting and a new willingness to come together and engage the US administration and the nationalist parties in Ireland, North and South. Irish America was waking up to the potential of a nationalist alliance which in association with an involved American President could encourage the IRA to end its violence and take its chances at the negotiating table.

O'Dowd wanted corporate America to lend weight and respectability to any mission to Belfast. Eight years earlier he had co-founded *Irish America* magazine, which published profiles of the top "Business 100" Irish Americans each year. He had become the chronicler of a phenomenon of modern America: the fact that one in four chairmen and chief executive officers in the country had Irish ancestry. In just over a century the impoverished Catholic Irish had progressed through several layers of society, excelling first in sports, then politics, and now in the boardrooms of America.

One of these whom he guessed might be prepared to get involved was New York insurance executive Bill Flynn, an Irish Catholic whose mother came from County Mayo and father from County Down. A pillar of respectability and a member of countless charitable and educational boards, Flynn had already dabbled in peace efforts. His company, Mutual of America, sponsored "the Williamsburg Charter," which addressed the principles of religious liberty in a pluralist society, and an "Anatomy of Hate" conference in Oslo on the effects of hatred on people and society; he had also helped organize a 1992 conference in Derry on conflict resolution. He had important friends in law enforcement, and had recruited into his company several ex-members of the FBI, which had been conducting an underground war with IRA gunrunners and fundraisers in America for twenty-five years. His personal bodyguard on trips abroad was Ted Kennedy's friend Bill Barry, an ex-FBI man who owned his own anti-terrorism security company and who had been Bobby Kennedy's bodyguard the day he was assassinated.

These connections made Flynn an unlikely emissary to Sinn Féin, but it was through an FBI event that the insurance chief got interested in personally trying to stop the violence in Northern Ireland.

In 1991 he attended an FBI training course for business executives at an air force base in New York State to learn about defensive driving. "After the training session we stopped for a couple of cokes and ham sandwiches," he said, "and a friend of mine from Syracuse, New York, the Chairman and CEO of United Mutual Life Insurance Company, Jack Mannion, got into a debate with some of the FBI people on the Irish situation, about terrorism being committed by both sides there. And to my absolute amazement he began to argue that the British provocations were so severe he wondered why people wouldn't understand the reaction. I was stunned. He was one of my closest friends and I had never known he entertained these views. I said, 'Jack, I just can't believe you have these views.' He said, 'Bill, why don't you see two fellows who run this organization and let them talk to you?' I said, 'You're on.'"

Two men from Noraid came to see Flynn at his Manhattan office. "I told them I was totally supportive of the concept of Ireland getting unified. My parents before me, my relatives were all of one mind on that. But I could not agree with using violence to achieve that end. And the group they represented had the taint, though I don't believe it was the fact, that money that was to be used for prisoners' families was also going to guns and bombs and bullets. Religious leaders and political leaders had said that. I said, 'I just can't go along with that.' They responded by saying 'Well if you feel so intensely about the reunification of Ireland then what the hell do you support? What are you doing about it?' And I said that was the first time I had been made to feel like a draft dodger. I said, 'You're right. I hear the bell.' In two weeks I was on my way to Ireland to find out how I could be of help."

In Northern Ireland he spent time with the Peace People but felt they did not have the answer. He spoke with Cardinal Daly and a British minister, Richard Needham.

In the end he went to West Belfast to meet Gerry Adams. He found the bearded, bespectacled leader of Sinn Féin to be a straight talker, he said. "He pulled no punches. If he couldn't answer a question he said so. I liked that about a person, rather than blarney." Adams brought him to Clonard Monastery where they talked with Father Alex Reid, the emissary between Sinn Féin and the Dublin government. "I'm a Catholic," said Flynn. "Adams is a Catholic, a communicant. I would see these priests and brothers, living there, trying to help people, under poor conditions. To see them, and their respect and friendliness for Adams, I knew he had to be a man of peace."

Flynn had also been breaking some new ground on his own by hosting British ministers visiting New York, for which he had attracted some criticism from Irish Americans. He presided over a business lunch for Sir Patrick Mayhew, the Northern Ireland Secretary, at New York's 21 Club and held a breakfast at the University Club for Richard Needham, whose family were landowners in Kilkeel, County Down.

On the latter occasion he had bantered with the British minister about their families' past. Needham said, "Bill, I should tell you, my dad used to own the Mountains of Mourne." Flynn replied, "You made conditions so impossible my father had to leave there and come here to make his way." Needham retorted, "Well Bill, the truth of it is your father didn't pay the rents," to which Flynn responded, "Well, dammit you're going to pay for this breakfast!"

When O'Dowd approached him, the chairman of Mutual of America hesitated, wondering was he just a newspaper publisher who wanted to do something to improve his circulation. "That proved to be the worst thought I ever had," he said later. O'Dowd has "a genuine, honest passion for a peaceful resolution."

O'Dowd also went to Charles "Chuck" Feeney, the reclusive New Jersey-born billionaire and co-founder with Robert Miller of DFS, Duty Free Shoppers Ltd, the largest duty-free shop operation in the world. Annually listed by *Forbes* magazine as one of the 400 richest Americans, Feeney and his partner's business empire spanned many countries and included oil, hotel and computer interests, but the billions came from selling duty-free cigarettes, liquor and designer goods to tourists all over the world, mainly Japanese. Feeney, who spoke Japanese, created an international retailing colossus four times larger than its nearest competitor. *Forbes* magazine said the 62-year-old entrepreneur was "a hyperactive man who values his family and their privacy and does not dress to impress." It quoted someone who worked for him as saying he saw him once with a safety pin holding up his pants. Married with five children,

Feeney also came from modest beginnings and supplemented his income when at Cornell University School of Hotel Administration in the mid-fifties by selling sandwiches to students.

He had been involved quietly in philanthropy north and south of the Irish border for many years. O'Dowd got to know him when Feeney contacted him at the *Irish Voice* one day to discuss what was happening in Ireland. After that they met occasionally for coffee or a meal. The publisher thought Feeney a fascinating and engaging businessman with a great sense of humor. He knew he was very wealthy but had no idea he was a billionaire until someone showed him a 1988 magazine profile. Feeney, who contributed generously to the campaign for immigrant visas, let O'Dowd know he was interested in promoting a peace process in Northern Ireland. He had family ties to County Fermanagh, and watched in horror on television the aftermath of the Enniskillen IRA bomb on 8 November 1987, which killed eleven people and injured sixty, mostly Protestants, as they gathered for a service at the town's war memorial. Viewers around the world heard the heart-wrenching story of how Marie Wilson died in the rubble telling her father, Gordon Wilson, "Daddy, I love you very much." Feeney said at the time, "This is ridiculous, I must do something." One of the things he did five years later was join Irish Americans for Clinton/Gore and he attended the meeting in Little Rock organized by Chris Hyland during the transition with the aim of getting the White House interested in Northern Ireland.

O'Dowd told Feeney his plans for Irish Americans to get involved as a bridge to Sinn Féin and said, "I want you to be a part of this." The duty-free magnate immediately agreed. "He turned out to be a rare example," O'Dowd said later, "of a major Irish-American figure prepared to put his reputation and his money on the line."

With Flynn and Feeney providing the respectability of corporate Irish America, O'Dowd sought out Raymond Flynn and Bruce Morrison to give political leadership to the group of amateur envoys. For personal reasons Morrison couldn't go to Ireland then, but made a commitment to take part in the future. O'Dowd arranged to talk to Raymond Flynn about the project and they met in a room in Fitzpatrick's Hotel on Lexington Avenue in Manhattan, a favorite haunt of visiting Irish politicians and journalists. Both he and Scannell had a high opinion of the Boston city boss and O'Dowd was impressed with the questions Flynn asked about his proposal. He told him a temporary IRA ceasefire would be in place when they got to Northern Ireland. They could open up a link between Sinn Féin and Irish America, and explore the possibility of internationalizing the conflict to bring Sinn Féin in from the political cold and thus help make an end to the armed conflict possible. Flynn finally agreed to go, saying with some enthusiasm, as O'Dowd recalled, the political risk was worth it if it brought peace to Ireland. They planned also to set up meetings with the two governments and the political parties but not until they were in Ireland. There could be problems if mainstream Irish politicians knew they were meeting Sinn Féin. When members of the respectable San Francisco Forum led by Pat Goggins visited Ireland ten years earlier, the Taoiseach Garret FitzGerald cancelled a meeting with them when he learned they had talked with Sinn Féin in Northern Ireland. The publisher also asked Chris Hyland to join them, to tie the group into the Clinton camp, but he was unable to do so.

O'Dowd told his Sinn Féin contact that they were about ready to go, and within a short time, confirmation came from Belfast that an informal seven-day ceasefire would be arranged to coincide with their arrival in Ireland. There would, however, be no announcement and nothing in writing. They would have to take the republican movement on trust. O'Dowd in turn had to ask the other members of the group to take him at his word.

A ceasefire of any kind was a big deal for the IRA, O'Dowd believed. Since the 1970s there had been no precedent for an IRA cessation of any kind, however short or informal, other than the annual three-day Christmas ceasefire. The IRA fixed the informal cessation for 4 May 1993.

Shortly before that, things started to go wrong. O'Dowd found one day that he could not contact Mayor Flynn. Mike Quinlan, the intermediary he used on Flynn's staff, had gone on holidays and the Mayor did not return his calls. It soon dawned on him that Ray Flynn was backing out of his agreement to lead the Irish-American delegation.

The Boston Mayor, an Irish diplomat later told me, had in fact been "warned off" by the Irish government. He had told the Dublin authorities what he intended to do and was advised in quite strong terms that the Irish side did not believe there should be official contact with Sinn Féin until there was an IRA cessation of violence. Mayor Flynn would undermine the government's position if he went ahead.

Albert Reynolds confirmed that this was the case. "I thought it was too soon," he told me. "Pressure would build on me. I didn't want anyone else taking the initiative."

The Dublin government had little option but to state its official view to the Boston Mayor once it had been notified "up front." Using a back channel, as O'Dowd routinely did through Brendan Scannell to let the Irish side know what was happening informally, was a different matter. Then Dublin didn't have to take a position. In fact the Irish-American initiative got quiet but important support from Seán Ó hUiginn, one of the most important architects of policy in the Department of Foreign Affairs in Dublin with whom Scannell was in close contact.

Later Mayor Flynn told me of another reason for backing out of the delegation. He had been nominated United States Ambassador to the Vatican by President Clinton on Saint Patrick's Day, but had not yet been confirmed by the US Senate. All ambassadors-designate are counselled by the State Department against potentially controversial action of any kind while their nomination is pending. When I spoke to him in Boston around this time, the Mayor, in shorts and dripping sweat after a jog around the city parks, said he had accepted the nomination to the Holy See, though he had wanted a post in the Clinton cabinet, and was now determined to go to Rome. To sit down with Gerry Adams in Belfast could put him in bad odor with Congress and the administration, it could give ammunition to members of the Senate Foreign Relations Sub-Committee like Jesse Helms who opposed the very existence of an American embassy at the Vatican, and it could embarrass the President. One of the major objections to his candidacy was that he was too pro-Irish, he told another reporter. It was best that he did not go to Northern Ireland over the objections of the State Department. "It wasn't going to do any good other than cause a big controversy," he believed.

Without political leadership, the group was just a bunch of businessmen. The project unravelled. O'Dowd tried to bring in Paul O'Dwyer at the last minute but the elder statesman of Irish America was not well enough to travel. The trip had to be called off. He got his Sinn Féin intermediary on the telephone and broke the news.

"You've no idea what this means," the contact said. "I have," O'Dowd replied. "I'm in the shit," the Sinn Féin man said.

O'Dowd's contact had gone out on a limb to assure Gerry Adams of the bona fides of the Irish-American group and would now have to tell him that the emissaries he promoted had failed to get their act together. O'Dowd had convinced his Sinn Féin contact that the American card could be played, but the persuasive New York publisher was not showing much competence. He had undertaken to bring a delegation to Belfast and it hadn't materialized. Getting the IRA to agree to a ceasefire for a visit by an amateur group whose members were still unknown to most republicans had been a difficult enough exercise for Adams. It had required much forward planning and explanation.

Ray Flynn did, however, go to Ireland on his own in early May. He asked to meet Church leaders as part of his preparation for the Vatican post. He tried to make private contact with Sinn Féin, but they did not want anything to do with a maverick operation.

The hesitation by conventional politicians like Mayor Flynn to meet publicly with Gerry Adams was understandable in the context of 1993. Those who came in contact with him found Adams a personable and articulate philosopher-politician and came away convinced he was trying to end the conflict, but to the British public he was a sinister apologist for IRA atrocities. He was loathed by unionist politicians and he was regarded as beyond the pale by all parties in the Irish parliament.

The eldest of ten brothers and sisters in a West Belfast republican family, Adams had been a 21-year-old housing rights activist and apprentice barman when the Troubles began in 1968. He almost certainly joined the Provisional IRA, though he later denied IRA membership. In 1972 he was interned on the *Maidstone*, a prison ship moored in Belfast Lough, and some months later became one of a seven-member delegation chosen by the IRA for secret but non-productive talks with the British—along with a close friend from Derry, a butcher's apprentice, Martin McGuinness. During four years in prison without trial, he studied, wrote, and gave lectures. In 1983 Adams and McGuinness and a handful of like-minded Northern activists, dedicated not just to guerrilla war but to a community-based political agenda, took over the republican movement from its Southern-based leaders. In the same year he was elected member of parliament for West Belfast but refused to take his seat. He lost it in 1993 to moderate nationalist Joe Hendron of the SDLP, who had the help of tactical voting by unionists. Adams had come to personify the Irish republican movement and in the ghettos of Belfast he was a folk hero. But as political representative of the IRA, doors were shut to him everywhere he turned. He was barred from travelling to Britain and his voice was banned from British—and Irish—radio and television. He was regularly denied a visa to visit the United States. Now the opportunity to engage the Americans on his home ground of Belfast had been squandered.

To maintain his credibility, especially if he was ever to try to repeat the exercise, O'Dowd had to explain personally what had happened. He flew to Dublin and drove to Belfast where a Sinn Féin driver picked him up at Duke's Hotel and drove him through dark streets past army patrols. He did not know what his reception would be, and was nervous and tense. "I looked down and found my knuckles were white holding my briefcase," he said.

"As I anticipated, it was a heavy meeting. They wanted to know what the hell I was up to," O'Dowd said. He explained exactly what had happened. Adams and his colleagues accepted he was serious and that events had been outside his control. They agreed to learn lessons from the fiasco, and start afresh.

As O'Dowd set out on the return journey he wondered if he had made an "eejit" of himself and if he really could pick up the pieces. "It was one of the worst weeks of my life," he said. On the flight back he said he almost fainted from nervous exhaustion.

The IRA's ad hoc ceasefire got under way on 4 May and lasted about thirty-six hours before word could be got to the units that it had been called off. It ended when a coffee jar bomb was thrown at a security forces patrol in Jamaica Street in Belfast, without causing any injuries. ('I wonder what kind of coffee it was?" I remarked to police press officer Sandy Johnston when checking IRA activity with the Royal Ulster Constabulary press office in Belfast. "I don't know," he replied, "but it was instant.")

The amateur American envoys were startled to discover later that year that they were not the only ones trying to negotiate an informal IRA ceasefire at this time. A proposal for a two-week cessation had also been the subject of secret negotiations between Sinn Féin and the British government. This emerged when details of the clandestine contacts were published by both the British and Sinn Féin in November after a leak to the London *Observer*. According to the documents, a two-week period of intensive negotiations between the two sides was planned for a neutral venue in May, possibly Scotland, Norway or Denmark, and the British contacts had proposed that the IRA reduce or suspend its campaign during that period to enhance the process. When interpreting the documents for the media, Martin McGuinness said, "Sinn Féin sought and was given a commitment by the IRA that it would create the conditions necessary to facilitate this round of talks and to enable us to explore the potential of the British government's assertion. This would have involved a fourteen-day suspension of operations. This was conveyed to the British government on 10 May." The British side backed away from the idea, however, and by August were demanding a complete end to violent activity before any process could begin.

Looking back, the Irish Americans realized that things were never quite what they seemed and no one could ever tell what was really happening in the murky world of paramilitary politics.

"There was clearly a whole other set of communications going on," said Bruce Morrison, "showing the British but doing it for the Americans."

7

Mission Accomplished

"Where is the Holy Ghost playing, forward or back?"
Code used by intermediaries to ask about the state of the peace process

Four months later Sinn Féin told the Irish Americans that the IRA was prepared to stage another informal ceasefire for their benefit. O'Dowd's contact informed him it would not be made public, and that nothing should be announced to the media by either side about any temporary cessation of violence. The aim as before was to demonstrate that the republican movement was serious about exploring political opportunities. It was directed primarily at influencing opinion in the United States. This time the ceasefire proposal was in writing.

Bruce Morrison, the former Connecticut Congressman, was now free to head the delegation and give it political leadership. There was still stalemate in Northern Ireland but in mid-June, President Mary Robinson had sent a tremor across the political landscape by shaking Gerry Adams's hand during a visit to Belfast, and new opportunities seemed to be opening up. Adams regarded the handshake as the first public sign that some elements in the Republic were trying to reach out to Sinn Féin. The party had done well in local government elections, strengthening its moves towards a political accommodation. O'Dowd told his colleagues that the time was right to bring the pressure of the business and political communities in Irish America to bear on the developing process in Northern Ireland. Once more O'Dowd briefed Brendan Scannell in the Irish embassy in Washington, and senior officials in Foreign Affairs again gave the group unofficial encouragement.

Morrison was an unlikely Irish-American leader. A tall man with a moustache and twinkling eyes, he looked more like a benevolent

British army colonel than an Irish-American "pol." Morrison was not a Catholic but a Lutheran and was more German than Irish. "I wasn't raised ethnic," he told me over lunch in a Washington restaurant. "I was adopted. My biological father was Irish-English and my biological mother was Austrian-American." To complicate matters his adoptive mother was German and his adoptive father Scots-Irish. He had been in Clinton's 1973 graduating class at Yale University Law School and worked on legal services projects with Hillary Rodham Clinton. In Congress as chairman of the House Judiciary Sub-Committee on Immigration, Refugees and International Law, he secured the "Morrison visas" which made him a hero in Irish America. Morrison was drawn to the Irish question through his interest in human rights and his Irish-American constituency groups. His staff told him "not to join the Biaggi crowd because they supported terrorism, but to stick with the Tom Foley group," he said, but he found the Friends of Ireland deficient in their concern for human rights violations in Northern Ireland. He travelled to Ireland under the auspices of the Irish American Unity Conference, which supported peaceful Irish reunification. In 1987 in Belfast he met Gerry Adams for the first time, despite the disapproval of the American consul there who told him, "If you meet these people, don't tell us, they're all terrorists." Adams, he concluded, "was not Daniel Ortega and he wasn't Fidel Castro but he was political through and through." He met John Hume too but did not hit it off with the SDLP leader. "I was always a minor player with Hume because I wasn't Foley and I wasn't Kennedy," he said, "I was this upstart Congressman." The British army did its bit to radicalize the mild-mannered legislator from Connecticut. While he was travelling through Derry with Gerry O'Hara of Sinn Féin their car was stopped by a military patrol. "I had my passport and I tried to write down all their numbers," he said, "but I had the paper snatched from my hand by a soldier and I was threatened with an offence for collecting information about the security forces." Morrison resigned his Congress seat in 1990 to make an unsuccessful bid for Governor of Connecticut. He was now practising law and eager for a place in the new administration.

Morrison, O'Dowd, Bill Flynn and Chuck Feeney travelled to Dublin on Monday 6 September 1993 to begin a round of meetings with politicians on both sides of the border. They arrived separately and met in the coffee shop in the Westbury Hotel at the top of Grafton Street. O'Dowd produced a document which he had secured from Sinn Féin. In it the IRA gave an undertaking to conduct a week-long ceasefire, starting at midnight on the previous Friday 3 September. It had already been in effect for more than forty-eight hours before they arrived. The North was at peace, if only for a few days.

They all read it closely. For the first time it hit them that this was for real, O'Dowd recalled. He then destroyed the document, concerned that while travelling around he could not fully guarantee that it would remain secret, as he had promised Sinn Féin.

Communications among the intermediaries involved in the peace process on both sides of the Atlantic had, of necessity, to be carefully protected. Documents were either destroyed or filed in unlikely places. The participants often spoke in Irish, in which O'Dowd and his Sinn Féin contact were fluent. A rough code was followed in letters and telephone calls in English. Letters were often phrased so that they looked like routine business communications. The attempt to get a ceasefire was simply "the project," and Gerry Adams "the chairman of the board." Letters were hand-delivered if possible, and often sent with airline passengers. On the telephone the IRA was referred to as "the local football team" and the peace process was known as "the Holy Ghost." The question, "Where is the Holy Ghost playing, forward or back?" was a way of asking how things stood. The reply "forward" meant they were good, "back" they were bad, and "on the sidelines" signified, as one of the participants put it, "we're screwed." Father Reid was always referred to as "An Sagart," the Irish word for priest. "The Sagart is travelling" was a real sign that things were moving. Jean Kennedy Smith, the American Ambassador to Dublin, was known as "Spéir-bhean," the poetic word for a woman seen in a vision of Ireland, or sometimes as "Strong Lady," and Senator Kennedy was known as "The Brother." Morrison and his companions from New York were sometimes referred to in telephone calls as the "Connolly House Group" because they met Adams in Sinn Féin headquarters in Belfast which was named after James Connolly, a leader of the 1916 Rising.

The lexicon was as simple as that used in the secret British–Sinn Féin communications published later that year, though the British side generally preferred less poetic and more prosaic code words. They referred to the London government as "the bank," a cabinet minister as "a member of the board" and negotiations with Sinn Féin as "the loan business."

The Connolly House Group spent two hours in Dublin with Taoiseach Albert Reynolds, from whom they received unexpected encouragement. "Albert just threw everyone else out of the office and conducted a two-hour seminar," said O'Dowd. Reynolds was making progress with his British counterpart, John Major, and was now more enthusiastic about finding ways of bringing Sinn Féin in from the cold and maximising American help. Bill Flynn was so jet-lagged that he spent the meeting standing up so that he would not fall asleep. They also went to see Jean Kennedy Smith at the US embassy, but she was still settling in and unsure of herself. "I thought she didn't know what she was talking about," one of the participants said. They got little sympathy for a proposal they put forward—that Gerry Adams should be given a US visa. She was not convinced that this would do any good.

In Northern Ireland, Ian Paisley, the most uncompromising Protestant leader, called Morrison a troublemaker and refused to see him. The Rev. Martin Smyth, David Trimble, Chris McGimpsey and Jim Wilson from the Ulster Unionist Party did receive them in their Glengall Street headquarters, still being repaired after an IRA bomb. The group argued they were not following a nationalist agenda and would encourage American investment in Northern Ireland. They had talks with John Hume in Derry, with John Alderdice, leader of the moderate Alliance Party, in Belfast, and with Northern Ireland Secretary Sir Patrick Mayhew at Stormont Castle. They had an "eye-opening session" with David Ervine and Gusty Spence on the loyalist side, finding them very serious about the peace process.

While in Belfast the group felt that they were under surveillance though they never discovered any firm evidence. In his room in Duke's Hotel, O'Dowd lifted the telephone once and heard a conversation between two strangers. On another occasion they suspected a hired driver was more than he said he was and communicated only by notes. It was brought home to Morrison just how untouchable Sinn Féin was even in some journalistic circles when he was advised privately by a reporter from the Republic that he should not go to see Gerry Adams as it would not be proper to do so. "We were warned not to talk to several groups as if somehow by listening to them we would be contaminated or somehow approve of their agenda," O'Dowd noted at the time. "In the end we talked to IRA and U[lster] V[olunteer] F[orce] representatives and found their motives and fears sincerely held. Far from being monsters they are men and women caught up in a historical cycle of rage and repression." During their six-day stay they thought most commentators in Ireland inhabited a different planet,

President Clinton with Irish President Mary Robinson.
(THE IRISH VOICE)

Candidate Bill Clinton with Irish-American activists at the forum in New York, 1992, when he promised a peace envoy and a visa for Gerry Adams. (JAMES HIGGINS)

President Clinton and Taoiseach Albert Reynolds and US Ambassador designate to Ireland, Jean Kennedy Smith, at the White House, March 1993. (JAMES HIGGINS)

Nancy Soderberg, President Clinton's special adviser on Ireland.

US Ambassador to Ireland, Jean Kennedy Smith. State Department officials accused her of putting Irish over US interests.

British Foreign Secretary, Douglas Hurd, who dismissed Sinn Féin President, Gerry Adams, as a "Mister Ten Per Cent."

US Secretary of State, Warren Christopher, who strongly opposed giving Gerry Adams a US visa.
(THE IRISH TIMES)

Sinn Féin President Gerry Adams with a New York taxi driver.
(POPPERFOTO)

President Bill Clinton and British Prime Minister John Major: smiles disguise transatlantic tensions.
(POPPERFOTO)

Heading towards a ceasefire: Senator George Mitchell, Taoiseach Albert Reynolds, President Clinton, Speaker Tom Foley and SDLP leader John Hume, on their way to the Speaker's Saint Patrick's Day lunch in 1994.
(POPPERFOTO)

Veteran Belfast republican Joe Cahill, whose support for the peace process carried great weight within the wider Provisional movement.

Niall O'Dowd, Bill Flynn and Bruce Morrison, arriving in Dublin prior to the IRA ceasefire of August 1994.
(THE IRISH TIMES)

recalled O'Dowd, the journalist-turned-insider. With some outstanding exceptions, many who reported and commented on Northern Ireland had made a cult of pessimism and saw little hope in any new initiatives.

At the heavily fortified Sinn Féin office, O'Dowd and his amateur peacemakers at last came face to face with Gerry Adams, who was accompanied by Martin McGuinness, Mairead Keane, the head of Sinn Féin's women's department, and the party's general secretary, Lucilita Bhreatnach. This was the main business of their trip. "It was a lengthy, very intense, session," said Morrison. The Americans emphasized how they could play a role in ensuring that any move towards peace was met with reciprocal political benefits in the United States, and that they had the best chance ever of involving the US administration in helping the parties in Northern Ireland move forward. The visitors left with a strong sense that a re-examination of the armed struggle was taking place.

The unofficial ceasefire took place as Adams promised, though it started over an hour late. At 1:19 a.m. on Friday 3 September, a huge IRA bomb wrecked the courthouse in Armagh. But from then until Monday 13 September, when an explosion devastated the Stormont Hotel in Belfast, there were no IRA bombings in Northern Ireland, or attacks on security forces. One shot was fired at Maghera police station in Belfast on 5 September and Woodburn police station in Belfast came under gunfire on 11 September but O'Dowd was assured by Sinn Féin that these were the work of the Irish National Liberation Army, a small but deadly left-wing paramilitary organization.

Later Gerry Adams told me that luck was on his and the Americans' side. The lull in activity was not like the Christmas three-day ceasefires, when all operations stopped. IRA commanders had told him that if an opportunity arose while the Americans were in Ireland to conduct a pre-planned operation, it would have to go ahead. They promised not to plan anything but not to stop anything, Adams said. The informal cessation had also not applied to England and some IRA units may not have got the word at all.

The story of the IRA pause in operations broke on Saturday 11 September, at the end of the visit by the New York group. Albert Reynolds was taken by surprise. He had not been aware of the informal ceasefire before it occurred. "It was purely between them," he said. "The first I knew of it was in *The Irish Times*."

One of the untold stories of this period is that the White House knew the precise details of the IRA cessation, even before it took place. Officials of the National Security Council were informed of every move that the Irish Americans were making, and knew days in advance of the deal between the Irish Americans and Sinn Féin.

It received the information through a channel which had been set up linking O'Dowd with the White House through the office of Senator Kennedy in Washington. As would so often be the case, Scannell had a hand in this. He advised O'Dowd to keep the White House informed of what his peace group was doing at all times. It was essential, he said, to establish a basis of trust and credibility with the administration if there ever was to be any meaningful engagement. The key official in the White House was Nancy Soderberg, staff director of the National Security Council whose brief included Northern Ireland. Access to the top people in the White House was extremely difficult for someone outside the political establishment, therefore a route to Soderberg had to be found, Scannell said. Senator Kennedy's office was the obvious conduit as she used to work there. Her successor as Kennedy's expert on Ireland, Trina Vargo, knew Soderberg exceptionally well as they had worked together for eight years as the Senator's foreign policy experts until Soderberg had joined Clinton's campaign in 1992. Scannell knew and trusted Vargo, a petite staffer with an infectious laugh who was acknowledged as the leading expert on Ireland on Capitol Hill. Almost nothing about Ireland got past Kennedy in the Senate and what got to Kennedy had to be run past her first. As it happened, Vargo and O'Dowd already knew each other. They had been introduced—by Scannell—during President Mary Robinson's visit to Boston in 1991.

The *Irish Voice* publisher was initially doubtful about working through Kennedy's office. The Senator was no friend of Sinn Féin, and O'Dowd had written critical commentaries about him in the *Irish Voice*. Scannell insisted the Senator's support was crucial in getting the United States involved because of his standing with President Clinton. "I at first thought Kennedy was useless," O'Dowd said, "but Brendan said, 'No, go to him. Go to Trina, she will validate everything you say.' "

O'Dowd and Vargo met early in July, as the publisher was again trying to put together a visit of his group to Ireland, to talk about how they would operate. "I told Trina I would tell her everything that was happening and she said she would pass the information on to Nancy," he said. Nothing would be held back.

From then on the calls went back and forth every day between Trina Vargo's office in the Senate Russell Building in Washington and O'Dowd's newspaper office or his apartment in Manhattan, sometimes several times a day.

O'Dowd always had a tough time convincing the Kennedy aide of a point of view but they developed a friendship which was to prove crucial in the days ahead. Vargo, a graduate of Pittsburgh and McGill universities with a reputation for utter discretion, initially didn't quite trust O'Dowd. "Bad enough that he was a journalist but at first she thought he was a Provo," said a friend of both. "But he never tried to oversell himself or what he was doing, or promise what he could not deliver, or lie to her." Born in a small mining town in Pennsylvania, she was one-quarter Irish—her mother's name was Daugherty—and a Protestant, which helped her establish cordial relations with Northern Ireland unionists who called to see the Senator.

Soderberg was also one-quarter Irish, having a Scots-Irish mother and a Swedish-American father. She was highly valued by Clinton as a foreign policy adviser. On her office wall was a framed photograph of the President on which he had written: "To Nancy, first you tell me what to say, then if I miss a beat you actually write it out word for word. Those who say I think for myself should never see this picture. Thanks." As the number three in the President's foreign policy team, she could often be found at dawn or late in the night in her office, spinning out decision-making until every angle had been dealt with. She had worked as a foreign policy adviser with Democratic candidates Walter Mondale and Michael Dukakis, and then as foreign policy director in the Clinton campaign. Her association with Kennedy, and a long-standing friendship with John Hume, created suspicions in London that Soderberg was a covert supporter of Irish causes. But on Capitol Hill, she was regarded by some Irish Americans as unsympathetic to nationalist causes, particularly the MacBride Principles. Some members of Congress blamed her for steering Kennedy away from involvement in the case of Joseph Doherty, the IRA man who won widespread Irish-American backing for his fight against deportation from New York to Belfast.

"When I was working in Kennedy's office," said Soderberg, interviewed in her White House office for this book, "there was a real division in Irish America between Noraid and other groups that would have been a lot closer to the IRA, and those who were what they call Friends of Ireland who were more closely allied with John Hume, and took a very strong line against violence. I was in that camp when working for Kennedy so I wouldn't talk to the other people, one of whom was Niall O'Dowd. He'd written a couple of critical articles about Kennedy, and I just didn't think he was worth the time. So when I wanted to get a better sense of whether or not an IRA ceasefire was coming, I talked to people on the Hill and the Irish government and other people I knew in Ireland. I talked to Trina. When it actually became something we were seriously considering and I needed some more information, she would talk to Niall O'Dowd and Niall O'Dowd would talk to his contacts around Adams."

Soderberg had been alerted by John Hume that things were moving in Ireland. "He's a master of many things, one of which is just keeping his finger on the pulse of everything that is happening," she said. "And I remember very distinctly that he said, 'I really think that the IRA is moving towards a ceasefire.' "

The arrangement whereby O'Dowd communicated with Soderberg only through Vargo suited everyone at the time. If things went wrong, Nancy Soderberg had deniability. She could legitimately say she was dealing only with Kennedy's office, not Sinn Féin. Vargo, by talking to both Soderberg and O'Dowd, could keep Senator Kennedy and his sister Jean fully informed of what was happening. Equally important, she could guarantee for O'Dowd that there would be straight dealing with the National Security Council: she could vouch for everything Soderberg said to him through her, and vice versa. If the National Security Council wanted to back away from something, it would have to justify itself to Senator Kennedy rather than just an ethnic New York activist. O'Dowd in turn provided the vital link to Adams, who was still a political pariah in Ireland, Britain and the United States, unable to make contact even with political aides in Washington. As someone who had left Ireland as an adult and lived many years in New York, the *Irish Voice* publisher understood the politics of both countries and knew many politicians and business personalities on both sides. He acted as a pathfinder for people who needed information about Ireland.

"My essential role was as an interpreter," he said. "In the United States people would trust my judgment about what was going on in Ireland and in Ireland I could interpret what was going on in America. I was able to interpret Adams to the White House, and the White House to Adams. But to be honest when I started talking to Trina as a way to the White House I had no idea what I was getting into."

In the next few hectic weeks he would find out.

8

THE PIZZA PARLOR PLOT

"This is bullshit." Joe Kennedy
"This is not bullshit." Tony Lake

New York Mayor David Dinkins held a press conference in October 1993 to boost his flagging re-election campaign. As it was winding down Chris O'Donoghue of WWOR TV turned to Ray O'Hanlon, editor of the *Irish Echo,* and asked him what would be a good Irish-issue question.

"Ask will he invite Adams to New York," replied O'Hanlon, without giving it much thought.

Dinkins, who was at the time fighting a losing battle for re-election on the Democratic ticket and was eager to court the Irish vote, committed himself on the spot to invite the Sinn Féin leader to New York to explain the Irish peace process to the Irish-American community. "I'll do it tomorrow," he promised.

There was no love lost between the African-American Mayor and the British, who would object to any invitation to Adams. Two months earlier he had an angry exchange of correspondence with the British consul in New York Alistair Hunter who accused him of undermining US–British action to combat the terrorist threat in Ireland by voicing support for IRA prisoner Joe Doherty. On 25 October the Mayor sent a letter to President Clinton asking for Adams's visa request to be reconsidered on the basis of the peace dialogue going on in Northern Ireland between Adams and John Hume.

"It is only by being open to change that change can occur," he wrote. "I know that certain considerations, in particular the special relationship between Britain and the United States will make what I ask difficult."

Adams had already applied for a visa in April 1993 through the US consulate in Belfast, to test the waters after Clinton's election.

He had been turned down, as he had expected, despite the pre-election promise given by Clinton in New York that he would give a visa to Adams or any other elected politician. Adams had since then lost his West Belfast seat at Westminster and technically the promise was compromised. He was found ineligible under Section 212 of the US Immigration and Nationality Act which prohibits the issue of a visa to any alien who has engaged in terrorist activity.

Clinton claimed to a reporter in the Rose Garden on 14 May that he had only promised to review the evidence if Adams applied for a visa.

"I said at the time, because he was a member of parliament, if I were President I would review that, and I thought that if there were no overwhelming evidence that he was connected to terrorists, if he was a duly elected member of parliament in a democratic country, we should have real pause before denying him a visa. I asked that his case be reviewed by the State Department and others, and everybody that reviewed it recommended that his visa not be granted and pointed out that he was no longer a member of parliament."

That decision provoked little reaction in the mainstream Irish and Irish-American media. But by October it might have been less easy to dismiss the campaign commitment. Dinkins was an important city boss in Clinton's own party. There were stirrings of political progress in Northern Ireland which enhanced Adams's case for access to Irish Americans.

However, Dinkins could not have picked a worse moment. On Saturday 23 October two IRA men carried a bomb into a fish shop on the Protestant Shankill Road in Belfast. It was designed to kill loyalist paramilitary leaders meeting in an upper room. But there were no loyalists there, and the bomb went off prematurely, killing nine people and one of the bombers, Thomas Begley. The scenes of carnage provoked outrage on both sides of the Atlantic. As the funeral cortège of Begley wound its way through the streets of Belfast, Adams took a turn carrying the coffin. Not to have done so would have provoked a split with the IRA which regarded Begley as a heroic volunteer, but this cut little ice with the politicians looking at the photograph in newspapers in Belfast, London, Dublin, New York and Washington.

Shortly afterwards the White House sent a reply to the Mayor of New York under the signature of the President. "Thank you for your letter regarding a visa for Gerry Adams," it said. "As you know, Adams has applied on several occasions over the past years for a US visa, and each time, he has been refused under US immigration law because of his involvement in terrorist activity. Adams's ineligibility could be waived by the Attorney General on the recommendation of the Secretary of State, but I supported her most recent decision not to do so in April of this year. Unfortunately, recent events provide no grounds for reconsidering Adams's visa request. The PIRA's 23 October bombing in Belfast that killed ten people—including two children—has underscored the brutal and terrorist nature of the organization and undermined efforts to resume the political dialogue among the parties. Neither the British nor the Irish Government favors granting Adams a visa. My administration's policy continues to support the early resumption of political talks as the most promising way to seek peace and reconciliation in Northern Ireland."

The President's National Security Adviser Tony Lake, Nancy Soderberg's boss, did consider the Dinkins letter, but only to dismiss the request almost immediately. "There was a brief discussion between myself and Tony Lake about whether to give Adams a visa," recalled Soderberg. "There was just no interest in it at all here. There was no sense that things were happening. No sense that there would be a ceasefire or anything."

The White House reply to Dinkins was leaked to *The Irish Times* Washington office. British diplomats were delighted at its contents, as were unionists in Northern Ireland. This President might have his priorities right after all. The bombing had appalled Clinton, Soderberg and everyone concerned with Ireland in the White House. There could be no support for letting Adams come to New York with the image of him carrying the coffin fresh in people's minds. The President voiced his outrage at the bombing and subsequent retaliation against Catholics, including the killing of seven customers in a bar at Greysteel, County Derry. Bruce Morrison called the Shankill bombing a "shocking, saddening and ultimately disgusting event." He knew how serious the setback was. "We have been given a bigger mountain to climb," he said.

But what the White House did not foresee was the angry reaction of Irish Americans, and of the Irish embassy in Washington, not to the visa refusal but to the wording of the letter to Dinkins. It referred to the Provisional IRA as PIRA, an abbreviation used by the British and the State Department and hardly anyone else. The tone and content of the letter, and especially the use of "PIRA," sent an unmistakable message: "The State Department is still in control." The reply had in fact been drafted from State Department materials by Jane Holl of the National Security Council, a colleague of

Nancy Soderberg's in the White House and an expert on foreign policy issues, whose brief included Cyprus and the former Yugoslavia. Holl, who later became executive director of the Carnegie Commission on Preventing Deadly Conflict, had no idea that the initials "PIRA" had such negative connotations among nationalists in Ireland. Nor did the wording of the letter ring alarm bells with Nancy Soderberg before it went to the President for his signature.

"It was our fault," Soderberg frankly admitted. "We'd always say "IRA" and the State Department always said "PIRA." I remember at the time thinking, why is it "IRA" sometimes and "PIRA" others. Once that letter blew up in our face we finally found out. "PIRA" got dropped. We should have stopped and thought. It was in our first six months [in office], we didn't have time to stop and think. We just wrote the letter. Then Dinkins released it. At the time we didn't realize he was going to use it in his campaign."

Those Irish Americans who thought that Soderberg was attuned to their concerns were furious. "We've been hung out to dry," said O'Dowd. Bruce Morrison called for the sacking of the political officer who drafted it. "I couldn't believe Nancy saw it," he said. The claim in the letter that neither the British nor Irish government favored granting a visa to Adams also did not go down well in Dublin. The Department of Foreign Affairs said it was "not aware of any approaches" from the Americans on the visa issue and Irish embassy officials in Washington denied that their guidance had been sought by the administration. Two administration officials separately told me that Dublin had in fact advised them during the year they were against issuing a visa to Adams. Irish Ambassador Dermot Gallagher was furious at being "ambushed" by the letter and made his feelings known to Soderberg over the word "PIRA." Adams wrote to Clinton protesting that the reply to Dinkins contained "the usual lies concocted by the British" and vowing, "I have no involvement in terrorist activity." The letter rejecting the visa request was read out to jeers from several dozen picketers outside the British consulate in New York.

Through his contacts, however, Niall O'Dowd was able to divine that the door had not been slammed shut. The political staff in the White House did not like to see a sector of the Irish-American community turning against them. It was politically damaging to snub publicly an important Democratic Mayor. And Clinton had all but promised a visa to Adams. Another attempt might bring about a rethink, if the circumstances were different.

Two things happened soon after that to bring about a different set of circumstances. The British government admitted that it had been conducting secret talks with Sinn Féin for a long time, which weakened their case against Adams being allowed to have open talks with Irish Americans, especially if he was promoting peace. And it was leaked in Dublin that the British and Irish governments were close to their long-awaited Joint Declaration on the future of Northern Ireland.

O'Dowd meanwhile was looking for further opportunities to bring the situation forward. He decided it was time he brought Bill Flynn and Ciarán Staunton together to explore what was possible. He went to see Flynn in his Manhattan club and told him, "I want you to meet someone." They set off in the insurance executive's limousine to Muldoon's pub on Third Avenue in Manhattan where Staunton worked.

"O'Dowd wanted me to meet Flynn," Staunton recalled about that evening. "He suggested going out for a meal but I couldn't get the time off so they came round by the bar where I worked." He managed to get away long enough for the three to go to a nearby pizza parlor at 688 Third Avenue, called "Famous Original Ray's Pizza."

"We went to the pizza parlor because we wanted to have a private discussion in a place where no one would know us, that would be absolutely secure," said O'Dowd.

"We had come back from Ireland. The IRA had delivered a temporary ceasefire. They were saying what now? I didn't know which way to play it. We had to come up with something new." Seated at the table O'Dowd began what was now an obsessive occupation, drawing boxes on paper napkins. They were all gridlocked inside the box, he told Flynn. If one party made a move, the other made a predictable countermove, and the gridlock remained. Only the United States could act as an outside force, and come at the box from the outside to change the dynamic of the interior workings.

To O'Dowd the prospect of an American visa for Adams was now becoming more attractive than a peace envoy, an idea which was clearly going nowhere. They could control the visa issue better. It would show the republican movement the immediate benefits of the political path. It would bring in Irish Americans behind the peace process. The Americans might also be more susceptible to the idea, now that the British had been caught secretly dealing with Sinn Féin. Staunton said that the Dinkins initiative had not been executed too well. He felt they could move things forward to Sinn Féin's benefit if they could find some other way of getting Gerry Adams into America. O'Dowd suggested trying again by inviting Adams to an Irish community event in New York. But that hadn't worked a month earlier. Flynn, who with the naivety of a businessman dabbling in politics hadn't realized before then that Adams couldn't get a US visa, said they would have to have Adams invited to some prestigious event to get the White House to change its mind.

The Mutual of America boss was in a position to do just that. One of his many roles was chairman of the National Committee on American Foreign Policy, a non-profit organization founded in 1974 by Professor Hans Morgenthau to stimulate debate on foreign policy in the United States. This reputable body could organize a Northern Ireland peace conference in New York to which all the Northern Ireland party leaders, including Adams, would be invited. It had in fact been considering such a conference for some time. Flynn himself had impeccable credentials for staging the event, having sponsored conflict resolution conferences on the Middle East and Ireland. The White House would find it harder to turn down a visa for a peace conference than for a Dinkins election ploy.

"We'll either go down in flames or make it work," Flynn told his two companions. "We're not going to fade into the wallpaper on this one."

Flynn put the proposal to the National Committee on American Foreign Policy in New York. It was strictly his own idea, he told me. "It was not a device. It was the right thing to do." There was some opposition from among his fellow-members to the idea of inviting the representative of a terrorist organization to the United States. The committee was by no means an Irish-American front. A few years earlier it had presented Margaret Thatcher with the Hans J. Morgenthau Award, a prestigious foreign policy award. One of its most prominent members was Ambassador Angier Biddle Duke who had been chief of protocol in the State Department and the White House. Its honorary chairman was Henry Kissinger, National Security Adviser and Secretary of State under Richard Nixon. Kissinger was not involved in the discussions but said he did not like the idea when he heard about it. Later, in Flynn's presence, he acknowledged that it had been a good decision and that he had been wrong.

All that was needed was to set the date and invite the party leaders.

The White House was now taking the Northern Ireland peace

process more seriously, a fact which was brought home to members of the Ad Hoc Committee on Irish Affairs not long after the Dinkins affair when National Security Adviser Anthony Lake arranged a private meeting with the committee's leaders, Ben Gilman, Peter King, Tom Manton and Richard Neal, and members Joe Kennedy, Hamilton Fish, Robert Menendez, Eliot Engle, Bill Coyne and Gary Ackerman. Nobody from the White House, much less the President's top foreign policy adviser, had ever bothered to speak to the group before. They had been beyond the pale, espousing goals such as the MacBride Principles and British withdrawal from Northern Ireland, from which the more respectable Friends of Ireland shied away.

"The meeting was held in one of those hidden rooms on the third or fourth floor of the Capitol," said Peter King, the Republican who had attended the Irish forum in New York and who had since been elected member of the US House of Representatives for Long Island. In his Capitol Hill office, King had hung pictures of himself with famous figures, George Bush, Ronald Reagan, Pope John Paul II, and his old friend, Gerry Adams—which was considered risqué at the time. He was regarded as hostile by the British. "The day of the Shankill bombing I got a fax from the British embassy along the lines of, 'We hope you now realize who you are dealing with,' " he said. "There were three or four faxes back and forth, with the last one ending '. . . there's no sense in talking to people like you.' "

Lake, who had influenza and a temperature, astonished the Ad Hoc Committee members by discussing Northern Ireland in dispassionate terms. He said he would not say "yes" to every initiative they came up with but he would be candid and in future give more attention to the subject, and the new Ambassador Jean Kennedy Smith would travel to the North regularly. King sensed that Lake was sincere.

"Before this, in Congress you felt you were a pain in the ass just bringing up Ireland," he said. "It was a fringe issue. This was the first time I ever heard the Irish issue addressed as part of policy in diplomatic terms. This was not feel-good Irish-American rhetoric. It wasn't a case of good guys or bad guys, but 'What do we have to do?' That showed me they were taking it seriously."

But Joe Kennedy, whose profile in the Congressional Quarterly's *Politics in America* begins with the words, "brash, impolitic, impetuous, impatient," didn't quite see it that way. "This is bullshit," the son of Robert Kennedy snapped at the polite and erudite National

Security Adviser. Lake was taken aback. "This is not bullshit," he retorted.

"It was quite a scene," said Nancy Soderberg, who accompanied him to the meeting. "I remember very distinctly Joe Kennedy jumping at Tony and saying you're just a lot of hot air. Tony doesn't take comments like that quietly. He took personal offence. Tony pushed him back and said, 'Give us a chance to prove ourselves.' I think Joe's come around since and realized it was inappropriate."

She and Lake had gone to the meeting, she said, "because we felt we were prepared to do things that others weren't and there was a lot of skepticism about, that we weren't serious about Ireland because we hadn't done the envoy, and we hadn't given Adams the visa. It was to correct that impression and to explain our policy, which was that we were actually considering an envoy if it was the right time, that we went. Both the Irish and British governments at the time said, 'Not now,' and we wanted to reassure them personally."

The Joint Declaration was finally produced by Albert Reynolds and John Major on 15 December, raising hopes of an early IRA ceasefire. It went further than any other British commitment on the question of self-determination in Ireland, a major goal of the IRA. It stated that Britain would uphold the democratic wishes of the majority in Northern Ireland, whether for the Union or for unity with the Republic; that the British had no selfish or strategic or economic interest in Northern Ireland, and that the role of the British would be to encourage, facilitate and enable the achievement of agreement. It also confirmed the right of the people of the island, by agreement between the two parts, to exercise the right of self-determination on the basis of consent and subject to the agreement of the people of Northern Ireland.

Suddenly the atmosphere was full of hope. With Britain declaring it had no intention of staying in Northern Ireland longer than it was wanted, the arguments were building for an IRA ceasefire to give the political process a chance to work.

The Joint Declaration caused some excitement in the White House. Jane Holl of the National Security Council and John Tefft, director of Northern European Affairs at the State Department, immediately began drafting an appropriate response for President Clinton to make, working together on linked computer terminals. It called on all those who embraced or justified violence "to cast off the works of darkness and put on the armor of light" and accept this "historic opportunity to end the tragic cycle of bloodshed."

Irish-American members of Congress also welcomed the Joint Declaration. Senator Kennedy said the two prime ministers had shown great vision and courage.

Practically the only discordant voice in Irish America was that of Martin Galvin of Noraid, who said it was "a disappointing recipe for further bloodshed in Ireland."

In early December I asked the White House for an interview with President Clinton on his Irish policy and was told by Nancy Soderberg that he would accept a number of written questions. I asked about the special relationship, the envoy promise and his response to the Joint Declaration. One of the questions I submitted was: "Given that the British government has established ongoing contacts with Sinn Féin with a view to establishing peace, is there not a case for granting a US visa to Mr. Adams now, so that Irish Americans can hear first-hand what his peace proposals are?"

The replies were drafted by Jane Holl, again in consultation with John Tefft in the State Department. White House communications chief Mark Gearan told me they would be ready on Friday 17 December, the day after the Joint Declaration was published. Early that Friday he informed me again that they were on the way and would be coming through my facsimile machine in a couple of hours. I alerted my newsdesk in Dublin and waited by the fax machine. Nothing came through. Late on Friday evening I reached Gearan who told me that there were problems of some sort. Afterwards I learned that soundings had been taken from the Irish and British embassies on the wording of the replies and that great care was being taken "with every syllable and comma" as written replies amounted to a review of US policy on Ireland and would shape US actions in future days and that the response to the question about the Adams visa was at the center of some particularly lengthy deliberations. Michael Collins, a senior diplomat at the Irish embassy—he had replaced Brendan Scannell who had returned to Dublin, pointed out to Soderberg that the version prepared differed little in essence from the letter to Dinkins, though the offending abbreviation "PIRA" for Provisional IRA had been dropped. He suggested that the reply as drafted would signal that the President was not responding in a positive way to the changed atmosphere brought about by the Joint Declaration and the rising hopes of an IRA ceasefire. The National Security Council staff looked at it again. Collins knew that the Taoiseach was keen to open doors to future possibilities. Reynolds was already considering moves in Ireland to encourage the IRA to call a ceasefire, such as lifting the ban on broadcasting interviews with Sinn Féin.

Jane Holl worked on the answers that Friday evening and throughout the weekend. It was Tuesday, just four days before Christmas, before the President "signed off" on the half-dozen replies. His central message was that "the time had come for all those who claim a legitimate stake in the future of Northern Ireland to stop the killing and the violence and pursue peace through constructive dialogue."

Regarding Adams, the President said, "As you know, Gerry Adams was refused a US visa earlier this year. That decision followed a careful review of his case and was consistent with our own immigration laws regarding terrorist activity. We will of course keep the issue under review as the developing situation warrants, especially in the light of events flowing from the 15 December Joint Declaration by Prime Minister Reynolds and Prime Minister Major."

This meant that for the first time the question was linked with political developments. The letter to Dinkins had simply said that Adams was banned under immigration law "because of his involvement in terrorist activity" and nothing about a possible review in new political circumstances. White House policy was clearly shifting.

The pizza parlor meeting had a slightly unnerving sequel for the visa plotters. Some weeks after Flynn, O'Dowd and Staunton met in the "Famous Original Ray's Pizza" to work out their plan, the US federal authorities raided the premises as part of a major anti-mafia sweep. They netted twenty-nine members of three organized crime groups from Italy, who were using the restaurant as the center for an international drugs ring. The organization, part of the Naples Camorra, was headed by Aniello Ambrosio, owner of the pizza parlor. For three years, while orders for pizza flowed in, Ambrosio used the restaurant phone to arrange drug shipments, and he collected money and stored narcotics in the basement. For months federal agents had been conducting a huge surveillance operation on his premises.

The place where the Irish Americans went so that they would be "absolutely secure" as they conspired how to get a notorious figure "involved in terrorist activity" into the country was in fact the most intensively bugged premises by the FBI in the whole of the United States.

"Probably the salt-shaker was bugged," said O'Dowd, laughing, when he found out.

9

Discussing the Business

"By visiting Ireland I don't mean a quick helicopter ride."
Joseph Biden

The first thing Jean Kennedy Smith did when she was confirmed as US Ambassador to Ireland was to get rid of the Dublin embassy's deputy chief of mission, Tom Tonkin, sight unseen.

"His analyses of the political situation gave us nightmares," a senior Irish official said bluntly. "He had to go."

"The Irish poured Jean Kennedy Smith's ear full of poison about him," said a US diplomat. "She didn't even ask to meet him."

A new American Ambassador has one absolute right, to select his or her deputy. Many incoming envoys hold on to the current deputy chief of mission to benefit from the officer's accumulated experience and knowledge of the country. Tonkin was two years in the Irish post and had assumed a great deal of responsibility for running the mission, as outgoing Ambassador William FitzGerald was over eighty years old and had no diplomatic experience. But Jean Kennedy Smith was told early on by Irish officials how unhappy they were with Tonkin's role at the embassy. He had not been a supporter of the Irish government initiatives on Northern Ireland. They were also critical of the strict application of American visa laws at the embassy, which meant many young people were refused short-term visas because they could not prove they did not plan to stay in the United States. Tonkin was doing no more than carrying out State Department orders. It was a question of tone and disposition. "He wasn't having a good time in Dublin. He wasn't appreciated," said a US official. Tonkin, who had come from the US embassy in Guatemala, was reassigned to Venezuela.

It was also the right of a new Ambassador to select any career officer as deputy chief of mission. After some discreet vetting of likely candidates by Senator Kennedy's office in Washington, Jean Kennedy Smith decided to ask Dennis Sandberg, deputy chief of mission in the American embassy in Copenhagen, to join her in the Dublin embassy. The tall, bearded diplomat from Minnesota was highly regarded by the Irish Ambassador to Denmark, Andrew O'Rourke, with whom he was friendly. Ireland would be his last post before retiring, a factor which left Sandberg less susceptible to State Department pressure to curb any unconventional moves by the new political appointee. He was an independent-minded official who appeared open to the new policy on Ireland evolving in Washington. He had also been head of the operations center in the State Department for two years and he knew how the system worked.

The incoming Ambassador asked Sandberg to come to New York from Copenhagen for an interview, before confirming his appointment as her deputy. When they finished talking, she suggested that he go on to Washington to have a further chat with her brother Ted. "How do I get there?" he asked. The American diplomat had to admit to Jean Kennedy Smith that up to then he had never been in New York in his life. She told him to get the shuttle from La Guardia airport to National airport in Washington. On Capitol Hill, in Senator Kennedy's office, Sandberg was asked why he wanted the job. "She needs me," he replied.

Sandberg later revised his opinion. She needed him for all sorts of reasons, but he found that Jean Kennedy Smith could be very single-minded, well able to stand up to pressure and get her own way, and determined to show that she merited the position, even if it was obtained through her younger brother. Arthur Schlesinger, the historian, commented once that "Jean may well be the best politician of all the Kennedys."

After her Senate confirmation and a going-away party with three hundred guests thrown by Mayor Dinkins, Jean Kennedy Smith arrived in Dublin in July 1993 to start her new career as Ambassador to Ireland. She brought a photograph of her nomination ceremony at the White House inscribed by her brother Ted: "For Jean, who is going back in the springtime," a reference to President Kennedy's remark before leaving Ireland in 1963, "I'll be back in the springtime." It was thirty years to the day since he had made that promise.

With the Kennedy aura and her enthusiastic embrace of all things Irish, she was an instant celebrity in Ireland, and almost immediately became the second most prominent woman in public life after President Mary Robinson. She also forged a special relationship with the Irish authorities. She received permission to set up a kennel for her dogs at the Phoenix Park residence, thus avoiding a six-month quarantine. She told the Minister for Foreign Affairs, Dick Spring, that the US was unhappy about plans for an Irish soccer team to play in Libya and the game was cancelled, but later she would move mountains to smooth the way for thousands of soccer fans travelling to the United States for the 1994 World Cup. Nevertheless, her habit of arriving late or cancelling appointments gave her a reputation of slight eccentricity and her inexperience in the minutiae of Irish politics made some of her earlier official visitors shake their heads in despair.

In August 1993, after only a few weeks on the job, Jean Kennedy Smith decided to make her first visit across the border into Northern Ireland. She went to Belfast, she said, "because I didn't know as much about the North as I should have, as the briefings in Washington were cursory, not in-depth." It was not unusual for US ambassadors in Dublin to cross the border, though Northern Ireland, as part of the United Kingdom, was in the territory of the US embassy in London. During the 1980s, Republican-appointed ambassadors Margaret Heckler and Richard Moore had made several trips to Northern Ireland to see for themselves what was going on there. But the State Department grew uneasy if it appeared an ambassador was interfering. The last envoy nominated by a Democrat, William Shannon, an Irish-American newspaper man from Boston, was rapped on the knuckles after just one visit. "We drove North one weekend in 1977 and stayed with the consul in Belfast and talked with some local politicians, John Hume of the SDLP and John Taylor of the Ulster Unionist Party," his widow Elizabeth told me. "Shortly afterwards, he was told by the State Department 'You will never go to Northern Ireland again.' And he didn't."

The US embassy in London, under Ambassador Raymond Seitz, did not want someone they regarded as a loose cannon like Jean Kennedy Smith travelling North. But it was harder to say no to a Kennedy, especially one on whom the President looked with favor and who had been encouraged by him to visit Northern Ireland frequently, as Tony Lake disclosed to members of the Congressional Ad Hoc Committee on Irish Affairs.

The young US consul in Belfast, Valentino Martinez, held a reception for her at his residence at Shaw's Bridge on a scenic stretch of the river Lagan outside Belfast. There she met a West

Belfast woman, Molly McMullan, who had been brought by a guest. She told Jean Kennedy Smith about the imprisonment of her son, a member of the "Ballymurphy Seven," seven Belfast teenagers incarcerated for two years before being brought to trial on charges of acting as IRA lookouts. Next day Jean Kennedy Smith went along to see the court proceedings for herself. It was in one of the Diplock Courts, special criminal courts with no jury set up by the British government in Belfast to hear cases of terrorist-type offences. It brought her face to face with the realities of Northern Ireland. The court was heavily guarded, and she and her secretary were searched before going in.

This visit to the Diplock Court was considered to be a breach of protocol at the US embassy in London, where some diplomats believed Jean Kennedy Smith to be the visible extension of a group of influential Irish Americans with a nationalist agenda, or at least to be prone to clientitis, State Department jargon for over-identifying with a host country. Ambassador Raymond Seitz in London, a career diplomat, was popular with the British, but had shown little interest in Northern Ireland, reflecting the priorities of the President who nominated him, George Bush. She was astonished to learn that on the one visit Seitz made to Northern Ireland, he rode around in a British army helicopter, and did not meet John Hume, a key player in Northern Ireland's politics. On that occasion Seitz visited British army headquarters in Lisburn, County Antrim, where he met an army officer whom he had befriended when both were stationed in the former Rhodesia. He accepted a lift with him in an army helicopter to north Belfast, a London embassy source said. Nationalists in Northern Ireland were not pleased.

The helicopter incident was referred to obliquely when Seitz's successor as Ambassador to London, Admiral William Crowe, was being questioned by the Senate Foreign Relations Sub-Committee in Washington some months later on how he would approach his new post. "I'd like to respectfully suggest that you consider the possibility of spending some time in Northern Ireland and become politically familiar with the landscape," said Senator Joseph Biden, adding dryly, "and by visiting Ireland I don't mean a quick helicopter ride."

Jean Kennedy Smith told friends that the President had sent her to Dublin "to help find a way to bring peace to Northern Ireland," and she made many more trips North. But she was quite happy to let the US consulate in Belfast handle the troublesome question of visa applications from Gerry Adams. Coming from a family in which two brothers had been gunned down by assassins, she had no reflexive Irish-American sympathy for the IRA or its political wing. When the delegation of Niall O'Dowd, Bruce Morrison, Bill Flynn and Chuck Feeney came to the embassy during their fact-finding mission in September 1993, she told them the question was a matter for Martinez in Belfast. "It's a British problem, not my problem," she said.

Then the Joint Declaration of 15 December changed the political landscape. Suddenly there was talk of an IRA ceasefire in the not-too-distant future. Albert Reynolds began to look for new ways of drawing Sinn Féin into constitutional politics. He had been open to what the Irish Americans were saying and began to think that a visa for Adams could be an important part of a peace dividend for the republicans.

Jean Kennedy Smith and Albert Reynolds got on well, and formed an alliance which would prove crucial in the days ahead. When not travelling round the country or visiting the North the Ambassador would drop into Government Buildings. "She was always coming into the office with daily bulletins if necessary, or ringing me at home, or I would go and see her," the Taoiseach recalled.

Reynolds told her that he was in favor in principle of a visa being given to Adams. She also knew that John Hume had been trying to work out a peace plan with the Sinn Féin leader and was of the strong opinion that Adams was trying to lead the IRA down the political road. Later she would tell friends that the one person who convinced her that Adams was worth supporting was John Hume. The SDLP leader had enormous influence on the Kennedys, so much so that her friend, Irish history professor, Joe Lee, once described Jean Kennedy Smith as Hume's ambassador to Dublin, where there needed to be pressure to reinforce Hume's ideas. Jean Kennedy Smith's friendship with the SDLP leader and his wife Pat went back to a weekend she and her children spent with them in 1974. His eloquent, passionate brand of constitutional nationalism endeared him to her family and a generation of powerful Irish-American legislators, so much so that Senator Kennedy and others would nominate him for the Nobel Peace Prize in 1995 and 1996.

At the end of December 1993 Ted Kennedy and his wife Vicky came to Dublin to spend the New Year with his "valiant friend and big sister," as Rose Kennedy described Jean in her autobiography. They were driven from the airport to the Phoenix Park residence for a shower and then went with Jean for dinner to the home of author and former *Irish Press* editor Tim Pat Coogan. Kennedy had grave doubts about the visa idea, according to Coogan's account of the conversation in his book *The Troubles*. The author argued over the meal that the visa would push Ireland up the American, and hence the British, agenda, and expose Adams to the vast groundswell in Irish America for a peaceful resolution of the conflict.

Reynolds recalled that Jean Kennedy Smith had by the end of December become a strong convert to the visa idea and was pressing it on her younger brother.

"She had a job with Ted to convince him, a big job," he said. "They had dinner at my apartment, himself and Vicky and the young Congressman, Patrick, he went out on the town with my kids, and we had a real family get-together up in the apartment in Ballsbridge. And we discussed the whole business that night." The Senator had doubts, he recalled, but he was coming round. "I think Jean had a big influence. I mean without her I don't think he would have swung behind it."

Senator Kennedy confirmed later how important his older sister's advice had been. He had been informed by John Hume of the nature of the contacts the SDLP leader had been having in the summer with the Sinn Féin leader, he told the *Boston Globe*. "But what impressed me was Jean's observation of the strong commitment that Adams had to ending violence."

"It all started with Jean," the Kennedy family friend, Bill Barry, told me. "She hates terrorism and terrorists. She said many times, though not of Adams, these are the kind of people who killed my brothers. She was the key. If she had said no to the visa application—forget it!"

To Reynolds the support of the Kennedy family for the visa idea could be a major political asset. The Taoiseach could not publicly advocate that Washington should give Adams a visa because of the unfavorable impression this would make with unionists and the British government. Jean Kennedy Smith was constrained as an Ambassador in what she could say. Somebody like the Senator could lobby openly where it counted when Adams applied once more to visit the United States.

By the time he left Ireland to return home, the Senator was familiar with the argument that it was important for Adams to be heard and that he was genuinely trying to bring an end to the IRA campaign. If he were to get involved in a campaign for a visa for Adams the whole question would be on a different plane. Clinton might reject a request from a city mayor on a controversial Irish issue but was less likely to do so from Kennedy, a key legislative ally, a long-time opponent of the IRA and a member of the family he admired and relaxed with; Clinton had sailed one day with the Kennedys off the Massachusetts coast during his first summer holiday as President.

As the New Year came in, Flynn and O'Dowd decided to force the pace. Flynn arranged for the National Committee on American Foreign Policy to set 1 February 1994 as the date for a one-day peace conference in New York's Waldorf Astoria Hotel, and to invite all five Northern Ireland party leaders: Jim Molyneaux of the Ulster Unionist Party, Ian Paisley of the Democratic Unionist Party, John Hume of the SDLP, John Alderdice of the Alliance Party and Gerry Adams of Sinn Féin. The news was splashed on the cover of the *Irish Voice* on 5 January.

Publicly John Hume was non-committal. He would consider his invitation when he received it, he said. Jean Kennedy Smith was put out, friends said. She thought they were being bounced into a fight on the issue too quickly and that they should have waited until Sinn Féin had given its response to the Joint Declaration. She made her views known. O'Dowd got a phone call from someone who quoted her as saying that "John Hume thinks it's a dreadful idea and so do I." Reynolds recalled that the Ambassador's reaction at the time was that "she thought they were pushing her too fast." Bill Flynn remarked to a friend that no one had accused him of interfering when he forked out a large donation for the conflict resolution conference in Derry.

However the key supporters of the peace process had to make up their mind quickly what to do. Jean Kennedy Smith went to consult Reynolds in his office. "She asked me about it," he said. "I told her, 'Why not?' "

The pizza parlor trio waited anxiously for the Senator's reaction. "If Kennedy didn't move on the issue, it wouldn't happen. We knew that now," O'Dowd said. On the other hand, Kennedy did not go into a fight without going all out to win.

The key player on the Irish side was, as always, John Hume. The SDLP leader was not easily rushed into something over which he had no control. Reynolds said he asked Jean Kennedy Smith to get Hume to support the visa for Adams. "She told me that she was having problems to get John to go down the road with them. Unless we were all united on this, she didn't see it working," he said.

By supporting a visa for Adams, Hume would be opening the American door to a rival nationalist with enormous media appeal.

The Sinn Féin leader wanted to travel to the New York conference to strengthen his argument with the IRA that the republican movement would make great gains from the US by ending their campaign. The argument was irresistible to Hume but for the Derry man it was a moment of truth. Adams would gain in political stature at his expense. But he had no choice. Hume came to the same conclusion, that it should be done.

"He did drop his opposition," Reynolds said, referring to Hume, "But not until the very last minute."

The SDLP politician said he supported the visa idea from the beginning. "I argued very strongly that it was very necessary for Adams to go to America," he told me. "It was essential that he would go to them and explain the whole background and approach to a ceasefire. That's what it was about. That it was a genuine peace movement. I knew it was central because Adams told me it was central in our dialogue." He acknowledged that "I would have preferred the reaction to the Joint Declaration first, everybody would, but I realized that he needed to persuade people. If he didn't get the visa it would have been a very serious setback."

Early in January former Speaker Thomas "Tip" O'Neill died, and at the funeral in Boston John Hume had a critical conversation with Ted Kennedy.

"Are you going for the visa or not?" asked Kennedy, Hume told me later.

"Yes," he replied.

"Right, that's it," said the Senator.

10

Revolt in an American Embassy

"This is just a case of Lilliputians firing their arrows at the emissary of Gulliver."
John Treacy

US Ambassador Jean Kennedy Smith worried that Gerry Adams would arrive at the US embassy in Dublin with a noisy entourage and stage a political demonstration when he applied for a visa to attend the foreign policy conference in New York. But Sinn Féin had no intention of embarrassing the woman they knew as "Spéir-bhean." Adams arrived at the embassy on his own on the morning of Friday 14 January 1994, with no media presence, and was directed by a Marine guard to the consular office in Hume House, across the road from the embassy proper. There, at the information window, the consular official, an Irish national, pointed out the "drop box" for non-immigrant visa applications. The Sinn Féin leader posted an envelope containing his passport and visa application, and left without encountering any of the embassy diplomats.

Jean Kennedy Smith had actually hoped that Adams would apply at the American consulate in Belfast, where he lived. She had been taken aback to be told over lunch that he was coming her way by the chairman of Dublin's Abbey Theatre, film producer Noel Pearson. Pearson, a strong supporter of the peace process, had been given this intelligence by O'Dowd in New York. The idea, yet again, could be traced back to the Irish diplomat Brendan Scannell, now based in Dublin, who suggested that the recommendation made by the Ambassador in the jurisdiction where Adams applied would be critical in deciding which way it would go. There was not the remotest chance that Ambassador Raymond Seitz in London would advocate that Adams should be allowed into the United States. Though his residence was within the jurisdiction of the United Kingdom, Adams could apply in Dublin because that was where his party had its official headquarters.

Immediately after Adams's envelope was opened later that morning, Jean Kennedy Smith prepared a cable recommending to the State Department that it should waive the visa ban on Adams on the grounds that the United States could play a positive role in breaking the deadlock in Northern Ireland by allowing him to attend the New York conference.

Her decision brought to a head a simmering rebellion among some of the diplomatic staff, and touched off the most serious internal crisis ever in an embassy which always had a rather uneasy relationship with its host city.

Because of the British–American special relationship, under which the State Department in Washington regarded Northern Ireland as England's problem, the American embassy in Dublin was traditionally considered by Irish governments to be "more under the influence of London than independent," as Albert Reynolds put it. The perception was that trying to change that would be to engage in "a battle that you couldn't win, and you certainly couldn't win it against national security interests in Washington," he said.

Ireland's neutrality also meant that American diplomats sometimes considered themselves in less than friendly territory when they were posted to Dublin. There were still memories in the Irish capital of attempts by the US minister in Ireland, David Grey, to push the country into war on the side of the allies in the 1940–45 period. There was considerable US resentment of Irish neutrality at a time when thousands of Americans were dying in the struggle against Nazi Germany. Grey and the Taoiseach Eamon de Valera became bitter foes, and the American diplomat highlighted claims that the German and Japanese embassies in Dublin were being used as centers of espionage. It reached the point where de Valera asked, unsuccessfully, for Grey's recall.

In postwar Ireland, American diplomats made it a priority to refute any public expressions of disapproval of US foreign policy, and to dampen public and media criticism of US support for right-wing governments in central and southern America from where Catholic priests and nuns from Ireland regularly reported human rights abuses.

"We felt we were so close to the United States we could voice such opinions as differences within the family, but these people thought we were reds under the bed," said an Irish official.

Many American career officers also resented being posted to a backwater like Ireland. As an unhappy diplomat put it in a leaked letter in 1981 Ireland was "pretty small potatoes compared to other countries of Europe" and no great issues burned up the wires between Dublin and Washington. The embassy in Ireland had also been used as a political booby prize. In October 1985 Ronald Reagan made Margaret Heckler Ambassador to Ireland when he wanted to move her from Secretary of Health and Human Services after a highly publicized divorce. His successor, George Bush, also regarded Ireland as small potatoes. Near the end of his term in office, he nominated an 82-year-old Republican crony, William FitzGerald, as Ambassador. At his Senate confirmation hearing, FitzGerald mixed up unionists and nationalists and insisted on giving the senators the result of a referendum in Ireland which had not then taken place. For some Irish Americans this was the last straw. Calling for the withdrawal of his nomination, the *Irish Voice* complained that Bush had insulted not just Irish Americans but all Americans. The *Irish Echo* said the appointment reinforced the view that the administration paid little heed to the problems of Ireland or the concerns of Irish Americans.

The public affairs officer of the American embassy in Dublin, John Treacy, dismissed the complaints in a revealing retort to *The New York Times.* "No blow is too low," he said. "No shot is too cheap. This is just a case of Lilliputians firing their arrows at the emissary of Gulliver."

But the constant turnover of do-nothing elderly appointees sent to Ireland as political reward had left its legacy. The embassy which Jean Kennedy Smith took over in the summer of 1993 was "dead in the water" according to Albert Reynolds, and "basically non-productive with very low output" in the words of her deputy Dennis Sandberg.

Jean Kennedy Smith shook the place up a bit. Sandberg told *The Washington Post* that she started out by saying the President had sent her to find a way to bring peace to Northern Ireland. "All these suits looked around, like, *what*?" he said. "I had them stumbling into my office later saying, 'She can't be serious.' It was a big shock for them, people who'd spent their days playing computer games and having four-hour martini lunches."

According to a still-classified report drawn up by the inspector general of the US State Department on the conduct of the embassy under Jean Kennedy Smith, several officers reported that she and Sandberg inherited a quiet post and that the pace "quickened significantly after their arrival." But the direction they were taking the embassy was unpalatable to some of the career diplomats, it said. There was open friction between the two at the top and the staff members at the next level. The highly critical report found that a cause of friction was the conclusion drawn by some employees that the embassy under Ambassador Smith "was more attuned to Irish rather than US interests."

"The ambassador wished to avoid confrontation with the Government of Ireland and the Irish, whether with regard to policy difference or with visa issuance," said the report, which noted that she also expressed an appreciation for Irish culture, cultural exchanges and US business promotion. The report found that differences between the Irish-American Ambassador and a small number of senior diplomats became so acute that her relationship with one official could only be described as "dysfunctional."

A major controversy concerned the determination by the Ambassador and Sandberg to minimize short-term visas as an irritant in US–Irish relations.

This had become a problem because the Republic was the only west European country, other than Portugal, not in the US visa waiver program which allowed people to take business or tourist trips to the United States without a visa. Young, unemployed Irish applicants were likely to be refused permission to travel to the United States. A US law classified all visa applicants as potential immigrants, unless the consular official was satisfied otherwise. It also stipulated that unless the visa refusal rate was lower than two percent for two consecutive years, then the country did not qualify for the visa waiver program. The rate of applicants being turned down at the Dublin embassy was more than double that, and there were regular complaints of harsh decisions by consular officers which kept it up around five percent.

Jean Kennedy Smith told government ministers in Dublin that she was determined to bring Ireland under the visa waiver program, and undertook to have all visa refusals reviewed and applicants given the benefit of the doubt. The rate of refusals dropped dramatically and, with the help of revised legislation in Congress, Ireland eventually qualified for the program. This made her very popular in Ireland and brought about an improvement in US–Irish relations, but the introduction of the new policy caused severe strain within the embassy where a number of officials believed that US law was being compromised.

Dennis Sandberg pointed out to State Department inspectors "that there were those of the embassy staff who did not 'get on board' with the new Clinton policies, which led to problems."

One of those who did not "get on board" was John Treacy, the defender of FitzGerald's appointment, who was well known to Dublin newspaper editors for his frequent and lengthy letters pointing out what he saw as unfair or incorrect criticisms of the United States. Like Tonkin, he had come from the US embassy in Guatemala. His relationship with Jean Kennedy Smith was already poor, according to the report, by the time she recommended to the State Department that it grant a visa to Gerry Adams, something with which he strongly disagreed.

For Treacy and Jim Callahan, head of the consular section, it was a visa too far. They expressed vehement opposition to what she was doing. They recommended strongly to the Ambassador that she should not support Adams's request to enter the United States because of his long-standing ineligibility "due to his association with IRA terrorist activities." When she made it clear that she would, they requested that their dissenting views be represented in the Ambassador's cable. She responded by inserting in her cable a single line saying there was dissent within the embassy.

This was considered inadequate by the dissenters. Treacy, Callahan and two other embassy officials drafted dissent cable "Dublin 0190" to express their opposition in greater detail and with maximum force. Under State Department rules dating back to the Vietnam era, diplomats could use a dissent channel to present to senior officials in Washington dissenting views on substantive foreign policy issues. The inspector general's report found that, "The officers stated that they were assured by the ambassador and DCM [deputy chief of mission] that their views would be fairly reported to the Department. The officers involved in sending the cable were not satisfied with the cursory statement in the ambassador's cable: 'There is, however, dissent within my country team over this issue.' As a result they joined together in drafting and sending the dissent channel cable. The cable stated in relevant part that the dissenters opposed granting the visa until Adams and Sinn Féin renounced violence as a political tool, a position that frequently had been espoused by the Department until that time."

In arguing that Adams should not be recommended for a visa until he and Sinn Féin renounced violence, the embassy's publicity and consular officers and their colleagues were at one with the most senior officials in the State Department, who took the view that Adams should be kept out of the United States, but that if not, the issue of a visa to him could, and should, be used to extract concessions from Sinn Féin. They were also at one with the British government. For over twenty years London and Washington had adamantly insisted on never making what would look like a concession to terrorism. The action of the rebel diplomats was consequently welcomed in the State Department in Washington. Indeed Treacy and his colleagues received an acknowledgment from a top official of their "thoughtful dissent message [which] raises a timely and sensitive issue which we need to consider carefully."

Treacy and Callahan did not however show the contents of the dissent cable to the Ambassador before sending it; nor did Sandberg see it as he had just gone for two weeks to the United States. The relevant dissent regulation, 11 FAM 243.3, encouraged its users "to discuss issues with supervisors and show messages to them," but it required no clearance. It was transmitted that same Friday, after Jean Kennedy Smith left the embassy late in the morning. Treacy said later he acted quickly because he feared a decision on Adams would be taken that weekend, and he did not show it to the Ambassador because she did not return to the embassy on the day in question.

However, the Ambassador and her subordinate were now at daggers drawn. When Jean Kennedy Smith returned to the embassy the following Monday the atmosphere in the mission was evidently extremely unpleasant. The two protagonists confronted each other. "The ambassador reportedly told Treacy she considered the dissent cable an unhelpful attempt to undercut her with the Department," the report said. "She said that she could not run an embassy if her employees were to contradict her policy decisions and she made it clear that she expected her officers to support her decisions."

The State Department inspector general conducted a formal investigation into the incident because Treacy and Callahan subsequently complained that they were forced to leave the embassy because of retaliatory measures taken against them by the Ambassador, such as being excluded from embassy functions and being given poor performance ratings. The inspector general upheld the complaint and two years later Jean Kennedy Smith was formally reprimanded by the Secretary of State, Warren Christopher.

The Kennedy sister denied that she had retaliated against the two officials and protested when the report came out that the other two who dissented remained at the embassy and received promotion. Privately she told friends that the real problem in the embassy was that there was resentment against her "because I am a woman and a Kennedy."

11

Visa War One

"We really thought that a country which was concerned about terrorism would not set aside principles to which it was wedded for Irish Americans."
British government source

Though it was not known at the time, British Prime Minister John Major was well aware that Albert Reynolds was privately in favor of Gerry Adams getting an American visa to travel to New York and that Reynolds himself was lobbying for it to be granted.

This was because the Taoiseach rang No. 10 Downing Street and told him. "I told Major then I was going to support the visa, oh yes, I did!" Reynolds said, laughing at his own audacity. "He didn't like it and he said, 'I'm going to oppose it with all I have.' I says, 'Fine John, that's OK.' We did our business up on the table like. I just told him straight up, this is where we're coming from, you know."

Only a few weeks earlier Reynolds had been against letting the Sinn Féin leader gain such a political advance. He changed his mind, he said, because he thought it would help lead to peace in light of the Joint Declaration.

"We were trying to put together an unarmed strategy to replace the violence, and we had to demonstrate that it was going to be successful as against twenty-five years of violence, which was futile and hadn't made any progress," he said. "Consequently it was necessary to demonstrate this, so that Adams could make his case to the IRA. And there was a series of initiatives. The visa was one. The abolition of Section 31 [the ban on Sinn Féin interviews on Irish radio and television] was another."

The Taoiseach also lobbied President Clinton. "I went on direct to the White House after he applied for the visa," he said. "Jean

Kennedy Smith gave me the names and the telephone numbers of Nancy Soderberg, Tony Lake and the President. I felt that this was one issue that would make a huge difference in persuading them [the IRA] away from violence and into peace. We did the business with Nancy first. Jean was pushing it hard through her own connections, there's no question about that. Nancy didn't think it would run. So we kept at it."

Reynolds eventually got the President on the line and pressed the case for letting Adams into the United States. "I told him the Downing Street Declaration was a big leap forward," he said. "He was very reluctant for a while and we talked it through and I said, 'Look, you can give him a short-term visa.' And he talked about fundraising and I said, 'No fundraising, short-term visa, send him home with a message, that you want him to join the peace train and leave violence behind and that if he doesn't he'll never get another one.' "

The fight over the visa began in Washington within twenty-four hours of Jean Kennedy Smith's recommendation arriving in the US State Department headquarters at Foggy Bottom in Washington, on 14 January. Next day, a Saturday, her brother, Senator Edward Kennedy, sent a letter to the President, signed by himself and three Democratic Senate colleagues, John Kerry, Chris Dodd and Daniel Patrick Moynihan. They said they supported the visa application on the grounds that it would strengthen Adams in his dialogue with IRA militants. Adams had a critical role to play in advancing the all-important peace process in Northern Ireland. "While no one can be certain that a visa for Mr. Adams will result in the IRA's accepting the conditions established by Ireland and Great Britain for participation in the peace process," they argued, "the United States cannot afford to ignore this possibility and miss this rare opportunity for our country to contribute to peace in Northern Ireland." It was important for the United States to facilitate the emerging dialogue as an alternative to violence.

Such a letter could not easily be ignored. The 61-year-old Senator, the fourth-longest serving member of the upper chamber, was one of the most influential legislators on Capitol Hill. He had proved himself a powerful ally and friend of the Democratic President in his first troubled year in the White House. He was pushing as hard as he could to get the health care reforms the President sought. If Clinton was going to rely on anyone for advice on Ireland it would most likely be Kennedy, and the Massachusetts Senator was providing the President with political cover to keep a controversial Irish promise. And Kennedy was not alone. Senator

Chris Dodd was working just as hard to rally support for the visa. His officials were constantly on the telephone, ringing the State Department and the White House. Irish diplomats in Washington and New York were quietly lobbying for it. Behind the scenes, Jean Kennedy Smith was pushing it strongly from Dublin. John Hume had given his blessing. Other leading Congress members began joining the crusade. Thirty-six more eventually signed the Senator's letter, including two crucial Clinton allies on Capitol Hill, Senate majority leader George Mitchell and the chairman of the Senate Foreign Relations Committee, Clairborne Pell.

There were other factors which helped to create a climate in Washington which favored Adams. When British diplomats argued on Capitol Hill that it was in no one's interest to take the pressure off Sinn Féin, they found Congress members citing against them the British government's own secret contacts with the Irish party, exposed a few weeks previously in the media. Opinion in Washington against anyone tainted with terrorism was also changing. The Palestinian leader Yassir Arafat had shaken hands with Israeli Prime Minister Yitzhak Rabin on the White House lawn the previous autumn, and Clinton had met Syrian President Assad, whose regime the State Department accused of promoting terrorism. *The New York Times*, once a staunch ally of the British, deserted them on this issue. In an editorial it urged Clinton to honor the wider principles of free speech and allow Adams into the US, noting that "a broad spectrum of Irish Americans now see an opportunity for engaging Mr. Adams in serious discussion of joining a promising peace initiative." This was important in shaping public attitudes. The newspaper also carried a full page advertisement from the National Committee on American Foreign Policy, at a cost of some $25,000, claiming that "forty-four million Irish Americans" were convinced it was time for peace. It was signed by the chairmen or CEOs of eighty-five leading American corporations, and over one hundred other prominent Irish Americans.

The alarm bells began ringing in the British embassy in Washington. For Ambassador Sir Robin Renwick, a visa for Adams would be a diplomatic catastrophe unless they could get the Americans to persuade Adams to go further than he had ever done before and renounce violence. In British eyes the Sinn Féin leader stood to gain unprecedented publicity and enhanced stature in a country where many people still had romantic notions about the conflict in Northern Ireland and had not directly experienced the terrorism of the IRA. Such an act would strain relations between the two countries intolerably. It would reflect badly on the largest and best-connected embassy in Washington if it could not rally its friends in the establishment to nip this idea in the bud.

As always on Irish issues, the British had only one prominent ally in Congress, House Speaker Tom Foley. They had others of course, less concerned about Ireland as such, but worried about the wisdom of offending America's staunchest ally over a matter that might have emotional appeal but was not a vital American national interest. On this issue, however, those with reservations chose not to defy publicly the powerful Irish-American lobby.

Foley was appalled at the idea of allowing the Sinn Féin leader into the country while the IRA campaign continued. He met Jean Kennedy Smith, when she was on a brief visit to Washington, at a reception on the eighth floor of the State Department building. "She started kinda sounding me out on it," he said. "I had heard from Ted that she favored it. As politely as I could, I told her I thought it was a dreadful idea. Until there was something concrete and meaningful in terms of the IRA's commitment to stop violence it would be a pretty bad idea. He would be given a hero's welcome in the United States by all the people who, as far as I am concerned, have been on the wrong side of this. This would only reinforce them and undo the work which had been done by a lot of people who for years have worked to de-legitimize this particular aspect of it. She listened, but obviously she was trying to get me to agree it might be worth doing."

Washington Post columnist Mary McGrory, who had been covering the White House since President Kennedy's time and who shared Foley's views on the visa issue, recalled Foley raising his voice on this occasion, an astonishing thing for a member of Congress addressing an Ambassador. "It was hard to figure out the Speaker," she told me. "He had the whole business of the House to worry about but the only thing I ever saw him get passionate about was Ireland." In her column that week she detailed another revealing incident about Foley, describing how "at a private dinner party he amazed guests by shouting at someone who tried to defend Kennedy's curious move for playing parlor games with people's lives." This wasn't the only case of frayed tempers at Washington dinner tables over Adams. The President's adviser, George Stephanopoulos, told me how sometime later British actor Hugh Grant rudely interrupted a speech he was giving at a private dinner, about a different subject, to shout something about the White House encouraging terrorists. Grant, who was in the news at the time for consorting with a prostitute in Hollywood, had just come from a reception in the British embassy.

The gathering storm went virtually unreported in the mainstream American media. To most Washington reporters, Gerry Adams was an "ethnic" Irish story best left to the London bureaus. They did not expect that the Sinn Féin leader would ever be allowed to come to the United States in any event. When I turned up at Speaker Foley's daily news briefing four days before President Clinton was to make his decision, and asked for his opinion on Kennedy's lobbying campaign, the Congressional correspondents didn't know what I was talking about.

That day as it turned out Foley had intervened personally with the White House, advising the President not to go down a "slippery slope" by granting the visa. He had not been consulted by the President's advisers, though as he conceded, "There was no reason to involve me because I was clearly against it, I was on the other side of the river and I wasn't going to help build rafts." It was a big thing for the Speaker to use up political capital in this way. In reply to my question, he said, "I disagree that the visa ban on Gerry Adams should be lifted until such time as Sinn Féin accepts the notion of abandoning violence, the support of violence, as a manner of resolving problems in Ireland."

The British government wanted the White House to get a renunciation of violence from the Sinn Féin leader as a condition for even considering a visa. Adams and O'Dowd, who now sometimes spoke directly to each other on the telephone, discussed the possibility that the British might lay a trap by trying to get the Americans to force him to go so far in denouncing violence that there would be a split between Sinn Féin and the IRA, and then deny him the visa in any event. Adams issued a statement in Belfast on 24 January to head off White House pressure for a denunciation of violence. He said Sinn Féin sought an end to all armed actions, and had been "actively engaged in initiating and developing unarmed strategies for struggle." He also promised that his public utterances in New York would be confined to the peace process.

In the office of the National Security Council, Tony Lake and Nancy Soderberg prepared to present the arguments to the President. Lake was open-minded on the question and Soderberg was coming round, a White House official told me later. John Hume had been in touch with Soderberg and given the idea his imprimatur, something which she knew the Catholic leader would not do lightly.

"John Hume played an extraordinarily important role in sensitizing me that things on the ground were changing, and he had my antenna raised," she said. But she had to overcome personal misgivings.

"I just never had any brief for the IRA or what it did," she said. "I have a personal revulsion for any kind of terrorism, blowing up people. There's no excuse for it. Anyone who is involved in that, I have no sympathy for. And therefore I wasn't particularly interested in reaching out to anyone. Initially I thought we could open up our channels of communication. We still had a ban on communications. That was our first idea—we can't possibly let him in because he's a terrorist but maybe we should open up a dialogue with him. We needed to reach out somehow. It was a question of how. And ultimately it came down to the visa as the only way to do it."

But outside the White House the big guns of Clinton's own administration were turned against them. Secretary of State Warren Christopher was against a visa, and he was backed by the American Ambassador to London, Raymond Seitz, by four diplomats in the Dublin embassy who had defied their Ambassador and by practically everyone else in the State Department. The ultra-careful Christopher would have to pick up the pieces if the special relationship was wrecked by allowing Britain's most hated supporter of terrorism into the United States. Attorney General Janet Reno, the tough Florida judge whose department was responsible for administering the immigration laws, was very strongly against giving any concessions to the representative of a banned guerrilla group. Her argument referred to Section 212 of the Immigration and Nationality Act prohibiting the issuance of a visa to any alien who had engaged in terrorist activity, though the Act also gave her the authority to waive the prohibition. The head of the FBI, Louis Freeh, who had an Irish-American wife, Marlyn, and a son called Conor, was also strongly against it, though he had been a guest at dinners in the Irish embassy residence and had heard both sides of the case. Freeh's agents had spent more than a quarter of a century combating IRA fundraising and gunrunning. Even within the National Security Council staff there was dissension. Jenonne Walker, who oversaw European affairs and later became US Ambassador to Prague, was not happy about giving Adams a visa, according to a National Security Council insider, and the British had been informed that National Security Council officials responsible for intelligence issues were not enthusiastic. The British Prime Minister was also weighing in from London. John Major's foreign policy adviser, Roderic Lyne, telephoned Tony Lake a number of times to say how upset John Major would be if the President authorized a visa.

The White House officials had to respond to the demands that Adams at least be asked to renounce violence. On Wednesday 26 January, with the clock now ticking away—the decision had to be made in time to let Adams get to New York by 1 February—they decided to have Adams call into the US embassy in Dublin to respond to two specific questions on his attitude to violence and the political process. The interview was to be conducted in the embassy on 27 January by Jim Callahan, who had signed the cable dissenting from his Ambassador's support for a visa. The request was relayed by Soderberg to Trina Vargo in Senator Kennedy's office. She passed it on to Niall O'Dowd in New York who got in touch with Adams in Belfast. The Sinn Féin President, who carried the bullet scars on his neck, shoulder and arm of an attempted assassination in 1984 by members of the Ulster Defence Association, said he could not travel at short notice on the basis of a telephone call on an open line, and he would need more time to arrange security for the hundred-mile road journey to Dublin.

This message went back to the White House on the same back-channel and it was agreed Adams would call instead on Friday morning at the American consulate in Queen Street, Belfast, located at the bottom of the nationalist Falls Road not far from Adams's home. The US consul in Belfast, Val Martinez, was instructed to conduct the interview.

As Martinez read his papers that morning before the meeting he was surprised to see an account in *The Irish Times* of the questions he was to ask. It quoted a White House spokesman as saying: "After consulting with the Irish and British Governments, we have instructed our embassy . . . to determine whether Mr. Adams will publicly renounce violence and support the Joint Declaration. Our decision on whether to provide him with a visa will depend on his response." It looked to Martinez as if the White House was heading towards a refusal. Why else put Adams in a box by making the questions public?

The wording of the questions had arisen from a tense dialogue between the White House and the State Department. "There was a genuine disbelief in the State Department that we would actually be seriously considering giving Adams a visa," explained Nancy Soderberg. "Finally the State Department started to notice that we were serious about this, and in an effort to flesh out the policy we talked among ourselves about what types of thing would be helpful to know Adams's views on in making this decision."

Martinez met Adams in his office at 9 a.m. and read him the questions from the cable. He asked the Sinn Féin President if he would publicly renounce violence and support the Joint Declaration. He knew what the answers would likely be. Martinez had a good appreciation of Sinn Féin politics and its precise lexicon. He also knew the political scene in Belfast exceptionally well. A devout Catholic, he went to Mass on Sundays in Clonard Monastery in Ardoyne in north Belfast, where Adams was also a member of the congregation. He regularly went walking along the Catholic Falls Road and the Protestant Shankill Road, talking to people and making contacts. He once joked to the Catholic MP for West Belfast, Joe Hendron, that he was the only person who could stroll along the Shankill with rosary beads in his pocket and not feel nervous.

Martinez and Adams discussed the questions for an hour and a half, at the end of which the Belfast man told the US consul he could not say what the administration wanted him to say. Martinez was so convinced that the visa application would be refused, he gave Adams back his passport and as the Belfast man left, presented him with a copy of the State Department cable on which the questions were printed as a souvenir. In the street outside, the Sinn Féin leader was detained and questioned briefly by RUC officers. It was not a good omen. Convinced he had lost the battle, Adams began drafting a statement when he got back to his office thanking those Irish Americans who had backed him.

But his supporters in the United States had spotted that while the White House had said that the visa depended on Adams's responses, it did not specify what those responses should be. Vargo rang O'Dowd and told him to get Adams to put out a statement of what he had told Martinez so that the White House would at least have two "balancing" accounts of the meeting, not simply the one from the US consul. O'Dowd had a frustrating time trying to get through to Adams in Belfast. When he did, the *Irish Voice* publisher told him not to give up. He impressed upon the Sinn Féin leader the importance of getting out his version of the conversation, and "ran by him" several critical comments on violence to see what he could live with. "The State Department is not the President," insisted O'Dowd. "Wait until Clinton makes his judgment call."

The statement Adams eventually produced came as close as possible to meeting the White House needs. "My sole purpose in coming to the United States is to advance the cause of peace and move the process forward," he said. "I want to see an end to all violence and an end to this conflict. I don't advocate violence. It is my personal and political priority to see an end to the IRA and an end to all other organizations involved in armed actions. I am willing to seek to persuade the IRA to make definitive decisions on the conduct of its campaign." As for the Joint Declaration, it was a "first step" and he was "anxious to be persuaded" that it could provide the basis for peace. He ended by saying he was prepared to go the extra mile to bridge the gap between what was required and what was on offer.

Adams faxed this statement to the *Irish Voice* office. O'Dowd sent it on to Vargo on Capitol Hill who in turn transmitted it to Soderberg in the White House. Vargo also sent word back to Adams that he should make the statement public to increase pressure on the White House. Sinn Féin promptly put it out on a press release.

"The truth is that when those questions were posed to him, we never assumed that he was going to give definitive answers to them but we thought they would be instructive in defining and helping us work within our own government to get the decision," Soderberg told me. "I think the State Department viewed it as two preconditions he had to meet before he'd get the visa. And they took it a little further than we had intended it. And so Val Martinez asked him these questions and sent back answers that were helpful but not definitive. We took them as helpful. They took them as him failing the test. Our bureaucracy wanted to immediately assume he had flunked the test and wouldn't give it to him, so we had to walk it back a little bit."

The State Department officials took a more jaundiced view. "The National Security Council wanted cover," said one official. "Posing the questions was clearly a mistake by them which made it more difficult to grant the visa."

It was now approaching time for the President to make a decision. Two of his most senior officials in the National Security Council, Tony Lake and Nancy Soderberg, recommended that Adams should be given the visa to allow him to attend the New York peace conference. They had the support of Jane Holl, the European affairs official in the National Security Council who had come a long way since her unfortunate experience with the word "PIRA." They said they felt that a unique opportunity had arisen to allow the President to hasten peace in Northern Ireland. Backing them were the US ambassadors in Dublin and the Vatican—Ray Flynn had been confirmed, had taken up his post and he now weighed in with his support—and the Vice President, Al Gore. Gore, who had an Irish grandmother called Margie Denny, was an admirer of John Hume, who was later told by a very senior White House insider of a conversation between the Vice President and British Foreign Secretary Douglas Hurd, who arrived at the White House with a bundle of documents to argue against concessions to Adams. Gore asked Hurd from whom he took his advice on Northern Ireland. "The Northern Ireland Office," Hurd replied. "Well, we have taken advice from John Hume and he has not misled us in twenty years," responded Gore. George Stephanopoulos was also on their side. He had not forgotten how the British Tories had tried to damage Clinton in the 1992 election, and an anonymous quotation from a White House official after the visa was issued was later attributed widely to him: "It obviously ticks off the Brits but equally obviously that is acceptable to a lot of us."

The political counsellor at the British embassy, Peter Westmacott, sensed that the dynamic of the case was turning against them. A former press officer to Prince Charles, Westmacott spent a lot of his time in the final hours before the decision talking on the telephone to Soderberg and arguing the British case that it was too early to give Adams any concessions as he had not renounced violence or endorsed the Joint Declaration. Westmacott was a highly rated professional whose own family had been touched by the Troubles: his cousin, British army SAS officer, Herbert Westmacott, was killed in 1980 by an IRA unit in Belfast. One of the IRA men was Joe Doherty, who became a celebrity among Irish Americans in his losing battle against deportation from New York to Belfast in 1992.

Nevertheless, there was a strong sense among the British that it would be unconscionable to give a visa to someone associated with terrorism, who only three months before had carried the coffin of the Shankill Road bomber. "It was wrong in principle, insulting to people in Britain, and unhelpful," a British government source told me. "We had worked our butts off to get the Joint Agreement. We had gone down the path of saying the British government was neutral on the issue of the Union, and they were going to give this guy everything he wanted in exchange for nothing. We really thought that a country which was concerned about terrorism would not set aside principles to which it was wedded for Irish Americans."

They also believed that it could be a disastrous decision for Clinton. The first year of his presidency had been plagued by controversies over Supreme Court appointments, gays in the military, the sacking of the White House travel staff, the Whitewater affair and the suicide of White House counsel Vincent Foster. Relations with Britain were deteriorating over Bosnia. The President didn't need another controversy, much less a crisis with the United States' oldest and most trusted ally.

Jonathan Powell, a high-ranking diplomat at the British embassy, was convinced up to the end that they would prevail. On the day before the decision was expected, he struck a wager with Vargo. "I bet you a lunch Adams gets turned down," said Powell, who later became chief of staff to British Labor Party leader Tony Blair. "Sure," replied Vargo, though not without some misgivings.

12

Crossing the Rubicon

"Does this mean I have to apologize every time an Irishman gets into a fight with an Englishman in a pub?"
Gerry Adams

O'Dowd was taking a shower in his tenth-floor Manhattan apartment at 7 o'clock in the evening when his telephone rang. Grabbing a towel he picked up the receiver. It was Trina Vargo in Washington sounding unusually agitated.

"They are leaning in favor, but something has come up," he later recalled the Kennedy aide saying. "Put the phone down immediately. The White House wants to make contact with you."

As soon as he replaced the receiver, the telephone rang again. It was Nancy Soderberg from the White House. They had never spoken before. She introduced herself briskly and told him: "We brought the Adams issue to the President. He feels good about it."

That afternoon, Saturday 29 January 1994, three days before the New York conference to which Gerry Adams and other Northern Ireland political leaders had been invited, President Clinton had called a meeting in the Oval Office to discuss Adams's request for a visa. Nancy Soderberg, Tony Lake and George Stephanopoulos came in and stood facing the President across the desk. Clinton had just arrived back from a lengthy lunch with German Chancellor Helmut Kohl in an Italian restaurant in Georgetown, where he had been working hard at a new special relationship with Germany. He had already received a memo from the National Security Council recommending the visa be granted.

"We looked at it as a win–win decision," recalled Soderberg. "If we were to give him a visa and it did help deliver a ceasefire, that's obviously a plus for getting involved. If we gave him a visa and he didn't deliver on the ceasefire, it would help expose him as a fraud, as someone who's not seriously working for peace. It would help us push back Irish America which was funding this movement and organization in a way that would, I think, also advance the peace process. Ultimately we didn't see the down side. The down side at the time was, well it makes us look not serious on terrorism, but no one really said that this individual was a threat to America in any way." Adams had also gone down the road towards peace by saying he did not advocate violence and that he regarded the Joint Declaration of the British and Irish governments in December as a stepping stone to a ceasefire.

There was also the all-important domestic consideration. Senator Kennedy and other powerful politicians and trade union leaders in Irish America had gone all out for a visa, arguing that it would help the peace process. They were inundating the White House with telephone calls. Senate majority leader George Mitchell had spoken to the President. Tom Donahue, deputy head of the country's biggest trade union organization, the AFL-CIO, had gone to see Sandy Berger, Lake's deputy, to press the case. Other labor leaders with Irish-American connections were ringing the White House. Kennedy was working the telephone from Palm Beach, Florida, where he was spending the weekend at the family compound, "the summer White House" of JFK. A refusal would produce a groundswell of ill-will from Irish America and a political setback for Kennedy. And there was the promise Clinton had made in the Sheraton Hotel in Manhattan during the New York primary.

The President and his advisers talked through the consequences of giving Adams a visa, and its effect on the alliance with the United Kingdom. "We knew we would be going against Britain but on the other hand we figured the special relationship was strong enough to weather a disagreement on Northern Ireland," said Soderberg.

The President said he agreed with their analysis. There was just one final issue to be dealt with. A wire story had come to the White House reporting that hoax bombs had been placed in British stores in the southern California city of San Diego, with a warning that there would be trouble if Adams did not get the visa. They had been claimed by the previously unheard of "South California IRA." It raised the possibility that they could be seen as bowing to the threat of terrorism if a visa was issued to Adams, and it highlighted the risk of importing Northern Ireland terrorism into the United

States, where the FBI was already on edge after the World Trade Center bombing. Some Justice officials had "freaked out" at the San Diego report, one insider said.

"We decided we would try and get Adams to denounce the bombs," said Nancy Soderberg. "I was told not to promise him the visa if he denounced them, but to get him to do that to make a decision." A renunciation by Adams of the bomb threats would move the Sinn Féin leader closer to renouncing violence, and if he refused, then the game was up for him. Clinton asked the National Security Council officials to report back to him that evening.

She now told O'Dowd on the telephone, "You need to talk to Adams about the San Diego incident." She said the President required a public disavowal by Adams of the hoax bombs in the form of a statement to the wire services and in language acceptable to the White House. O'Dowd was stunned.

"I think she wanted to find out how much influence I had with Adams and if he would respond," he reflected later. He wondered how the Sinn Féin leader would react and if the long weeks of tense and nervy negotiations could be upset by this bizarre last-minute twist. "I really believed this was crazy and wondered where the whole thing was going," he said.

O'Dowd replaced the receiver. At least the White House, by talking to him directly, had brought him closer to the source of decision-making. "I had a feeling Nancy was crossing the Rubicon. She would not talk to me before because she had to have her deniability. Every step of the way she wanted cover so that if anything went wrong, it was just Senator Kennedy's office she was dealing with," O'Dowd said. Direct contact had now been established and the White House had moved one step closer to Sinn Féin.

Soderberg said that she came to the conclusion it was "absurd" to continue keeping O'Dowd at arm's length and as this issue was going down to the wire she decided to talk directly with him. She had also concluded she could trust him. "At this point we'd had so many back-and-forths with him through Trina, and it had never leaked, he'd been very straightforward, he always said what he was going to do, and I began to realize he was someone who was dealing with us straight-up and that he wasn't trying to get himself publicity," she told me.

The telephone rang again almost immediately. This time it was Senator Kennedy, calling from Palm Beach. "I can't believe this nonsense about San Diego," he said. The Senator wanted to know how Adams would react, and asked O'Dowd "to tell Adams I personally say he can trust me" and that the visa was there for the taking if he would respond positively.

O'Dowd worked out a form of words which he thought would be acceptable and telephoned the Sinn Féin leader at home in Belfast, where it was now 2 o'clock on Sunday morning. Adams was taken aback to receive the White House request.

"Actually he was quite funny," O'Dowd recalled. "He said, 'Does this mean I have to apologize every time an Irishman gets into a fight with an Englishman in a pub?' "

The Sinn Féin leader obligingly condemned the bomb threats. "I unreservedly condemn these incidents as I do all attacks on innocent civilians everywhere. It is absurd to even associate the incident with Irish republicans," he said, taking his cue from O'Dowd. "It appears to be the work of elements who seek to sabotage efforts to rally support in the United States for the peace process in Ireland."

Now the *Irish Voice* publisher had the problem of getting the Adams statement out on the wire services as promised. Not having dealt with news agencies before, he telephoned me for advice in Washington late in the evening. I took the call at the house of Stella O'Leary and Tom Halton, a popular Irish couple who live in the Washington suburb of Chevy Chase. A small dinner party was in progress, with Irish Ambassador Dermot Gallagher one of the guests. Our hosts knew something was going on as Gallagher and I kept excusing ourselves to make and take telephone calls.

"How do I get a statement from Adams out to the wires?" O'Dowd asked me. I suggested he contact the wire services in London, as they looked after Belfast stories. The publisher went to his newspaper office a few blocks away and faxed the text of the agreed denunciation by Adams back across the Atlantic to the Belfast home of Sinn Féin press officer Richard McAuley who eventually got it out on the Associated Press. McAuley also faxed a copy to the National Security Council in the White House. Nancy Soderberg rang O'Dowd shortly afterwards to inform him she had received the statement. "She was quite taken aback. It was like—'My God! I got a fax from Sinn Féin,' " said O'Dowd.

By this time the President had gone to a dinner at the Alfalfa Club in Washington. To the consternation of those supporting the visa, Clinton was seated at the top table between Warren Christopher and Tom Foley, their two most formidable opponents. "I did raise it with him," the Speaker said. "He indicated pretty much to me their reading of it. He understood my objections." Foley concluded that the President had already made up his mind.

When Clinton climbed into the White House limousine after the dinner, he was handed Adams's statement by National Security Council official Sandy Berger.

Next morning at 9:30, the President dropped by Tony Lake's office. It was Sunday, and the White House was otherwise almost deserted. Clinton thought the statement was strong enough. He got on the phone to Warren Christopher who for the next thirty minutes argued against what the President was about to do. "Christopher made a very hard pitch not to give him the visa, as it would send a bad signal on terrorism, and would basically undermine our relationship with Britain," said Soderberg. She and Lake then explained their reasoning to the Secretary of State, and "talked through what we'd got in the statement the night before." They also spoke on the telephone with Janet Reno who was extremely unhappy to hear the news.

At about 10:30 a.m., the President said, "Let's do it." He issued an order to grant Adams a visa waiver allowing him into the United States for forty-eight hours to attend the one-day peace conference on Northern Ireland, and restricting him to twenty-five miles from New York.

For Clinton the decision was instinctive. "It was a gut thing," said Stephanopoulos. "When it's a close call you take the extra step for peace."

"I talked to Tony and Nancy and then to people around the country and I listened to all the arguments pro and con," President Clinton said when I and Washington-based colleagues, Susan Flavella-Geraghty of the *Irish Echo,* Martin Fletcher of *The Times* and Jack Farrell of the *Boston Globe* interviewed him later in the White House. "I also listened to people in the administration who thought I shouldn't do it. And it occurred to me that it was one of those points where there had to be some tangible evidence that there could be a reward for the renunciation of violence and beginning to walk toward peace. Those kinds of things are always a judgment call. There's no rule book to tell you when this or that or the other thing happens. I believe it was the right judgment."

Jack Farrell wrote that the visa saga was "a case of classic Clinton, of a president who brooded and temporized, and weighed the political ups and downs, and then followed his heart down a risky path."

For the Secretary of State it was a humiliation, though not a resigning matter. He never regarded Northern Ireland as a priority. The Arab–Israel conflict was his major preoccupation, earning him the reputation of "Secretary of State for the Middle East." Nevertheless his advice on Ireland, and that of his vast State Department—with the exception of two Irish-American political appointees—had been overruled. The White House had also in effect hijacked Irish policy, taking it away from the State Department and lodging it with the National Security Council. From then on, the Irish desk in the State Department would be largely irrelevant to the peace process. Everything would center on the offices of Tony Lake and Nancy Soderberg in the West Wing of the White House and in the Oval Office down the corridor.

It was already dark in Washington that Sunday evening and past midnight on the other side of the Atlantic when a conference call was set up by the State Department operations center at Foggy Bottom to clear the way for the visa to be issued. It linked Peter Tarnoff, Christopher's Under Secretary for Political Affairs, with Val Martinez in Belfast and Jim Callahan in the Dublin embassy. Tarnoff advised the two officials that the President had decided to allow Adams into the country on a restricted visa. He instructed Martinez to bring Adams in and issue the visa.

By this time, however, Adams was already on his way to Dublin, so that he would be in a position to catch the midday flight to New York if he was given a visa. He had supplied a contact number in the Irish capital to Val Martinez, who now suggested to Callahan, "Jim, you issue the visa." Callahan could do nothing else but comply. The operations center arranged for a State Department telegram with the stamped signature of Warren Christopher to be sent to the Dublin embassy early on Monday morning authorising a forty-eight-hour visa. Callahan telephoned Adams at the Dublin number—it was the home of Sinn Féin official Rita O'Hare—and told him the news and where to collect his visa.

Adams called at the embassy early next morning, picked up his passport, and with only a couple of hours to spare, caught the midday plane to New York, the last possible flight that could bring him to the United States in time for the Tuesday conference.

By now the story was big international news, propelled to the front pages by a sudden outburst of angry speculation in the media in Britain about Clinton's decision. The reports accurately reflected the fury of the British government. British diplomats in Washington had good reason to feel cheated. Not only had they been rebuffed, but the first they heard of the decision was through a Reuters news agency report some hours after it had been made. The British Ambassador and his two senior diplomats dealing with Irish-related affairs, Jonathan Powell and Peter Westmacott, had been in regular contact with the National Security Council, but no one bothered to call them. "We were mad as hell," a British source said when describing reaction to the decision. Westmacott rang Soderberg and told her how "unimpressed" he had been to learn the news from the media. Renwick called Lake with a similar angry complaint. Powell in particular was infuriated. He blamed Soderberg for the debacle, pointing out to British journalists that she had worked for Kennedy's office. (He later honored his bet with Trina Vargo.)

"The British Ambassador made it very clear to Tony that they were not pleased with this," said Soderberg. "I don't think that they thought we were seriously considering it, and I think they were genuinely surprised that we would do this. It was the first time the United States had ever gone against Britain on an issue relating to Northern Ireland. I don't think that they ever really felt that we were going to do it. They had kind of talked to us before that, saying, 'Well, of course you're not going to give Adams a visa?' And we'd sort of mumble," she said, laughing at the recollection.

National Security Council officials privately blamed Janet Reno's Justice Department for leaking the news of the decision before it could be communicated to the parties. "There was a leak almost immediately," said Soderberg. "Then we heard it was on the wire. And the wire started to run at 2 o'clock. We hadn't time to call the British or anything."

In Dublin, the Taoiseach was jubilant. Major was upset now, but the Adams visa would advance the peace process, Reynolds told the government press secretary Sean Duignan. "Sinn Féin will pay a price for going to Capitol Hill. A lot of powerful people went out on a limb for Adams. If he doesn't deliver they'll have him back in the house with the steel shutters [Sinn Féin headquarters in Belfast] so fast his feet won't touch the ground. We're slowly putting the squeeze on them, pulling them in, boxing them in, cutting off their lines of retreat."

Some days later, after Adams had come and gone, I tried to find out what had been going on in San Diego. The incident had started when the receptionist at San Diego radio station KFMB was called by a male with an Irish accent who said three bombs had been placed round the southern California city. The caller said the devices had been planted in protest at the refusal to give Gerry Adams a visa. I located a San Diego law enforcement agent who was on the case. He said that after the warning they located three blue, pineapple-shaped, practise grenades at the "Shakespeare Pub and

Grille," a curio shop called "All Things Bright and British," and the federal courthouse, all of which had to be evacuated until the devices were declared safe. The incident made little impact in the city. It was accorded only a brief mention in the San Diego daily newspaper, the *Union Tribune.* The federal official told me that he thought the whole thing was very odd and raised intriguing questions about who might be behind it and who stood to benefit. He said there were no known militant Irish groups in the city, though many years previously two men were convicted for buying AR15 rifles for the IRA. The inert grenades were standard issue for military maneuvers—all training ordnance is blue—and not generally available to the public. "A dirty trick is a good possibility," he agreed, implying that pro-British or US agents had planted the devices to put the wind up the White House, "but it could have just as easily been a patriot sending a message." Joe Hughes, the *Union Tribune*'s crime reporter, told me, "We get a lot of bomb hoaxes in San Diego, though nothing before with an Irish connection."

Val Martinez spent a worrying few days in Belfast after the decision to grant Adams a visa became known and the anger of some unionist and loyalist politicians grew as they watched on television the Sinn Féin leader being feted in New York. He received a tip-off that a branch of the Ulster Volunteer Force, the most ruthless of the loyalist paramilitary organizations, were blaming him, assuming that as Belfast consul he had made the decision to issue the visa. Martinez put the word out along the Shankill Road through his contacts, who included a reformed double-murderer who had become a fundamentalist pastor, that the decision had nothing to do with him. After a few days he was told that there was no longer any threat to his life.

13

SHLOMO BREZHNEV

"What we had to do was de-demonize Gerry Adams and I believe we did it."
Ciarán Staunton

The limousine taking Gerry Adams into Manhattan carried an unlikely escort for the political representative of the IRA. It was driven by a chauffeur provided by Bill Flynn, a giant of corporate America and friend of many top FBI officials. In the front during the forty-five-minute journey was Flynn's trusted bodyguard Bill Barry, a former FBI man and president of his own security firm, Barry Security, specialising in anti-terrorism measures at nuclear plants. Sharing the back seat with the Sinn Féin leader was a former member of the 1940s Stern gang, Dr. George D. Schwab, now a professor at the City University of New York and president of the National Committee on American Foreign Policy which had invited Adams and other Northern Ireland party leaders to the peace conference the next day. A pillar of respectability in New York, Schwab, like Adams, had been branded a terrorist in his younger days. He had been involved in gunrunning in the United States for the Jewish resistance. He was fourteen at the time, having made his way from his native Latvia in 1947 to New York, where he joined a cell of the Stern gang for a year and a half, smuggling arms and ammunition to Jerusalem, then under British control. "I told Adams in the limousine of my underground activities and we had a very friendly conversation," he recalled later. "I had the impression we could do business with him. We understood each other. We spoke the same language." Barry, who described himself as "definitely not pro-IRA," said he found Adams "a decent sort, a reserved gentleman." He admonished Schwab for not giving

Adams a chance to look at the sights from the car window on his first-ever visit to New York.

Adams's plane, Aer Lingus flight EI 105, had touched down at Kennedy airport at 4:30 p.m. on Monday 31 January, and he was whisked through customs and into a room packed with TV cameras and reporters. There were television crews from many countries to cover what was suddenly the world's biggest story that day, though not from the Republic of Ireland: RTE was still forbidden by law from carrying the voices of Sinn Féin members on the air and decided not to bother covering the event. Bruce Morrison and Adams's old friend, Republican Congressman Peter King, were there to greet him among dozens of fans, some screaming Adams's name.

"The media didn't know what to expect," said King. "They seemed to think he would come through the door with a gun at each hip. Here was a guy who had been confined to West Belfast and they treated him like Elvis. We had only the British to thank for that." Adams gave a brief press conference and was escorted to the limousine, leaving a Noraid delegation led by Martin Galvin to make its own way back to the city.

The Adams party arrived at the Waldorf Astoria Hotel, where the conference participants were being put up in $315-a-night rooms. It was an appropriate destination for Adams. Eamon de Valera, also called a terrorist in his day, had stayed there when he came to New York as the President of Sinn Féin seventy-five years earlier. The ornate, high-ceiling hotel lobby and the corridors outside Adams's room were patrolled by several bulky men in plain clothes. Most were off-duty Irish-American officers of the New York police department. They had been deployed by Bill Barry, whom Flynn had put in charge of security. As a further security measure Adams was registered as Shlomo Brezhnev and checked in under that name. John Hume was also given a code name, but nobody could remember what it was so that when the Derry politician arrived to register, he had to check into a different room under his own name. Hume had been understandably reluctant to come in the first place and this did not help. Adams was going to be the star turn after a quarter of a century during which the SDLP leader had been unchallenged in America as the voice of constitutional Irish nationalism.

Adams and Hume attended a small private reception held by Bill Flynn in a room of the Waldorf Astoria to which two journalists were invited, myself and Pulitzer Prize winning columnist Jim

Dwyer of *New York Newsday*. The two politicians from Northern Ireland chatted amicably, reflecting the trust which had grown up between them in years of dialogue. The Sinn Féin leader then left for a meeting with Trina Vargo set up by Niall O'Dowd in a separate room. This was kept secret because Adams was still regarded as untouchable by political figures like her boss, Senator Edward Kennedy, as long as the IRA campaign continued. Vargo brought a message from the Massachusetts Senator: that his views on violence and the IRA had not changed, but that he believed that Adams's had changed and that many benefits would flow from an IRA ceasefire. O'Dowd then went to Adams's room to help him with his speech. The Belfast man had only a short time to adjust to some of the puzzling things about America, like the advertisement on the Magnavox television in his room for "Free IRA fact kit," which was a commercial for "Individual Retirement Accounts" rather than the organization with which he was more familiar. Adams was thirsty but for some reason neither he nor O'Dowd could open the drinks cabinet. Nor could they get through on the telephone to room service. Downstairs Martin Galvin of Noraid hung around in the foyer, looking forlorn, a clear signal to long-time observers of Irish America how much things were changing. Galvin, who came across on television as sharp and uncompromising, was being upstaged as the only spokesman of Irish republicanism in the United States by the bearded, academic-looking figure in neat suit and buttoned-down shirt who left the Waldorf later that evening to appear on *Larry King Live* on Cable Network News.

"Tonight," began Larry King, dramatically as he went on air, "the New York visit of a man so controversial, his very voice is barred from British television. I should point out that it is against the law in Britain to put Adams's voice on television. CNN and many British broadcasters are challenging the law, but meanwhile we are abiding by it. This show is not being seen on our European satellite." For Adams this exposure in America of the British ban was a good start. His appearance on the CNN program, a career goal for politicians and celebrities in the US, was itself a major coup. King's style was non-confrontational, which helped Adams portray himself as an Irish Nelson Mandela. The program helped to humanize the head of the political wing of the IRA in a city where terrorism made people think of swarthy figures in masks and blind Middle Eastern clerics. Adams portrayed himself as a victim of violence who was shot, interned and beaten up. He was a peacemaker who wanted "to see an end to all violence." He was a conciliator prepared to say about those who tried to kill him, "I would shake their hands to move the situation forward."

"Could CNN come to Belfast to host a program with all the political parties?" asked Larry King, peering at Adams through his thick glasses. "I'd buy you a pint of Guinness on the Falls Road," replied Adams. "I wouldn't be shot though?" asked King. "No, you'd have your pint of Guinness," said the Sinn Féin man. CNN rebroadcast the program to Europe later with an American actor reading Adams's responses.

Banal as they were, such exchanges infuriated the British.

"The press just went wild in Britain," said Nancy Soderberg. "There were quotes from government officials as if the western world was going to fall apart."

Conservative members of parliament were furious. "In recent years, few sights have more nauseated the public than the Americans' feting and flattering of Adams, particularly on that visit before the ceasefire," Andrew Hunter, chairman of the Tory Backbench Committee on Northern Ireland, told me. "The granting of a visa, the welcome he received, revolted us. They combined to give him a level of credibility and a platform which he did not deserve. Adams was the leading apologist for IRA violence for the greater part of the twenty-five years of the Troubles. He sought to justify the evil which the IRA perpetrated. Adams and his cronies are not genuine democrats. For them the ballot box is a tactic, not a commitment. Adams is no Mandela or Arafat, a leader of a downtrodden minority. He represents a minority within a minority in Northern Ireland."

However, any criticisms Adams made of London were readily accepted by an American television audience which was instinctively skeptical about British policy in Northern Ireland. American newspapers ridiculed the voice ban. "Adams makes the most of British mistakes without expressing a single new thought," said *The New York Times.* "For millions of Americans the novelty was in seeing a real live Irishman express such views . . . Censorship and visa blacklists are not the answer. Clinton was right to let Americans hear and question Gerry Adams." The *New York Daily News* said: "Adams reaped more publicity in two days than in two decades of resisting British rule in Northern Ireland." Columnist Denis Hamill concluded that the visit illustrated why the British did not want Adams on TV. He had "charisma, intellect, language, humor and passion."

"The idea was to make as much use of the forty-eight hours as possible," said Ciarán Staunton, who acted throughout as Adams's fixer and adviser. "The target was to bring him into every home through the talk shows, Larry King, Donahue and Pozner, Charlie Rose, the morning network shows. Quite a number of people didn't know who Gerry Adams was. What we had to do was de-demonize Gerry Adams and I believe we did it."

What really upset the British was the coverage of the visit by *The New York Times,* which sets the agenda for much of the American press. *The Times* had for many years been regarded by Irish Americans as pro-British. In a controversial incident during the 1980s a reporter was withdrawn from London after British complaints that her coverage was weighted towards the Irish side. Things had changed since then, partly because of successful lobbying of senior editorial staff by Dermot Brangan, a New York based Irish diplomat who had the task of putting his government's view to editorial boards across the United States, and partly because *The Times* had established a resident correspondent, James Clarity, in Dublin, thus becoming the first American newspaper ever to break with the practice of reporting Ireland from London. There had also been major changes in the editorial-writing staff and the paper had steadily become more sympathetic to the Irish interpretation of events as the peace process unfolded. It now played an influential role in portraying Adams as a peacemaker. On its front page, reporter Francis X. Clines welcomed him as "an articulate and enigmatic partisan leader in a centuries-old struggle." Its opinion page carried a profile of the 44-year-old Sinn Féin leader by the Irish author Edna O'Brien, who lived in London. She compared him to the hero of Ireland's War of Independence, Michael Collins. But "where Collins was outgoing and swashbuckling, Gerry Adams is thoughtful and reserved, a lithe handsome man with a native formality," wrote O'Brien. "Given a different incarnation in a different century, one could imagine him as one of those monks transcribing the gospels into Gaelic." To her, Adams was indeed Nelson Mandela, and "no doubt on his journey from violence to the negotiating table he sees parallels." I asked Edna O'Brien later if she had any problems with the British over her article. "Let me tell you, my dear, they think I'm the Barbara Cartland of Irish republicanism," she said, with a mischievous grin. *The New York Times* had telephoned her to do some fact-checking before the profile appeared, she said, but she had told them impatiently, "Treat it as literature."

On the day of the peace conference, about two hundred delegates from the American foreign policy establishment crowded into the Waldorf Astoria's Empire Room beneath crystal chandeliers to hear the three participants, Adams, Hume and John Alderdice, head of the Alliance Party, make their case for peace. As expected, the unionist leaders had not turned up because they would not share a platform with Adams. The dozens of reporters and camera crews were interested only in "the terrorist guy" as I heard one technician call him, and they crushed around the Sinn Féin leader, ignoring Hume sitting stony-faced just a few feet away. The speakers were introduced by Ambassador Angier Biddle Duke, a 78-year-old former American diplomat who had organized the protocol for world leaders at President Kennedy's funeral. "You are part of history," he told them.

In an impassioned speech, Hume criticized those who tried to solve problems by "waving our flags and draping them around us," a dig at sentimental Irish-American nationalists. The only sign of a border left in a unified Europe were British military checkpoints on the Irish border, he said. "What are they there for? To deal with people who want to get rid of the border."

Adams told them that if the Joint Declaration was "the first step" to peace, they needed to know what the second step would be so "I can sell the agreement to every Irish republican." It would have to involve the policy objective of Irish national self-determination, a timetable, consultations and guarantees for unionists, he said. Sinn Féin also wanted to know if Britain was willing to join the ranks of "persuaders" and tackle the issues of an amnesty for prisoners and the demilitarization of the conflict. He received a standing ovation from half the delegates as he ended his thirty-minute speech with the words: "It is our intention to see the gun removed permanently from Irish politics." John Alderdice, who went first and did not stay for Adams's speech, pointed out that the speakers represented less than half the population of Northern Ireland. The problem was perfectly simple from three thousand miles away, but was in truth "complex and difficult."

I rang Speaker Foley from the Waldorf Astoria at his Capitol Hill office and asked for his reaction to the arrival of the Sinn Féin leader in New York. Alone among Irish-American politicians, he had opposed the visa. If it helped lead to peace, he would be the first to say it was the right decision, he said, but he believed Adams had still not gone far enough in his statement for Clinton to justify a visa. In Washington, Clinton told reporters that he approved giving Adams a US visa in the hope it would help the peace process. "But I think he should also support the work being done by the prime ministers of both Ireland and Britain in pursuing the peace," he said. "The people who have to resolve this are the Irish and the British."

After the conference, which amounted to three speeches lasting about two hours, Adams was given a quick tour of Manhattan by former IRA prisoner Francis Gildernew. "What would you remember of New York?" someone asked him. "Lifts," he replied, "and nice rooms."

That evening it was bitterly cold and fresh snow dusted the window ledges of the Manhattan skyscrapers when Adams left his nice Waldorf Astoria room to greet over a thousand Irish-American supporters gathered for the only public meeting the Sinn Féin leader held during his two-day stay. News of the venue was spread by word of mouth—the Sheraton Hotel, just across the road from Rosie O'Grady's famous Irish bar. It was in the Sheraton that Clinton had promised a visa for Adams at an election forum twenty months earlier. By the time the Sinn Féin leader arrived, about three hundred people had been turned away and fire marshals had closed the doors of the ballroom. He was given a standing ovation, punctuated by cheers and yells, as he entered the packed room to the skirl of two dozen pipers from the Emerald Society Police Band, dressed in kilts and with revolvers strapped to their waists. The cheering gave way to a burst of *A Nation Once Again.* This was the moment most of the republican supporters in the crowd had been waiting for for twenty years. "It's sort of their 'Tiocfaidh ár lá,' " said one of the organizers, referring to the IRA slogan "Our day will come."

Despite the apparent spontaneity, the meeting was carefully choreographed. Under his limited visa, Adams was required to refrain from direct or indirect fundraising in the US. There could be no rallying of support for the IRA or Noraid in his public appearances. So no one from Noraid was allowed on the stage, which was flanked by the Tricolor and the Stars and Stripes. The banner draped from the wall was not that of Sinn Féin or the IRA, but of Americans for a New Irish Agenda, the lobbying group chaired by Bruce Morrison. The only two public figures on the platform were Morrison and the veteran Irish civil rights activist Paul O'Dwyer, now confined to a wheelchair.

Nor did the militants in the crowd get the speech they waited so long for. The Sinn Féin leader made no calls for support for the armed struggle. He did not appeal for backing for the republican movement. "I come here with a message of peace," he said. "We're going to have peace, not in forty or fifty years time, but in our time . . . We are moving into the final phase of the conflict. We have to move forward. It can only be good for the British as well as the Irish to move ahead." There were cheers when he ended, but some of the hard men did not join in. Adams's only reference to the armed struggle was an oblique one. He raised his glass of Coke to propose a toast "to absent friends and all those who have suffered in the long war—freedom, justice and peace."

"It's a watershed," said O'Dowd, watching from the body of the crowded ballroom. "The most powerful government in the world has said it will support Irish Americans if we support the peace process." Father James Kelly of Brooklyn, who came along out of curiosity, thought the politics of Irish America were changing as they watched. "Irish Americans are more involved in the peace process now," said the Limerick-born priest, who had gained some publicity in Ireland for his role in negotiating financial transactions between Bishop Eamonn Casey of Galway and his former American lover, Annie Murphy. "They can't betray the trust put in them by Senators Kennedy and Moynihan and President Clinton." John Hume, asked later what good could come of the Adams visit, replied, "He can go back home with a bit of encouragement, bolstered, strong enough to risk peace."

Before he left New York, Adams made a point of saying that he would not disappoint those "who stuck their neck out" for him to obtain the visa, including Clinton. In the limousine on the way to JFK airport, according to George Schwab, Adams said, "George, I promise you we will never return to the old ways."

Adams arrived back at Dublin airport on Thursday morning after a hectic forty-eight hours during which he gave seven television interviews and five press conferences. Two dozen protestors from Families Against Intimidation and Terror, the anti-paramilitary organization partly sponsored by the Northern Ireland Office, booed the Sinn Féin man as he came through the terminal building. "Gerry Adams got a forty-eight hour visa and he was a free man to come back again," said Nancy Gracey, whose son Patrick was shot in the leg by an IRA punishment squad in 1990. "What about the hundreds of people in exile because of the republican movement? When are they coming home?"

Travelling on the same plane as Adams were Bill Flynn and Bill Barry. They had taken up an offer he made to come to Belfast. On 12 February, they drove north, with Flynn behind the wheel, and turned off the M1 motorway at Belfast to make their way to Sinn Féin headquarters in Connolly House.

They were about an hour behind time and were not sure of directions.

"We had to stop when we came to a burning building with tanks, and soldiers with machine guns," said Barry. "We eventually drove on, but decided the best way to find Sinn Féin headquarters was to take a taxi." They parked their Mercedes and flagged down one of the London-style black taxis which serve as people's transport in Belfast.

"When we opened the door there were people inside and we thought it was taken, but they shouted, 'No. No. Hop in!' " said Barry. "We squeezed in. We are both six-foot-two Americans but they were smiling as if they knew us. I said we're looking for Sinn Féin headquarters. The driver braked. We had only gone one hundred yards. 'There it is,' he said. The door was covered with graffiti. When we knocked, it flew open. 'Thank God you're all right,' said the man inside."

It turned out that the Americans were at another Sinn Féin office on the Falls Road. The burning building was Connolly House. It had been hit by an RPG7 rocket fired by loyalist paramilitaries wearing red, white and blue scarves. No one was injured though it damaged an upstairs office and the roof.

Gerry Adams took the visitors to Clonard Monastery where the attitude of the priests convinced Barry, just as it had Flynn, that the Sinn Féin leader was intent on peace. "That really turned me round," he said. "They loved this guy. There was nothing phoney or obsequious about it. I thought he can't be the monster depicted in the British press." Adams took them for a walk round West Belfast. "I got the impression," said Barry, "that he wasn't showing Belfast to us. He was showing us to Belfast."

14

Not So Special

"When I listen to Gerry Adams, I think, as we all do, it's reminiscent of Dr. Goebbels."
Sir Robin Renwick

The worst rift since Suez," said the *Daily Telegraph*, summing up a view from London of the effect on the long-standing special relationship between the United Kingdom and the United States of the Adams visit to New York. "The Lion Whines About Mr. Adams," retorted a headline over a *New York Times* editorial castigating Britain for "throwing a fit" over the publicity coup for the Sinn Féin leader. London was, in diplomatic terms, doing just that. Prime Minister John Major called in the US Ambassador in London, Raymond Seitz, to complain about the decision, marking a low point in the affairs of the two countries, though it was probably a reasonably civil encounter as Major knew that the US Ambassador was equally put out by Clinton's decision. The State Department in Washington tried to put a brave face on it. Spokesman Mike McCurry said that the relationship was still special, "reflecting the very unique understanding that these two countries have of each other, reflecting also the co-operation that we have on so many issues of importance globally."

At first the British kept a stiff upper lip over their diplomatic setback. An embassy official in Washington said coldly when the Adams decision was announced that it was an internal matter for the US authorities and that Adams and the IRA would ultimately be judged by their deeds rather than by their "evasive statements." But Douglas Hurd was in the United States that week and when interviewed on television, the white-haired Foreign Minister with parchment-dry voice could barely hide his anger. On CNN, Hurd called Adams "Mr. Ten Percent" to emphasize the smallness of the Northern Ireland vote of Sinn Féin and asked why CNN did not interview Joe Hendron of the SDLP, who had won Adams's seat in the House of Commons. "No, he's just a successful elected politician," Hurd said bitterly. "He's not a man who connives at and excuses terrorism and the killing and bombing of innocent people." The point was taken up by Sir Robin Renwick who also criticized the US media for not giving as much attention to Hendron.

The British Ambassador told viewers of CNN that Adams could be compared to Hitler's propaganda chief. "When I listen to Gerry Adams, I think, as we all do, it's reminiscent of Dr. Goebbels," he said. "It's an extraordinary propaganda line. The line is 'I want peace but only after we've won.' And the line is also that 'I'm not prepared to call on the IRA to end the shootings, the bombings, the killings of innocent people in Northern Ireland and Great Britain.' " A man of great charm, the 57-year-old envoy was never a fan of Bill Clinton. He had come to Washington from South Africa where he was praised for his contribution to the ending of apartheid and now in his last posting he was undoubtedly the best-connected diplomat in Washington. But the many senior members of the administration who were regular guests at his dinner parties in the magnificent embassy residence on Massachusetts Avenue had been unable to prevent a decision which had left British diplomacy in disarray.

"The problem," said one astute observer, "is that the British have always tended to rely on the security network, Janet Reno and all that, they get these people to do things blindly for them, and then they get a shock when they find out something doesn't carry through the system."

Some London newspapers struck a more moderate note. The *Guardian* considered Adams's visit to be a necessary part of the peace process and denounced the British establishment for insisting that American politicians were now "soft" on the IRA. "That's a misleading, simplistic and falsely comforting nonsense," it said. "The notion that New York and Boston are riddled with respectable apologists for the bombers who know nothing of unionist concerns or who are unacquainted with the nuances of the current Northern Irish situation is a myth which neither hard-line republicans nor hard-line unionists should allow themselves to swallow." The London *Independent* denounced the British government as "foolish" for objecting to Adams's trip. "New York will give him a taste of what is on offer if he can earn respectability," it forecast. This view was broadly reflected in the Irish media. *The Irish Times* declared the visa decision to be "a moderate victory for common sense and good judgment."

However, the British tabloids and the conservative broadsheets expressed contempt for Clinton and the Irish Americans. The *Sun* demanded that "the Yanks keep their noses out of Ulster." The *Daily Express* described Clinton's decision as "a coarse insult from a country we thought was our friend," and insisted that Adams's presence would excite the "thoughtless passions" of Irish Americans. The *Daily Telegraph* published a cartoon depicting a desperate Adams struggling to crawl through a desert as Clinton quickly ran to him with bottles of oxygen, and called the trip a "snub" to the British government.

There were personal attacks in the British press on Nancy Soderberg which the White House found offensive. (One which really annoyed her, a friend said, described her as in her "late thirties"— she was in her mid-thirties.) The *Sunday Times* said she was a "staunch supporter of a united Ireland" who was guilty of "deception" and who "was being held responsible for a foreign relations fiasco that has embarrassed the American Government."

"They were unbelievable," Soderberg recalled. "There's this misperception that I ran around and rammed it through everybody all by myself. Anyone who says that doesn't know how the White House works. Even this one. I mean it just seemed so absurd. Part of it was ridiculous. I was viewed as having pushed this through for Ted Kennedy. What was surprising about it was the vehemence. Pretty much the whole White House supported the decision, the President, the Vice President, George Stephanopoulos, the President's advisers, they were all for it. The Vice President actually was crucial to the whole decision. And Tony Lake. We'd never have gone anywhere had any of those people gone against it."

The *Sunday Times* particularly angered Clinton for its suggestion that he disliked Major and was determined to end the special relationship and was himself guilty of "shamefaced deceit." "The President was angry and extremely exercised by the reports," said Lake. When Kennedy telephoned the President to thank him for his decision on the visa, Clinton told him, according to a White House aide, "See what the Brits are saying about me?" The Senator replied, "Don't worry about it. That's what the Brits have been saying about the Kennedys for years."

The "worst crisis since Suez" was a failure at a personal level. The special relationship flourished when the two leaders were of one mind and admired each other, as with Ronald Reagan and Margaret Thatcher. This could not be said about the former Arkansas Governor, who was often depicted in the British press as a bumbling incompetent in foreign affairs, and the colorless British Prime Minister. Some of the White House staff still smarted over Tory attempts to prevent Clinton's election in 1992. On the day he decided to issue a visa to Adams, Clinton was courting German Chancellor Helmut Kohl in a Washington restaurant, sending a strong signal of America's shifting concept of who was important among European powers. By contrast, when Major dined in a Washington restaurant, Clinton only dropped by for the dessert and that was on his way home from an evening with the Kennedys.

The situation was exacerbated by unpleasant differences over Bosnia. The previous year when Warren Christopher went to London with Clinton's proposal to help arm the Bosnian Muslims, the British not only dismissed the idea, they leaked their rejection before Christopher had left the country. The view in London was that Christopher was weak and could not prevail over Lake.

All this helped bring tempers to the boil over the Adams visa. "At some levels, I think there was quite a sense of bitterness," said Speaker Foley, Britain's ally on Capitol Hill, who believed the row raised the question "of whether the special relationship exists and to what extent it exists . . . in the general conditions of the post Cold War world."

The term "special relationship" had in fact already fallen out of favor with the fall of the Soviet Union. Ambassador Seitz avoided using the term in the US embassy in London. The British Ambassador in Washington had more or less proclaimed the special relationship non-existent by banning outright the use of the words among his diplomats. "You will not hear the term from me or anyone in this embassy," Sir Robin said.

Nevertheless the very size of his embassy testified to the fact that Britain still devoted more diplomatic resources to America than anywhere else. It was the largest embassy in the US capital and the biggest British embassy in the world. It had 460 staff, half of them military personnel whose job was to liaise with their opposite numbers in the American armed and intelligence services. A senior State Department official assured me the CIA did not monitor Northern Ireland from the Irish Republic as this was regarded as the legitimate sphere of interest of Britain's MI6. The term "special relationship" "smacked of arrogance and nostalgia and exclusivity, and taking things for granted," a British government source told me. "The relationship is special but it isn't *the* special relationship. It is one of extraordinary depth and breadth however one looks at it. Britain is the biggest investor in the US, the two countries share information in defence and intelligence which they share with no one else in the world. There are legal, constitutional, linguistic and cultural ties. We are allies in NATO. We stood shoulder to shoulder not long before in the Gulf War. There was a strong feeling after the Adams decision that this was a bad business but substantially it didn't make a vast difference to the relationship. What made it worse was that throughout all this we were disagreeing on Bosnia. This together with the Adams visa made it a bit more serious."

The special relationship went back to the aftermath of the 1812 war between the two countries, when they agreed that they did not need to protect the Canadian border against each other. Ironically, its first real crisis came over the Irish question. In 1866 President Andrew Johnson courted electoral support from Irish Americans in New York, considered a key constituency in that year's mid-term elections, by allowing Irish rebels to use the United States as a launching ground for a Fenian invasion of Canada. In later years the bonds were strengthened through the marriages of impoverished members of the British aristocracy to rich Americans.

The special relationship was practically institutionalized in 1939 when President Franklin Roosevelt wrote to the First Lord of the Admiralty Winston Churchill, suggesting they keep in touch "about anything you want me to know about," an invitation which produced 1,700 cables between them, and a state visit by King George VI and Queen Elizabeth to Washington, the first by a reigning British monarch since America's war of independence. Churchill, himself the product of a transatlantic marriage, pursued the alliance arduously, if only as a way of circumventing the reports to Washington of the US Ambassador to London, Joe Kennedy, who was scathing about Britain's capacity to fight the Germans. The old cigar-smoking British warrior came to stay with Roosevelt for three weeks after Pearl Harbor. The President once came upon Churchill completely naked in the guest room in the White House; as he withdrew, embarrassed, Churchill called out, so the story goes, "The Prime Minister of Great Britain has nothing to conceal from the President of the United States." But the Americans drove a hard bargain with the British, causing Churchill to complain that their business-like extraction of reparations for war aid was like "the sheriff collecting the last assets of a helpless debtor." The alliance also came under great strain over

America's refusal to push past Berlin at the end of the war and contain the Soviet advance.

In the postwar British depression, historian Max Beloff called the special relationship an agreeable British myth to help cushion the shock of national decline, and on the American side Secretary of State Dean Acheson denounced it as a dangerous intellectual obstacle to the acceptance by Britain of its European role. But it endured at many levels. In the early 1960s, the personal chemistry of Harold Macmillan and John F. Kennedy made it a very special alliance, and the British Ambassador David Ormsby Gore became a close adviser and almost a cabinet member in JFK's White House. President Kennedy, unlike his father twenty-five years earlier or his brother Ted and sister Jean over a quarter of a century later, was not willing to upset the British.

A 1963 report from the Irish Ambassador to Washington, Dr. J. T. Kiernan, just before Kennedy visited Ireland, revealed that this extended to Irish affairs. President Kennedy turned down a request from Irish Foreign Minister Frank Aiken that he suggest to the British that they should indicate publicly that they were not opposed to the unity of Ireland. Kennedy "is convinced that no British minister would feel able to make a public statement of the kind suggested," wrote Kiernan in a cable. "He is by his education British inclined. And in the present international conjuncture he makes no secret of his firm attachment to Britain. So that to raise a new issue or raise an old issue now when Britain has so many pressing problems to solve is something he would avoid and seek an alternative."

In those days the Irish Ambassador was regularly invited to the White House on Saint Patrick's Day. Kiernan described how on 17 March 1963, Kennedy got up from his rocking chair and took him to the veranda, leaving his chief of protocol, Angier Biddle Duke, inside while they discussed Kennedy's forthcoming visit. Kiernan concluded that Kennedy's "undoubted goodwill to Ireland will be exercised in our favor so long as he is fully clear that he can take a line which can be persuasively put to the British, with a chance of leading to results."

The relationship was called "special" by Winston Churchill and Richard Nixon, "strong, intimate and reassuring" by Jack Kennedy, "close" by Harold Wilson and "very, very special" by Margaret Thatcher. It was not so special with Anthony Eden and Dwight D. Eisenhower, Harold Wilson and Lyndon Johnson, and Edward Heath and Richard Nixon. Its low point came over Suez, when

Washington refused to support the British pound after what it saw as a bungled, imperialist action in Egypt. Even under Margaret Thatcher and Ronald Reagan there were frictions. She opposed the US invasion of Grenada and Reagan's Star Wars initiative. But there was never any rancor between them. Thatcher also enjoyed a close alliance with George Bush, though Britain's increasing isolation in Europe had by then diminished its influence and value to the US as a European power. By 1989, President Bush was referring to the US and Germany as being partners in leadership, which didn't play well in Whitehall.

In a lecture in London after the Adams visa row, Senator Kennedy ventured the opinion that the controversy was just another crisis in a relationship which continued to be strong and secure, whether characterized as special or not. "Passing storms such as the present have always been followed by fairer weather," he said, adding that while some British journalists called President Clinton's decision on Adams the greatest crisis since Suez, this "was hard to take seriously, since British leaders had been talking with the IRA long before the visa was requested."

But the relationship was not the same, and fences were not mended as quickly as they would have been during the Cold War. With the decision of the President to take his advice on Ireland from Irish Americans, it had failed in another important aspect. One of the historical purposes of the special relationship was keeping the White House and the State Department above the influence of American political factions which might interfere with US foreign policy. Or, as the Washington-based writer Christopher Hitchens put it, "The special relationship was historically a way of thwarting the Irish and German lobbies in the US."

President Clinton defined the relationship as an "enduring partnership," in answer to a question I put to him in December 1993, just a month before he authorized the Adams visa. "As long as I am President, the United States' relationship with the United Kingdom will indeed be special," he said. "Our relationship with the United Kingdom is unique and historic and we continue to share a common strategic world vision and a commitment to acting on common values. We are working together on issues ranging from trade negotiations to NATO reform." But he went on to say that his policy on Northern Ireland took into account another relationship: it was made "in the context of the deep ties of friendship and history the American people enjoy with the peoples of both Ireland and Britain."

The "Connolly House Group" with Sinn Féin officials before the IRA ceasefire. Billionaire Charles "Chuck" Feeney, who rarely allowed himself to be photographed, is behind Gerry Adams, on the right and looking directly at him.
(CRISPIN RODWELL)

Loyalist leaders Billy Hutchinson and David Ervine, who found unlikely allies among Irish Americans.
(THE IRISH TIMES)

Loyalist leader Joe English with Angier Biddle Duke and William Flynn of the National Committee on American Foreign policy, in New York. (POPPERFOTO)

Republican congressmen Peter King and Sinn Féin President Gerry Adams on their way to the Speaker's lunch on Capitol Hill, March 1995.

Northern Ireland Secretary of State, Sir Patrick Mayhew, who went to Washington in a futile bid to stop President Clinton allowing Gerry Adams to raise funds in the United States.
(THE IRISH TIMES)

Senator Edward Kennedy in Dublin, a year after the IRA ceasefire began.
(THE IRISH TIMES)

The Taoiseach, John Bruton (second from left), with Unionist MPs John Taylor, David Trimble and Ken Maginnis.
(THE IRISH TIMES)

Former US Senator George Mitchell with Sinn Féin President Gerry Adams.
(THE IRISH TIMES)

Senator Chris Dodd, who turned the tables on the British by taking President Clinton out golfing.
(JAMES HIGGINS)

Tony Lake, the National Security Adviser, confers with the President in the White House.

Sinn Féin President Gerry Adams, Irish Taoiseach Albert Reynolds and SDLP leader John Hume after their first meeting at Dublin's Government Buildings on September 6, 1994.
(THE IRISH TIMES)

Ireland's Ambassador to the US, Dermot Gallagher, with the President and Mrs. Clinton.

The author with President Clinton in March 1996.

Clinton appeared to have genuine regrets about offending John Major so deeply. He told a reporter it had been very tough to disappoint the British as he believed Major had stuck his own neck out to make peace, at least on the basis of what Albert Reynolds had told him. After the US embassy in London sent a cable to Washington warning of a high level of fury in the British capital, the President moved to limit the damage, upgrading a scheduled meeting with the British Prime Minister four weeks later by adding in a personal element. He arranged for Major to meet him in Pittsburgh, Pennsylvania, for a "roots" experience: the British Prime Minister's grandfather and father had lived there. With typical thoroughness, and quite taken with the unusual idea of helping an English leader find his origins in America rather than the other way round, US officials scoured the Pittsburgh archives for any trace of Major's family to present to him when he arrived. They came up empty-handed. The Western Pennsylvania Historical Society went through census records and church archives and drew a complete blank. The British embassy sent an urgent message to Downing Street seeking more information, but got none. Major's family had no record themselves of their Pennsylvania days. His grandfather, Abraham Ball, laid bricks for blast furnaces in Andrew Carnegie's steel mills in Pennsylvania, but the company documents were destroyed half a century earlier. The British Prime Minister's family name was Ball, but his father Tom changed his surname to Major so that the circus act in which he was starring with Kitty Drum could be called "Drum and Major." A Pittsburgh newspaper criticized the whole exercise. "Why Is This Man Coming Here?" asked the *Pittsburgh Post Gazette*, which concluded that "no one on either side of the Atlantic seems able to establish where in Pittsburgh Major's ancestors resided or even to prove conclusively that they resided in Pittsburgh at all."

Nevertheless Clinton took his guest for a tour of the metropolis and treated him to a fireworks display which they watched from a restaurant overlooking the old coal-and-steel town. The President wore a tie with the British and American flags gaudily entwined, which Tony Lake described delightedly as "the tie that binds."

Back in Washington Major and Sir Robin Renwick did the rounds of Congressional offices. At one session, Republican Peter King, long distrusted by the British as a friend of Adams, thought he detected for the first time a less harsh attitude towards Irish-American legislators, despite all the dust kicked up by the storm over Adams. "I was all set to say, 'Congratulations!' to Major for taking these courageous steps towards peace when a Florida member said, 'Mister Prime Minister, on behalf of the people of the United States, I want to apologize for what the President did,'" said King. "When he came to me, I said, 'I'm not going to apologize for what the President did.' But we had thirty seconds alone after that and Major said, 'Maybe we can make this thing work.' Robin Renwick came over, also very friendly." It seemed to King the British were rethinking their tactics on Capitol Hill.

The President kept up the heavy-handed courtship of Major, putting him up in the Lincoln bedroom in the White House, the first British leader to be so honored since Churchill. But it didn't appear to work. Clinton went jogging alone in the morning, while Major slumbered in the pale-yellow and green bedroom with its huge bed. The atmosphere between the two men seemed as frigid as the weather when the President bade goodbye at a hastily arranged open-air press conference at the back of the White House. The answers to questions shouted by reporters through the damp snowflakes were drowned out by passenger jets screaming overhead to and from National airport. We just managed to hear Clinton saying, "It is a great mistake to overstate the occasional disagreements and to understate the incredible depth of our shared interests and shared values. It is still a profoundly important relationship for our two countries and the future of the world."

Clinton waved goodbye to Major's limousine as if at a hearse and appeared relieved that it was all over.

15

THE GREENING OF THE WHITE HOUSE

"We all had a feeling of finally arriving."
Don Keough

Early in March 1994, a series of mortar shells burst from a parked car at the Excelsior Hotel near the northern security fence round London's Heathrow airport. Two mortars landed on a runway while two others fell short. But none went off. Two days later another four mortars burst from tubes hidden in the ground south of the airport and landed near Terminal Four, Heathrow's main terminal for international flights. Again they did not explode. Incredibly, two days later another four mortars hissed skyward from rough ground outside the perimeter fence and this time one crashed onto the roof of Terminal Four. Yet again none exploded.

The mortaring of Heathrow may have been a deliberate attempt to intimidate rather than destroy. It was unlikely that all the mortar fuses could have been defective. But with echoes of the terrorist attack on an American airliner over Lockerbie in Scotland, this did not matter much in Washington, where those who thought the peace process had been a fraud said it was now over. Some members of Congress who had been persuaded to go out on a limb for Adams were angry and puzzled.

Senator Daniel Patrick Moynihan, who had reluctantly joined Senator Kennedy's campaign for the Adams visa, wrote Kennedy a four-word note. It said: "Have we been had?"

Moynihan, Kennedy, Chris Dodd, Speaker Foley and a dozen other members of Congress condemned the bombing and issued a statement appealing to Sinn Féin and the IRA to accept the Joint

Declaration. White House officials by this stage were well enough briefed to know that Sinn Féin and the IRA's decision-making process was painfully slow, and despite the feeling of anger, Lake and Soderberg remained quiet, never publicly expressing any doubts that things were moving in the right direction. In Clinton's words, they had made an "objective call" to try and encourage the IRA to move towards the Joint Declaration and make peace and they would see it through.

Nancy Soderberg recalled that when she heard about the Heathrow mortars she thought, "Well, maybe this is their last hurrah." But she was beginning to wonder when the IRA would call a ceasefire. "Everyone at the time thought it would be late spring or early summer," she said. "So I wasn't so surprised." But time was slipping by.

Despite the dent in the euphoria among Irish Americans, who now believed after the Adams visit that American involvement would bring a peaceful settlement nearer, a new special relationship between President Clinton and the Irish had been forged, as became clear at about 11 o'clock on the evening of 17 March 1994. At that moment, President Clinton stood up to say a few words to four hundred people crowded into the East Room during the first ever Saint Patrick's night party in the White House. Dressed in tuxedo and dark green bow tie, Clinton was about to start speaking when someone standing against the golden-draped windows shouted "Bravo!" Suddenly the chandeliers of the ornate room were shaken by a thunderous outburst of whoops and cheers and more shouts of "Bravo!" It went on and on, a spontaneous outburst of affection for the first President ever to stand up to the British on Northern Ireland. Clinton shook his head in amazement as he looked round the cheering room. "Céad míle fáilte," he said, "A hundred thousand welcomes," prompting another round of cheers.

The whole of the second floor of the White House had been put at the disposal of Irish and Irish-American guests who wandered in and out of drawing rooms with magnificent views overlooking the Washington Mall. There were politicians, movie stars, impresarios, trade union leaders, diplomats, writers, city bosses and community activists. The guest of honor was Albert Reynolds, who in response to Clinton's invitation to bring the family had arrived with his wife, seven children and two other relatives. The Taoiseach had insisted on the Dublin political correspondents being admitted as well, and when Jim Dougal of the BBC in Belfast was left out he went back to the President to get him in. "I had to intervene again at the highest level," said Reynolds. "I told Clinton we can't show division between North and South."

In the crowded rooms, Hollywood celebrities like Michael Keaton, Paul Newman, Joanne Woodward and Richard Harris mingled with Belfast flautist James Galway, talk-show host Conan O'Brien and film producer Jim Sheridan, whose movie *In the Name of the Father* about the Guildford Four was embarrassing Britain in cinemas across the United States. Derry-born actress Roma Downey, who played Jacqueline Kennedy on television, looked so striking that Clinton nudged Reynolds to ask admiringly who she was. People queued to shake the hand of John Hume and Paul O'Dwyer, the civil rights activist, now eighty-seven, who was last invited to the White House in 1933 and then couldn't make it. Senators Edward Kennedy and George Mitchell talked with "the peacemakers" Niall O'Dowd, Bruce Morrison, Bill Flynn and Chuck Feeney, while Irish officials chatted with Tony Lake and Nancy Soderberg, who wore a long green dress. In the East Room a concert of Irish music, which featured the haunting and romantic Mise Éire and the 1798 rebel song Boolavogue, ended with a performance by the Derry man whose appearances were now synonymous with the peace process in America, the musician Phil Coulter, who this time parodied Ian Paisley with a song ending "You can tell the President, from this Belfast resident, that Belfast says, 'No!' " He told the gathering that if the Irish Prime Minister and the American President, one who started out in dance halls, the other who played the saxophone, had followed these careers there might be a poster in Dublin that day advertising an Albert Reynolds production of Bill Clinton and his Arkansas Blues Band. Then, concert-hall fashion, he had the First Couple join in *The Town I Love So Well*, with its near-rebel lines about Derry's experience at the hand of the British: "But with their tanks and guns, Oh my God what have they done, To the town I love so well." Clinton's eyes glistened with tears.

The evening ended with an equally extraordinary sight, that of the trio of Reynolds, Clinton and Hume, standing together on the tiny stage, hands clasped behind their backs, swaying from side to side, singing *When Irish Eyes Are Smiling*. The President went off to bed hand in hand with Hillary, leaving everyone to finish off the Blarney cheese, the chocolate bowler hats, colored green and filled with ice cream, and the Irish coffee cake.

"Astonishing White House bash," Reynolds's press secretary Sean Duignan wrote in his diary. "Room after massive room taken over with eating, drinking, siamsa and craic . . . Raw green power, not just shamrockry. What must unionists think of it? Can Sinn Féin resist all of this?"

Don Keough, the former head of Coca Cola, said, "It's like the end of a journey. We all had a feeling of finally arriving." Said a wide-eyed guest, "John F. Kennedy never did anything like this for the Irish. The American Irish have always had their noses pressed against the window, looking into the White House from the outside. Now they are inside and nothing will ever be the same again."

Dermot Gallagher, a native of County Leitrim, felt that Ireland was now enjoying most favored nation status. As Irish Ambassador he found the White House more accessible than did the representatives of many larger countries. Every prominent political visitor to the United States wanted to meet the President and many were unable to do so, yet Clinton had five high-level meetings with the Irish in his first sixteen months in office before he ever met the Prime Minister of neighboring Canada. The Irish Foreign Minister, Dick Spring, was given a crucial fifteen minutes with the President on 16 November 1993 to canvass for his support in the final drafting of the Joint Declaration. That was one of the most hectic days of Clinton's presidency, when he was frantically lobbying Congress to pass the North American Free Trade Agreement, which it did. John Major rang to congratulate him on this but Clinton was unable to get back to the British Prime Minister for several days—and when he did he urged Major "to go the extra mile" for peace in Northern Ireland. On a number of other occasions Clinton would find time for the Foreign Minister of this "small potatoes" European country of his ancestors, and never once for British Foreign Secretary Douglas Hurd.

Perhaps the most remarkable example of "the most favored" status came a few weeks after the party when Clinton agreed to meet Reynolds at twenty-four hours' notice in Indianapolis, Indiana, in the unlikely setting of Mount Helm Baptist Church where the President was making his weekly radio address. Reynolds, who flew in from Chicago, conferred with the President in the pastor's tiny robing room, with books along one side, a teddy bear on a shelf, and a high-security telephone taped to the floor. Leaning forward on a brown couch and facing Clinton who sat in a hard armchair, the Taoiseach told him that the peace process looked stalled but was moving along. Ceasefire hopes had fallen after demands by Sinn Féin for clarification of the Joint Declaration were turned down by the British government. But he confided to the President that he had been quietly editing the Sinn Féin questions and virtually writing the British answers and the issue would be resolved soon. "I was explaining all that to Clinton behind the scenes in the sacristy of that little church wherever it was," he said. "That's real politics. Just sitting there on a couch. Just to assure him that it was on track and that it was moving forward."

Around that time, the Finnish President, Mauno Koizijto, a distinguished European statesman, failed to get in to see Clinton in the White House, which caused much critical comment in the Finnish press. The previous month the Turkish Prime Minister, Tansu Ciller could not attract any administration official to a banquet she held in Washington. The Czech Prime Minister could only manage to see Vice President Gore. The Dutch Prime Minister, Ruud Lubbers, refused to go to Washington because he could not arrange a meeting with the President. King Juan Carlos of Spain telephoned the White House three times without getting anyone to take his calls, though he eventually got a cup of tea with the Clintons.

During the transition, Gallagher had travelled to Little Rock, without an appointment, and managed to get to Clinton by guessing correctly which of several receptions he would attend, and then positioning himself at the top of a flight of stairs to waylay him as he came by. He and his wife Maeve identified and befriended several of the many senior officials in the administration with Irish connections. They included communications director Mark Gearan; legislative affairs aide Susan Brophy; the President's scheduler Marcia Hale; Education Secretary Dick Riley; the President's lawyer-friend from Denver, Jim Lyons; golfing partner Kevin O'Keefe; cabinet secretary Kitty Higgins; press advance director Anne Edwards, and Al Gore's chief of staff Jack Quinn. This networking helped to establish the credibility of the Irish operation. The Irish embassy had only six diplomats on its staff, compared to over seventy in the British embassy, but it was focused on one issue over all others, the peace process, and the President had made it known it was fine with him to spoil the Irish. Jack Quinn, for example, helped ensure that Spring got to see Clinton on the day of the NAFTA vote.

Despite the extraordinary "feel-good" aspect of the Saint Patrick's night party, there were concerns in the administration over the pace of events in Northern Ireland. The IRA and loyalist campaigns were continuing, despite the optimism generated by the Joint Declaration and the hopes that the Adams visa would accelerate the peace process. The IRA rockets at Heathrow set everyone back a little. During his remarks at the Saint Patrick's Day party, President Clinton said in a puzzled tone, "It is difficult to know what to make of the latest attacks at Heathrow. As in Hebron, reactionary forces will always attempt to kill the peace." In private he expressed concern about Heathrow to Reynolds, who told me later, "There was a lot of apprehension around in Washington. This was high profile, international."

At the party Soderberg and Lake got their first chance to take the measure of O'Dowd. "This is the contact with Adams," Soderberg said as she introduced him to Tony Lake. The President's National Security Adviser stepped back. "Should I be talking to him?" he asked. The three ended up in a corner where O'Dowd recalled Lake asking, "You're giving us all this advice, how do we know you are levelling with us?" He said they should trust him and pointed out that he had never given them wrong advice or misled them.

John Hume showed signs in Washington of the immense strain he was under as one of the most exposed figures in the process. Still above criticism in America for his courage as the leading constitutional nationalist in Ireland, he had been attacked at home by columnists in a Dublin Sunday newspaper for talking with Gerry Adams, and he chain-smoked nervously throughout the week. In the United States he was a moral compass for the Irish-American politicians who elevated him as a champion of peace. Now he was asking old friends like Tom Foley to trust him as he went down a controversial path with the paramilitaries. His frayed nerves showed in his uncharacteristic irritation over a *Boston Globe* headline "Ulster Leader, Backing IRA, Prods British," which appeared over his assertion that an IRA statement on Heathrow was actually an olive branch, and that Britain should clarify the Joint Declaration for Sinn Féin. Such a headline, Hume angrily told the paper's editorial board, could endanger his party colleagues' lives in Northern Ireland. But President Clinton, who received a message from Adams on Saint Patrick's Day, accepted his analysis that the situation was moving forward, and that Sinn Féin would be more isolated than ever if it did not take the opportunity offered for peace.

Two weeks later, Adams wrote to the White House explaining that a three-day Easter ceasefire the IRA had called from 5 April to 8 April was a genuine signal of intent. This was the first public ceasefire since the 1970s and was a major decision for the IRA, but to people in Washington it was derisory. Tony Lake wrote back to urge Sinn Féin to renounce violence.

Lake had now taken full responsibility for the administration's Northern Ireland policy. He made it clear he would not tolerate expressions of doubt about what they were doing from inside the administration. When an American diplomat in London, speaking as "a senior official," claimed to reporters that Adams had not responded to an expectation in Washington that he should do something in return for the visa, and that Washington now accepted that the issuing of a visa was a mistake, the mild-mannered Lake told a group of European correspondents in his office, "I am also a senior official, and he is wrong." Lake told us he thought the visa had offered Gerry Adams "a welcome opportunity to hear from many Americans, including many Irish Americans, of their very strongly held views that peace is both attainable and extremely important," and they had not expected Adams to make any immediate concessions. It had been a very difficult decision for President Clinton to take and the British did not agree, but the disagreement was "tactical, not strategic," said Lake.

Privately, the British Ambassador was offering a very different analysis. During an off-the-record briefing for British journalists in the embassy, Sir Robin Renwick said that the visa decision had been manifestly a bad one, that the conditions laid down by the US administration for a visa had not been met by Adams and that the US State Department and the FBI were now saying "I told you so." He advised the correspondents to read the syndicated column by Mary McGrory in the next day's *Washington Post,* of which he had advance knowledge. McGrory, who alone among liberal commentators took Speaker Foley's side in the visa argument, wrote that Adams "failed to renounce terrorism, encouraged all the wrong people in the United States and Ireland, and brought Clinton eight days of coruscating stories in the British press . . . The upshot of it all is that the cause of peace in Ireland was not advanced by a centimeter."

Having taken over Irish policy, Tony Lake's spacious corner office in the West Wing of the White House, with its portrait of a Hereford bull, Russian matryoshka dolls and rows of books on foreign policy, became a place of pilgrimage for Irish politicians, from North and South, who came to Washington in increasing numbers as the United States got more deeply involved in the British–Irish process. From the time of the Adams visa, party leaders from Northern Ireland found they could walk into the White House to confer with the President's most important foreign policy adviser.

Lake was not the first National Security Adviser to annex territory from the State Department on a particular policy issue. Henry Kissinger rode roughshod over Nixon's Secretary of State William Rogers on Vietnam and China. In the Carter administration, Zbigniew Brzezinski battled for turf on every Cold War front with Secretary of State Cyrus Vance.

But confrontation was not Lake's style. An inside operator with a dry sense of humor, he took over Northern Ireland policy because his boss wanted it that way. It was President Clinton who put Ireland near the top of the list of US foreign policy priorities, and entrusted it to the one senior official who spent "face-time" with him every day. It was an extraordinary decision, one based on the President's personal preference, and, as one British observer put it, responding to the aspirations of a section of the American population, rather than the national security interests of the United States.

The National Security Adviser was not entirely new to the Irish problem. Lake remembered his father, a British-born textile executive with a hot temper, arguing with his mother, a *Reader's Digest* editor with Irish ancestry, about the troubled history of Ireland. But it had not intruded on his lifetime in foreign policy, though he was now becoming fascinated by the complexities of the Irish peace process and its effect on relations among Britain, Ireland and the United States. He had a classic WASP—White Anglo-Saxon Protestant—upbringing in New England, and studied international economics at Cambridge. "There is the Yankee aristocrat there," a neighbor in Massachusetts once said. Lake joined Kissinger's team at the White House in 1969 but resigned when Nixon ordered the secret bombing of Cambodia and two weeks later Kissinger ordered that his telephone be tapped. In the Carter administration, he found himself on the other side of the foreign policy axis, serving as aide to Secretary of State Vance, where he witnessed the non-stop campaign by Brzezinski to usurp his boss. After Carter was defeated in 1980, Lake quit Washington and bought a 140-acre cattle-farm in Massachusetts—hence the picture of a bull in his office. He came back to serve Clinton only because the price of beef was down, he joked. The President considered Lake "one really smart dude," according to a friend. Diffident, efficient and private, with a distaste for the limelight and self-promotion, his aides labelled his first public speech after nine months in office: "Garbo Talks," comparing him with the publicity-shy film star. Opponents quickly found that he was also highly competitive. "People have the impression of him as a laid back guy," said Nancy Soderberg. "Tony is not a laid back guy."

There were setbacks in the early months. Lake offered to resign after eighteen American servicemen died in Somalia in 1993. But the National Security Adviser enjoyed the confidence of his commander-in-chief and when airman Scott O'Grady was rescued in a daring operation by US forces from Bosnia, it was Lake whom the President invited onto the White House balcony to smoke a celebratory Cuban cigar.

Despite his backing of the Adams visa, Lake was never a pushover for the Irish Americans. "Every time we engaged him on an issue, we had to start from ground zero," Niall O'Dowd said. As time went by, the National Security Adviser listened carefully to the Irish Americans, the Irish, the British, the State Department, and the President, before making a decision. His inclination was to be as even-handed as possible within the confines of the policy the President laid down. And having given an opening to the nationalists, he now turned to engage the unionists.

The Ulster unionists had never been eager to go to Washington. Over the years they had tended to demonize Irish-American politicians and did not see much sense in wasting time and money travelling to America to lobby Congress members the way John Hume had. In any event, they had a powerful British embassy to look after their interests in alliance with the State Department. There was also no political group in the US capital with whom they could associate to form a recognizable lobby. Where the Catholic Irish had preserved their identity in America through a sense of national grievance against the British, the Ulster Scots had scattered all across the United States and had assimilated to the point that, with few exceptions, they were no longer recognizable as an ethnic group. When the CNN program *Crossfire* decided to feature an exchange on Northern Ireland in December 1993, they could not find a single person in the lobbying capital of the western world to put the unionist case. They finally got Maureen Mercker, president of the small northern Virginia Ulster-Scots Society, a pleasant, middle-aged Ulster woman originally from Hillsborough, County Down, who had never before appeared on television. She almost gave apoplexy to co-host Pat Buchanan, there to put the Irish nationalist side along with Father Sean McManus of the Irish National Caucus, a Washington-based lobbyist for the MacBride Principles, when she asserted that the problem was poor Catholic education and that the Republic of Ireland was an imperialist nation.

Jim Molyneaux, who as leader of the Ulster Unionist Party for twenty-two years was one of Europe's longest-serving political leaders, never felt the need to travel to Washington. His party was attached to the British Conservative Party, which had the full title of "Conservative and Unionist Party," and he acknowledged he did not feel the same independence of spirit in foreign matters as John Hume. If they had gone to Washington, the Prime Minister of the day might have thought they were going on a holiday, said Molyneaux, looking back after he resigned as party leader in 1995. "We would have had no standing. As an opposition party we would have been expected to work through Her Majesty's Government."

For many decades the unionists were right. They were not needed in Washington. US policy since the partition of Ireland had been strictly one of non-interference, or support for a status quo which favored the Union of Northern Ireland with Britain. When, for example, the American League for an Undivided Ireland collected two hundred thousand signatures asking President Truman to help end Irish partition in the late 1940s, the State Department advised him to ignore it, and he did. When Eamon de Valera paid a courtesy call on the Democratic President in 1948, during an anti-partition tour of North America, the State Department reminded the White House that partition was the concern of the Irish and United Kingdom governments alone. In 1949, as Sean Cronin details in his book, *Washington's Irish Policy 1916–1986*, when Ireland declared itself a republic, the State Department asked the views of the British government on how it should respond—leading many Irish Americans to conclude that in its relations with Ireland the US preferred to work through the British government. The unionists did occasionally get alarmed at Irish propagandising in America. Northern Ireland Prime Minister, Sir Basil Brooke, called a press conference in London to counter de Valera's American anti-partitionist campaign, saying that partition was not the cause of the conflict, it was merely a symptom. The Northern Ireland government, before the disbandment of the Stormont parliament in 1972, saw the United States almost exclusively in terms of commerce. Unionist ministers crossed the Atlantic to seek investment rather than political support, and with some success: by 1969 they had attracted thirty American firms, including Du Pont, Monsanto and Goodyear.

After the Troubles began and internment without trial was introduced in Northern Ireland in 1971, the State Department looked after the unionists' interests. When Minister for Foreign Affairs Patrick Hillery went to the United States to call for the withdrawal of British troops from the six Northern counties, the Secretary of State William Rogers gave him a cold reception. A reporter who asked Rogers about Senator Kennedy's suggestion that the US act as a mediator in the North was told that the idea was "outrageous." Washington's view of Northern Ireland only began to change in the mid 1970s, and then almost exclusively in the Democratic ranks in Congress which had a heavy proportion of Irish-American legislators. Northern Ireland became an issue during the presidential campaign in 1976 of Jimmy Carter, who said it was a mistake for the US to stand quiet "on the struggle of the Irish for peace, for the respect of human rights, for unifying Ireland." Unionists were outraged. Jim Molyneaux declared at the time that the "irresponsible opportunism of this peanut politician has undone much of what has been achieved in persuading Americans to stop supplying arms to the IRA." But though Carter pressed London to take new initiatives in Northern Ireland and promised financial backing for any settlement, he did little more. Ironically, the first real setback for the unionists came under a Republican administration, when President Reagan backed the Anglo-Irish Agreement in 1985 which allowed the Republic of Ireland consultative rights on Northern Ireland. Lobbying by John Hume and Irish diplomats of Democrats like Speaker Tip O'Neill, Ted Kennedy and Tom Foley ensured US support for the agreement through an annual contribution of $20 million to an International Fund for Ireland. Reagan gave his endorsement because London and Dublin were acting together: when they did, American approval across the board was automatic.

The British government and the unionists still shared a strategic interest, however, in ensuring that the American administration took a tough line against IRA-related activity, from fundraising to arms smuggling. Margaret Thatcher and the Republican Presidents Ronald Reagan and George Bush worked closely together on this issue. The end of the Cold War changed that too. It came as a shock to some unionists when the British embassy, with all its powerful connections, proved unable to keep Gerry Adams out of America. Their anger was expressed by John Taylor, MP for Strangford, who called the decision to give Adams a visa "despicable" and blamed an "Irish mafia" led by Senator Kennedy. "We know that not only does the IRA get most of its funding for its murder gangs from the USA," he said, "but the White House now wishes to facilitate the apologists of the IRA murder campaign."

Privately some unionists saw the benefits of drawing Adams into the political process. Molyneaux told me, "It didn't seem to be an outrageous thing to do, especially after the Joint Declaration. The more you get Adams implicated in it, wrapped up in it, the more you're removing him from the hands of the gunmen." Letting him into the US could "do nothing but good."

With Washington now involved directly in the British–Irish process, the unionists for the first time saw the necessity to engage the Americans. Shortly after the Saint Patrick's Day party in the White House, Molyneaux accepted an invitation from Tony Lake to come to Washington. Lake and Vice President Gore received him in the White House. The unionist leader told Gore, "I had to lay my head on the chopping block," referring to the risk he took in working with John Major and Albert Reynolds on the draft of the Joint Declaration, "but it gives me great satisfaction that the two governments are locked together on it and underpinned by the one superstate present in Europe." Gore replied, "Yes, that's right." For the unionist leader the important thing was that the Americans were backing the Joint Declaration which enshrined the principle of consent. It was a turning point for unionists, he said. Adams was not "carrying all before him." The acceptance by the Americans of the Joint Declaration "laid the foundation for the linkage by the unionists with Washington."

Molyneaux, a slight, courteous man known affectionately to some of his constituents as "Big Jim" who had served under the command of the American 9th Army in Normandy during the war, was somewhat surprised at the fact that Senator Kennedy also accepted the Joint Declaration, and the hospitable way the Senator received him on Capitol Hill. There was no "carping, no opening up of old sores," he said. The unionist leader was experiencing one of the by-products of the peace process, a willingness by Irish-American politicians to play their part and reach out to unionists in the spirit of conflict resolution. This would have been less likely if Adams was still muzzled in America. The most optimistic of Irish Americans also hoped the unionist lobbying was a two-way street, because while in America unionists were also exposed to blunt American opinions on compromise and talking to one's enemies. David Trimble would acknowledge after a number of trips to Washington that Irish America was "complex, politically" and "part of the reason why the Clinton administration became more evenhanded is not just simply due to our advocacy, it's also because they've come in contact with reality."

"I never thought I would see the day," Molyneaux remarked as he emerged from the Senate Office Building on that visit, "that Senator Edward Kennedy would sit across a table from me and ask, 'Mr. Molyneaux, what can we do for you?' "

The unionists also received an assurance that the White House did not have an anti-unionist agenda.

"Part of the problem was that given the links with Irish America and the Catholic community, the Protestants tend to think that America doesn't care about them," Nancy Soderberg told me. "That was offset by the government basically keeping out of it and not getting involved." Now that the White House had reached out to Adams "there was a lot of suspicion. And one of the things we were concerned about was that the unionist community didn't trust us. They thought that we had a secret agenda to get a united Ireland in our back pocket. The truth is we don't and I don't know whether there'll ever be a united Ireland or not. I don't really care whether there is a united Ireland or not. All I care about is that there not be violence and that the North gets developed economically and politically so that it's a functioning society."

16

Listen For the Angelus Bell

"As of midnight . . . there will be a complete cessation of military operations. All our units have been instructed accordingly."
The IRA

One foggy summer evening in Dublin, around the middle of August 1994, a man stood waiting outside the *Irish Independent* office in Middle Abbey Street. Out of the mist, an attractive woman appeared and approached him. She asked, "Do you think Dublin will win on Sunday?" Recognising the code words, he handed her a document and they both walked off in different directions.

The woman was from Sinn Féin, and the document she was given was one drafted by Niall O'Dowd which the IRA urgently required. Sinn Féin had sent an enigmatic message to O'Dowd in New York, by hand, on 10 August to say that events were moving at a steady pace towards a "new situation" and the IRA wanted immediate amplification of what the Irish Americans were saying they could guarantee after a ceasefire. The Irish-American response would be a key element in determining their decision. O'Dowd asked a friend in Dublin to find a "safe" fax machine to which he could transmit a summary of what was on offer. The friend was then told that he should go to a specific location in the center of Dublin at a certain time, and that he should give the document to a person who would approach him and ask about the outcome of the match the following Sunday between Dublin and Leitrim in the all-Ireland Gaelic football semi-final. He did so and everything worked according to plan (and Dublin did win).

In the document, the Irish-American "peacemakers" committed themselves to a campaign to achieve certain goals if an unarmed strategy was pursued by the republican movement. The list of attainable goals included: unrestricted access to the United States for Gerry Adams and other Sinn Féin members; parity of treatment with other Northern Ireland leaders in Washington; early release or the transfer to Ireland of IRA prisoners in the United States and the end of FBI surveillance; the opening of a nationalist office in Washington; a major campaign to influence public opinion in the United States; United States government support for the peace process with the aim of getting Washington to act as a guarantor of any agreements in Northern Ireland, and the promotion of Irish-American business and investment in the North of Ireland.

These commitments carried considerable weight with the IRA. The Irish Americans had already delivered the visa for Adams and broken the grip the State Department had on Irish policy. Also implicit was the promise of considerable financial backing from figures like Chuck Feeney for the development of the Sinn Féin operation in the United States once the violence stopped.

That summer, as would later be revealed, the republican movement was debating a document which stated that the way to the movement's goal of a thirty-two-county democratic socialist republic was to "construct an Irish nationalist consensus with international support." To win the struggle they must strengthen it "from other nationalist constituencies led by SDLP, Dublin Government and the emerging Irish-American lobby." It noted that there was "potentially a very important Irish-American lobby not in hock to any particular party in Ireland or Britain" and that "Clinton is perhaps the first US president in decades to be substantially influenced by such a lobby."

For a time, however, it had looked as if the prospects for an IRA ceasefire on which this strategy was predicated were fading. A Sinn Féin conference held in the Donegal town of Letterkenny in June 1994 had taken decisions which were highly critical of the Joint Declaration of the British and Irish governments on the way ahead. This led many commentators to believe that the IRA was rejecting the idea of a cessation.

"There was an expectation that Letterkenny would see some kind of an announcement," Albert Reynolds said. "I don't know how that perception grew because it was never in my mind that there would be an announcement. The Sinn Féin conference was to be used to sort of bring the thing farther, to get a mandate from the floor as to what they were at. Some people expected an announcement before, some that it would be there, some thought it would be immediately afterwards. But they hadn't everything in place. They were worried. There was a leak, in the *Mail* in London, about an impending ceasefire and that postponed the announcement. It could have come earlier. Everything had to be strictly confidential. It had to be a tight ship, otherwise if these guys were put in a corner by the media they'd have walked away. You had to take them slowly, step by step."

In Washington, Nancy Soderberg was growing impatient. She too was concerned about the reports from Letterkenny, which were almost universally negative. One day her patience snapped. She rang O'Dowd, who was holidaying in County Kerry. Echoing Senator Moynihan's query to Kennedy after the Heathrow mortar bombs, she asked was the administration being taken for a ride. "Where's the ceasefire you promised me?" she demanded sharply.

"I was really at that point very depressed," Soderberg said, "well not depressed, but I was beginning to think the ceasefire was not going to come. By July the people who opposed it were all saying, 'See we told you so,' every time a bomb went off. It got sort of annoying after a certain point. O'Dowd had told me ahead of time to watch, there's going to be some very important announcement coming out of this party conference. And he basically ginned me up to think something was going to happen. We kept in touch with him during this period and he was saying, prior to Letterkenny, that the ceasefire was still coming, it was going to work. We should have some positive statements coming out of it about the ceasefire, watch it carefully. And then when the statements came they were very hard-line. There was nothing new."

"She came on pretty strong," recalled O'Dowd who said he had never given her any reason to suppose there would be an actual ceasefire announcement at Letterkenny. "There was clearly pressure on her. I said I could only tell her what I knew. I had not been told there would be a ceasefire out of Letterkenny. The media was useless, misreading everything. They had tagged this as the time of the ceasefire. I had not given that impression to her and I told her that it did not change anything."

Bill Flynn and his security consultant, Bill Barry, meanwhile made another private visit to Ireland in mid-summer. They drove to meet Adams in a hotel in the border town of Dundalk. Barry claimed there was some tough talking at the meeting, which was guarded by men he thought were from the IRA. "We met Adams with another man who didn't introduce himself," he said. "Gerry Adams was telling Bill Flynn what he would like him to do. I said, 'I don't think you understand who Bill Flynn is, he can't do your public relations for you.' Flynn said to Adams, 'Look, you've got to understand where I'm coming from. If one more person is killed, we're out of here. You're going to lose corporate America.' I think Adams was visibly shaken, Bill was so direct." The Sinn Féin leader had a hard time figuring Flynn out, a source close to Adams said. "We thought he was a bit of a loose cannon, a wild card, more Catholic than Irish, and a really complex character," he said.

Back in New York a few weeks later, O'Dowd received the message about the urgent need for the Irish-American proposals in written form. In a hand-delivered letter, his contact also asked the Connolly House Group to be ready to return to Belfast to lend visible support to what was about to happen. The *Irish Voice* publisher got him on the telephone and asked what would be the appropriate time to come. "When should I take my holidays?" was how he put it. The contact replied, "Why don't you try the last week in August?" The message was clear.

The American group prepared to return to Ireland on 25 August. It included the original four, O'Dowd, Morrison, Flynn and Feeney, plus trade union executives Joe Jamison and Bill Lenihan representing the American labor movement, an addition which broadened it to embrace the worlds of politics, big business and labor. Bill Flynn brought Barry with him for personal security.

O'Dowd was convinced that without the Americans, and the guarantees outlined in the document he had compiled, there would be no ceasefire. Apart from being the visible guarantors of Irish-American support, the presence of the group served a vitally important function for the republican movement in Ireland. It identified Irish America with an IRA ceasefire decision, thus making the possibility of a split in the United States, a prospect which haunted republicans, less likely. It reinforced the American dimension to those in the IRA army council who were about to make what was to them a momentous decision to call off their war, to end voluntarily a tradition of physical force nationalism dating back to Fenian times. It brought the promise of influential Irish-American support for an unarmed strategy.

The Irish Americans had already delivered much. Before the peace process, the republican movement's top-level contact in the United States had been Martin Galvin of Noraid; now it included important representatives of American business, politics and trade unions, and could go all the way to the President of the United States. This was the group, the amateur emissaries of Gulliver, which had already helped win the visa for Gerry Adams and had opened up lines to the White House. They represented a crucial point of reference in the broadening of the nationalist debate, the others being the government of Albert Reynolds and the constitutional nationalists of the North represented by John Hume. In his view, Joe Jamison said, it would be in the interests of everyone concerned to pursue an unarmed struggle as "we have a very green White House and President Clinton wants to play a constructive role regarding Northern Ireland." Also, "the Dublin government has moved the issue up to the top of its agenda and to his great credit John Hume has moved the two strands of Irish nationalism to his approach."

On Thursday 25 August the members of the Connolly House Group arrived back in Dublin. Reporters were told that this time they were private citizens who had come to Ireland at the invitation of Sinn Féin, which wished to solicit their views in relation to various decisions that might be taken in the future, views which they would relay back to the White House and Congress. If there was a substantive move by the IRA in terms of a ceasefire, said Morrison, then he believed the White House would be responsive. This did not mean the group was taking sides. "Sinn Féin views us as having things to say and here we are on that basis," he said. "We believe the IRA is considering a long-term ceasefire and that would be a wonderful thing." In Belfast, Sinn Féin said it regarded the forthcoming meeting with the group as a "significant and important element in the ongoing peace process."

While they were keyed up to receive exciting news, the group did not know any details of the promised ceasefire. There had been rumors that it would be limited in duration, or that the IRA would go on to what they called a "defensive posture," an idea based on the South African model which the Irish Americans had come up with. They discovered however when they met Albert Reynolds and Minister for Foreign Affairs, Dick Spring, in the Taoiseach's office that Reynolds was taking an all-or-nothing attitude. The meeting was quite tense. O'Dowd recalled how he thought the hostile body language between the two Irish leaders betrayed tensions which foreshadowed the break-up of the Fianna Fáil–Labor coalition that winter. The Taoiseach insisted on the group taking a blunt message to Sinn Féin in Belfast. Dublin wanted a permanent cessation of violence, he said. That was the only basis on which Sinn Féin could become involved in the political process. No reserving the right to defend nationalist communities. No limits of six months or a year. It had to be an all-out IRA ceasefire or nothing.

"The Americans came over and they were talking about a six-months ceasefire," said Reynolds. "They thought that was possible. I think they took the view about Letterkenny that it was a setback, and that maybe I was looking for too much, that we were all looking for too much. They were leaving me to go to Belfast and I told them straight out—if you go to Belfast I said, and you come out talking about a three- or a six-months ceasefire, I'm not with you, it's not acceptable. It's either all or nothing."

"I could see all their faces looking at me around the table," Reynolds said. "And Bill Flynn said nothing. And Chuck Feeney said nothing. Niall O'Dowd and Bruce Morrison I think were a bit taken aback with the ferocity of the opposition to a limited ceasefire."

Someone asked him how he could turn down a limited cessation of the IRA campaign. "I said, it simply won't work, it's not on. Bruce Morrison said, 'How are you going to do that in public?' I said, 'I'm going to do it, I'm telling you. Anybody goes into that meeting up there with Gerry Adams and says that a short-term ceasefire is on the cards, it's not, not as far as I'm concerned. For them and you maybe, but not for me.' "

Reynolds insisted that he did not know there would be a total cessation at that time, though O'Dowd left convinced that the Taoiseach was even then working out the final wording of the ceasefire announcement with Sinn Féin intermediaries.

On the hundred-mile drive to Belfast next day, Bill Flynn took the wheel. Barry sat beside him. "The whole time we were talking about how to get these guys to agree to a complete cessation," Barry recalled. Their reception in Belfast was not universally welcoming. The fact that the Americans had come at the invitation of Sinn Féin rankled with some SDLP members and the unionists. To many people they were identified with Sinn Féin. "Some Sinn Féin members would make the same mistake," said O'Dowd. "We would have to tell them to back off."

In the Wellington Park Hotel near Queen's University, before going to Sinn Féin headquarters, O'Dowd gave each a copy of the document he had drawn up for the IRA and asked them in turn what they thought Gerry Adams would tell them. Chuck Feeney, with his instincts for the deal sharpened by high-level international business, predicted confidently that it would be a total cessation of violence. But they were split down the middle. They decided that the best approach was to ask straightforward questions, such as "When will the ceasefire start and for how long?" That day Belfast was full of rumors of a ceasefire of limited duration or a shift to a "defensive posture." Feeney also thought that the republicans would have a problem with a passing reference in the document to the Joint Declaration, which Sinn Féin had not accepted.

A Sinn Féin driver, who had gone to the wrong hotel, eventually came to pick them up. They arrived through a crush of media at Connolly House to find Gerry Adams waiting for them with Martin McGuinness, Mairead Keane, Lucilita Bhreatnach and another official. O'Dowd guessed Bhreatnach was the attractive woman who collected the document in Dublin's Middle Abbey Street. He was impressed at how relaxed and in control Adams was as they sat round a large wooden conference table in a wood-panelled room with a television suspended above a curtained window. As a press photographer took pictures, Feeney stayed outside the door, only coming in when the cameraman had gone. The billionaire was so camera-shy, he engaged a photographer to take pictures when he met people on private visits to Ireland—with instructions never to develop the film.

"It was the biggest media scrum I ever saw in my life," said O'Dowd. "We had to battle our way in. We were very tense, jumpy and nervous. People were shouting questions. We were hot and sweaty when we got in. Then Adams came into the room looking so cool. Better than I had ever seen him. So calm. I knew something had happened. He had made a decision and a good one."

The Sinn Féin leader said immediately, O'Dowd recalled, "The army is going to call a complete cessation."

Bill Barry remembered how they crowded into a small room and immediately sat down for what they thought would be a difficult session. Adams said, "We're talking about a complete cessation."

"I thought, woah!" recalled Barry. "Everyone immediately relaxed."

Martin McGuinness and O'Dowd's Sinn Féin contact—whom he declined to identify—started to go through the document painstakingly. Feeney had been right; there was a problem with the wording.

"They went out to discuss it," said O'Dowd. "I thought it was nitpicking but they are like that with documents." When they came back they said it would not be a problem.

Bill Barry remembered being intrigued to hear Adams refer to the IRA as "the army." Adams said, he recalled, there was still one outstanding problem to be resolved. "If not, the army feels there is no way they can go forward."

"Adams then told us it was time to make a public statement," said O'Dowd. "He asked us to say nothing to the media. We went out. Chuck Feeney as usual was trying to duck the limelight. He's one of the most brilliant people I ever met but he hates publicity and never gives interviews. But a photographer climbed on some railings and there he was in the next day's *Irish Times.*"

"When we came out to face the press and television cameras, I had a feeling he [Adams] was showing to "the army" American people in positions of influence who were prepared to help and were in fact real," said Barry. "It was show and tell."

Gerry Adams told the reporters of the importance of American involvement in terms which sounded intriguingly like O'Dowd's box theory. "If you have a situation where the two governments cannot move, surely someone from outside that frame can be signalling the need for the situation to advance," he said. "That is what happened in the Palestinian–Israeli situation." Standing beside Adams, Bill Flynn came as close as possible to announcing what they knew, while giving nothing away. He said, enigmatically, that he had learned nothing from the meeting that led him to believe that anything but a permanent cessation would be on offer, he said.

"You've been fooled," one journalist told them.

That evening, O'Dowd rang Trina Vargo, who was holidaying in Ireland, to brief her on what happened. He also relayed to Jean Kennedy Smith and his Irish diplomatic contact, Brendan Scannell, what Adams said. He wondered if Reynolds knew already what was about to happen.

On Monday 29 August, O'Dowd telephoned his contact in Sinn Féin from his room in Dublin's Berkeley Court Hotel. Three days had passed since the Belfast meeting. The media was now frantic with speculation. "When would it happen?" he asked. It would be on Wednesday, the contact said, "Listen for the Angelus Bell."

Having been brought up in Ireland O'Dowd knew the Angelus was a call to Catholics to pray which was broadcast over RTE radio at 12 noon, followed by a news summary.

On Wednesday morning, O'Dowd, a fitness enthusiast, went to the Berkeley Court gymnasium to work out on the treadmill. At 11:20 he was exercising on his own, with the radio playing in the background. The program was suddenly interrupted for a news flash. A scratchy recording by a female IRA volunteer announcing the IRA ceasefire was broadcast, followed by a bulletin from a breathless RTE reporter, Charlie Bird. All over the country people stopped what they were doing to listen as he repeated the words of the IRA statement: "Recognizing the potential of the current situation and in order to enhance the democratic peace process and underline our definitive commitment to its success, the leadership of Óglaigh na hÉireann [the Irish Volunteers] have decided that as of midnight, Wednesday 31 August, there will be a complete cessation of military operations. All our units have been instructed accordingly."

O'Dowd wept with joy. His passion for the political process had taken a huge toll, financially, emotionally and on his personal life. At that moment it was all worth it. He rang Adams from his room to congratulate him, and to his surprise he got through. Speaking in Irish he told the Sinn Féin leader that America would not let them down. "Tá a lán obair le déanamh," said Adams. "There is a lot of work to be done." Jean Kennedy Smith rang O'Dowd and said she, too, wanted to talk to the Sinn Féin leader, who was still *persona non grata* with US officials. "My office says not to call him but I want to do it," she said. O'Dowd gave her Adams's telephone number.

Senator Kennedy came on the line with congratulations from the United States, where it was breakfast time. RTE invited O'Dowd onto a news program. At the broadcasting station an hour later, Albert Reynolds came into the studio "pumped up" and shook O'Dowd's hand so hard that it hurt for days afterwards. "Albert grasped my hand," he said, "and hugged me in a bone-crushing embrace, fixing his gimlet eye on me, and exclaimed, 'They said it couldn't be done, but we showed them!'"

Bill Flynn and Bill Barry later went to the American embassy, a five-minute walk from the Berkeley Court Hotel, where the Ambassador had called the embassy staff together in the rotunda to make the announcement of the ceasefire. It was a triumphant moment for her after the internal battles over the Adams visa. The two men drank a glass of champagne with her. Flynn would not admit to being emotional. "It's a curious thing, one you will not understand, but O'Dowd was in tears, I wasn't," Bill Flynn told me later in New York. "To me that IRA decision was the most natural thing in the world. I looked on it as another good business decision. You know, in my business, we celebrate great victories, and then we'll have a Martini, and then we'll go back to work the next day. So I felt awfully, awfully, good about it, but the arguments were strongly in favor of this being the only reasonable solution." He emphasized each word by tapping a table hard with his forefinger. It was when he talked to his relatives in County Down, he said, that he realized "what it really meant to them and to their teenage girls and sons."

The following morning, Nancy Soderberg went into her office at 4:30 while Washington was asleep and the streets around the White House deserted. She placed several calls to Ireland, where it was already daylight, asking questions, checking developments, and accepting and offering congratulations. The really sweet calls, she said, were those which came later, from the State Department, telling her she had been right after all. Two hours later she was on her way to the airport to catch a 7 a.m. flight to Panama to arrange for Panamanian officials to accept Cuban refugees picked up by the US coast guard. Ireland was only one of her responsibilities.

House Speaker Tom Foley, who had promised to be the first to admit he was wrong on the Adams visa if it helped bring peace, said on Irish radio he thought Adams had delivered on the promises he had made and he would now be prepared to meet him in Washington. Ted Kennedy issued a statement calling it "a joyous and hopeful day for all of Ireland and for all the Irish people." The head of Noraid, Paul Murray, welcomed the announcement and commended the IRA for its courage. Again the only off-key note was struck by Martin Galvin who said Noraid remained prepared to back a resumption of "the military fight for Irish freedom" if the ceasefire broke down due to "British perfidy." Not long afterwards he was moved aside as spokesman for the organization.

Six weeks later, on 13 October, the combined loyalist military command announced its own ceasefire in Belfast. The political wings of the two loyalist paramilitary groups, the UVF and the UDA, had also produced new political thinkers in David Ervine of the Progressive Unionist Party and Gary McMichael of the Ulster Democratic Party who were keen to achieve peace. The statement was read to the press in a community center in north Belfast by Gusty Spence, who as a member of the UVF had served a murder sentence for the shooting dead of a Catholic barman in 1966, an act of sectarian murder which helped spark the Troubles. He had long since espoused the cause of peace and the wheel had come full circle for him. He and his comrades offered "the loved ones of all innocent victims over the past twenty-five years abject and true remorse," a note of apology which caught people in Northern Ireland by surprise.

The loyalists had told Bill Flynn in coded language over the telephone what they were planning to do, and asked him to come over from the United States for the occasion. The burly insurance executive was present in a back room, with the door locked, during the announcement, so that no one from the media could blunder in and discover he was there.

"I was the only Catholic invited," he said proudly. "The only nationalist or republican."

Flynn was serving a similar purpose for the loyalists as the full Irish-American peace group had for Sinn Féin. His presence was a guarantee of equal treatment for them in the United States. "They knew that I was an ardent nationalist but that I didn't want anyone killed for Irish unity to happen," he explained. "I agreed with the republican movement's assessment, absolutely, but it was not worth one life." Meeting them was an eye-opener for Flynn. He was astonished to discover that they had contempt for the mainstream unionist politicians. He recalled one saying to him: "These sons-of-bitches will fight to the last drop of our blood." He came to trust some of them as much as he did Adams. Gusty Spence, now a friendly, pipe-smoking pensioner, was, Flynn believed, "one of the most honorable men I've ever met in my life, a man who made a terrible mistake but who could have been a [Roman Catholic] monsignor in the United States."

The night before the press conference, a group of seven loyalist politicians, including Gusty Spence, had met in the Europa Hotel with Flynn in attendance to draw up the final version of their cease-fire statement. Flynn offered one piece of advice: not to change the one sentence in which they apologized.

"I wish the IRA had said that," he told them.

17

Visa War Two

"It was a bit like Nixon going to China."
Tony Lake

Unknown to the public, and to most of those celebrating the IRA ceasefire, the decision to end violence hung by a thread until the last minute over another request to the White House for a visa.

By late August, as the IRA army council approached decision time, Albert Reynolds had reached the point where he felt there was nothing more he could do to bring about peace. He had got the Joint Declaration with John Major, helped win a US visa for Gerry Adams, lifted the broadcasting ban on Sinn Féin, lobbied the President of the United States, and secured clarification of the Joint Declaration for Sinn Féin.

"I was at the end of the road," he said. "Were we going to get a decision or were we not going to get a decision? My time was running out on this project. There was nothing more we could do."

But there was. An urgent call came from Father Alex Reid of Clonard Monastery in Belfast, the intermediary between Sinn Féin and the Taoiseach. It was the week before the ceasefire. He said the IRA wanted to send an emissary to the United States to be there on the day of the ceasefire to explain the decision to republican supporters. This was the crunch issue, the priest said. The man they wanted to send was Joe Cahill.

Reynolds was disbelieving. Cahill, he knew, was a hard man in the IRA with a prison record. He would never get a US visa.

"They were coming to decision time and they wanted to know post-decision how they're going to sell this to their troops," recalled Reynolds. The IRA's message was it needed to get Cahill, nobody else but Cahill, into "the States, because he's the senior person, he has the credentials and if he says—look, here's the road we're going, it's a change of direction, a change of policy—they'll accept it from him. If not, there may not be any ceasefire."

Father Reid told him that the one thing the IRA would not do was risk a split in the organization. It could start in the United States and come over to Ireland. They did not want any risks from Irish America. "If this can't be organized it could be the end of it," he told Reynolds.

Joe Cahill was a 74-year-old Belfast republican whose association with the IRA went back to the late 1930s. In 1942, he and five other IRA men had been sentenced to death for shooting a Catholic Northern Ireland policeman. One was hanged, Cahill and the others were reprieved. When the IRA split in 1969, Cahill was one of the leaders of the faction which became the Provisional IRA. Shortly afterwards Cahill and Daithí Ó Conaill went to New York and sponsored the setting up of Noraid along with three other veteran IRA men, Michael Flannery, Jack McGowan and Jack McCarthy. In November and December 1970, Cahill toured New York, Chicago, San Francisco, Cleveland, Boston, Yonkers and Philadelphia rallying support for the provisional movement and for Noraid, which was registered that year as a support group for the dependants of IRA prisoners. Noraid funds were often hand-delivered to Cahill in Dublin. No accounts of expenditure were ever made public, and the American, British and Irish authorities became convinced that much of the money was going to the IRA to acquire weapons. Its organizers denied this, though individual members were tried and convicted of gun-running. Cahill was to suffer a similar fate. On 28 March 1973 he was arrested aboard the *MV Claudia* off the Waterford coast with five tons of arms and explosives donated by Colonel Ghadaffi, the Libyan dictator, and was sentenced to three years in prison by the special criminal court in Dublin, though he was released early due to ill-health. Barred from the United States since 1971 because of his activities, Cahill slipped across the Canadian border into the country in 1981 to rally financial support. He was tracked by the FBI but managed to evade arrest and return to Ireland. Like Gusty Spence, Cahill was now a pleasant old man with a sense of humor, whom Jean Kennedy Smith later found to be "lovable and funny."

Cahill had touched every generation of the IRA ranks. He was respected by the hardliners. Only he would do. "I had to be there to secure the base as the announcement was being made," Cahill said later. If there was no visa there would be no ceasefire.

But all those who could help Reynolds were away from their desks. It was high summer. Clinton was at Oyster Pond, a small estate on Martha's Vineyard off the Massachusetts coast. Nancy Soderberg was in Madrid. Trina Vargo was in Ireland. So too was O'Dowd. Jean Kennedy Smith was in the south of France, holidaying with the former Conservative Chief Whip Michael Jopling and his wife, and other Kennedy family members, including the actor Arnold Schwarzenegger who was married to her niece Maria Shriver.

Reynolds began calling Jean Kennedy Smith at her holiday home.

"Jean was below in the south of France on her holidays. I was on to her maybe a couple of hours," said Reynolds. He kept ringing her. A guest at the house recalls Jopling taking the telephone in some exasperation once and asking, "Who is this?" only to find the Taoiseach asking for Jean. "She said, look, the best thing I can do is go home, we can't operate the peace process like this," recalled Reynolds. "She came back to Dublin and told me that things were not going well."

Jean Kennedy Smith had located Nancy Soderberg and got her on the telephone but the White House official had dismissed the idea of a visa for Cahill as preposterous.

"I was in Madrid," Soderberg recalled. "I had been in Morocco for about ten days and was driving through southern Spain. I had gone out for dinner with a friend in Madrid and had gotten back from dinner and the phone was ringing. It was Jean, saying, 'I have to talk to you about another visa.' I said, 'Forget it, there's no ceasefire. I'm on vacation,' that was sort of my reaction. Then I left the following day and flew to Los Angeles for the christening of my nephew. We were staying in the hotel and again the phone rang and it was Jean. I said, 'No, let's see the ceasefire. We're not doing any more visas until we see the ceasefire.' I came back to my office on Sunday. Jean started calling there. You know, I give her credit. She just wouldn't quit."

Soderberg talked to Lake that weekend from Los Angeles and found that he too was in no mood to give any more visas. And still the Ambassador to Ireland kept calling. "She kept pushing," said Soderberg, "saying, 'We really need this.' "

Albert Reynolds recalled that when Jean Kennedy Smith came back to Dublin she set up a call for him with Soderberg.

"She said, 'Nancy claims she's 25 percent Irish, you'd better increase that to 75 percent and tell her to make the right recommendation.' "

Soderberg recalled that Jean Kennedy Smith had Albert Reynolds call her directly "and he basically walked through exactly what the IRA was going to say. He said, 'Now I know you're a quarter Irish and I want you to have that part of your brain working.' He was just very impassioned that this had to happen in order to get the ceasefire."

"I spoke to Nancy a number of times," said Reynolds. "She said it was very difficult to make any progress because the Justice Department was against it, the Attorney General's office had come in against it, national security was a huge thing. And of course the background of the guy himself. Everything was against it. I said, 'You'll just have to break every rule in the book to get this one.' She said, 'I just don't see this one running for you.' "

Reynolds made a final appeal on Monday evening, less than forty-eight hours before the scheduled announcement of the ceasefire. "In the end, in the last telephone contact I had with her, she said, 'Look, the President took a risk before, he's been criticized, nothing has happened.' I said, 'That's not strictly true. I know the ceasefire hasn't happened, and as far as you are concerned it's way down the line. But if this doesn't work, I don't believe there will be a ceasefire. And that's why I want you to recommend it and do the best you can.' I asked where the President was. She said, 'He's in Martha's Vineyard.' I said, 'Nancy, will you get into your car and take this file to him personally and ask him, if he's going to say no, will he phone me before he says no?' She said, 'Only he can make that decision. And there's nobody recommending it.' And I said, 'Nancy, what about you?' And she says, 'I'll do the best I can.' I said, 'Don't forget you're 25 percent Irish.' She said she'd take it up to him and that she would tell him."

Soderberg did not get in her car to drive to Martha's Vineyard, a road journey of some eighteen hours with a ferry ride at the end. But she sent a "must see" memo by secure line and the President did ring Reynolds.

"I was at home," said the Taoiseach. "The President called and said, 'Nancy has been bringing me up to date with this. It's extremely difficult. Did you read this man's CV?' I said I wouldn't have to." Reynolds laughed at the recollection. Everyone in Ireland knew all about Joe Cahill. "And then he said, 'This guy that's with him, you know he was turned back from New York only four or five days ago?' "

The President was referring to Pat Treanor, a councillor from County Monaghan. Sinn Féin had sent him to New York in advance to prepare the way for Cahill and to look after the old IRA man when he arrived. He had been stopped at immigration at JFK airport and sent back to Ireland. Treanor had served time in an Irish prison for IRA-related offences, which meant he was barred under the 1990 Immigration Act for association with terrorism. Now the IRA wanted Treanor to be allowed to return with Cahill. Reynolds was annoyed. He had not been told through his intermediaries that the Monaghan councillor had been sent to America in the first place. "They sent him out blind on his own," said Reynolds later. "He went to square up Noraid. I gave out to Sinn Féin, the way they handled it, they didn't even advise me and walked me into that problem."

Reynolds told the President that Cahill had a bad heart "and could drop dead on the way." That was why Treanor was needed, to look after him. "The President asked, 'But why pick a guy when the records are against him, as well as Cahill? It's bad enough trying to get Cahill through, now you want to get this other guy in that we sent back three or four days ago.' I said, 'That's all he's there for. He's there to accompany Cahill. I'm absolutely certain that this is going to bring a ceasefire. If we get no visa, I don't think we'll have a ceasefire, that's my honest opinion.' 'Are you sure?' he asked down the phone. I said, 'I am.' I said it was not a short-term ceasefire. I made it clear it was for good. He thought about it and he asked, 'Are you sure there are no "ands," "ifs" or "buts"?' I said, 'I've asked for it unconditionally and total.' He asked, 'What kind of words are going to be used in this public announcement that I could think about?' "

At this point, Reynolds said he would be back to the President in a few hours with the exact words that were going to be used in the ceasefire announcement. He got on to his intermediary, Father Reid, "and I drafted a couple of lines that would be used if everything fell into place." He transmitted them to Washington. The projected wording had a big impact on Soderberg. It promised a "complete cessation" of violence, not a limited ceasefire.

"I flipped," recalled Nancy Soderberg. "That was the moment of realization for me that it was going to happen." The Taoiseach "was basically saying that this was not a heavily caveated ceasefire. This was a very clear and unequivocal statement. He wanted us to take that text to the President. Ultimately what he did was convince me and he wanted me to convince Tony and the President that this was a real ceasefire. Until I heard it directly from him and the direct language they were going to use, we were not convinced. Without that language we would not have given a visa. I talked to Tony and I said I think this is for real, we should do it. He said OK and we sent a memo to the President with the text, by secure communications. I think I actually talked to the President myself."

Jean Kennedy Smith also rang Oyster Pond to say "Mister President, I am completely convinced this will work."

Reynolds and Clinton spoke again after Soderberg had sent him the words to be used in the ceasefire announcement.

"He asked, 'They will change?'" Reynolds recalled. "I said, 'No, they will not change.' He said, 'This guy is looking for a visa for two to three weeks.' I said, 'Give him a visa for a couple of days and if it doesn't happen, send him home. That's all I can tell you.' In the end, anyway, he said, 'OK, have these two gentlemen at the US embassy at 9 o'clock in the morning. They'll be all right.' I said, 'Thank you very much.'"

Reynolds told a relieved Father Reid, who was staying that night in the same house as Joe Cahill, waiting for word from America. But for the priest and the old IRA man, the drama was not quite over. During the night the alarm system went off in the house and the two men ran out into the street in their nightwear. It was a false alarm.

The next morning, Tuesday 30 August, Cahill collected his visa. He caught the midday Aer Lingus flight from Dublin to New York and was in Manhattan by late afternoon, late evening in Dublin. The IRA went ahead with its ceasefire statement the following morning.

"The President was the first man back on the phone on the Wednesday morning when the ceasefire announcement came," said Reynolds. "He came on to me in the office. He said, 'Well done!' He said he always believed it would happen. I said, 'It couldn't happen if we hadn't got people like you. If Cahill hadn't got that visa I don't believe we would have had a ceasefire.'"

Nancy Soderberg recollects that the Treanor visa request actually came the day after Cahill was granted permission to enter the United States. "I don't remember that being a big issue," she said. "It was sort of an 'add-on.'"

To Reynolds the Cahill visa incident underlined again the extraordinary importance of American involvement. The British had lost the battle over Adams and now they had to concede on Cahill too. The British embassy in Washington had asked the White

House to wait and see the content of the IRA announcement before making a decision on Cahill. The media knew nothing about the flap over Cahill until it leaked in Washington the day before the ceasefire, and then it made little impact because of the news that a twenty-five year campaign of bombing and shooting was—apparently—coming to an end.

Tony Lake confirmed that the White House took the advice of the Irish rather than the British over Cahill because IRA supporters in the United States needed to be convinced and only a trusted figure could pull it off. "It was a bit like Nixon going to China," said Lake with a grin, interviewed in his office a few days later. The American role now, he said, was that of "interested, active onlookers," and their mere involvement kept the peace process going "to a degree it might not if left to its own devices."

"Would we have had a ceasefire at all without American involvement?" mused Reynolds later. "Maybe we would but I have my doubts. It demonstrated to the IRA army council that it could get things done politically that they weren't able to get done otherwise. Adams couldn't get into the States for about twenty years. It was a part of that crucial strategy to put everything in place. Maybe it would have happened twelve months later, maybe, I don't know. It was part of a strategy where the issue was broadened out into an international one. We weren't just fighting this battle on our own. Diplomatically we were enlisting all the support we could get anywhere around the world, both in Europe and in the United States, and to me it was vitally important."

He said it could not have been done without Jean Kennedy Smith. "No ordinary Ambassador would have gone out on a limb as she did," he said. "She's more than an Ambassador. She has a great political brain. She has a great combination of diplomatic and political skills."

The cessation came about, Gerry Adams told an American reporter, "because influential opinion-makers in the Irish-American community came to an understanding, a consensus, that I was then able to take to the IRA and say, look, there's an alternative way forward to pursue equality of treatment here in Ireland while moving towards a negotiated settlement. I told them we had a sympathetic President and a similarly disposed Dublin administration."

When Pat Treanor stepped back on American soil to act as Joe Cahill's minder, one of his hosts asked about the bandages on his hand. "I was one of the last people shot by the IRA," he said, almost proudly. Just before the ceasefire he was showing foreign journalists a border crossing which had been blocked by the British army, when two RUC officers grabbed him and pulled him into a car. As they were driving him along a road inside Northern Ireland, IRA men in a lorry in front of them opened fire, not knowing Treanor was in the car, and nicked him. The two policemen escaped injury.

As the ceasefire held, Cahill had his five-day visa extended to fifteen so that he could make a tour of the major American cities. He travelled to New York, Philadelphia, Boston, Chicago, San Francisco, Los Angeles and Florida. All his meetings with IRA and Sinn Féin supporters were closed to journalists.

One was held in a Second Avenue Irish bar in Manhattan. It was attended by Gerry Adams's long-time friend, Congressman Peter King of New York, who recalled thinking, "All that's missing here are the trench-coats." The meeting was held in a back room reached by going up a long flight of stairs and down a long corridor, and was attended by twenty people, among them businessmen, lawyers and activists. There were no flags or banners. Cahill, balding and with a bulbous nose, sat at a table. He was introduced by Treanor. Though looking sickly and sometimes gasping for breath, the old IRA man came alive as he spoke. He emphasized that for the first time since 1920–21 the Irish nationalist movement was absolutely united. It was a real unity, not phoney, and the IRA did not want to squander that. Secondly, Adams had been working for seven years to bring about peace and every strand of the movement and every IRA active service unit now supported the ceasefire. Thirdly, President Clinton had changed Irish republican thinking. For the first time an American President was not automatically linked up with the British. They wanted to take advantage of that. President Clinton's interest helped to assure them that British Prime Minister John Major would negotiate in good faith. Fourthly, the ceasefire meant that there would now be regular US visas for Sinn Féin leaders such as Gerry Adams and Martin McGuinness, the British would no longer have exclusive access to United States leaders, and Sinn Féin might open an office in Washington. Fifthly, there was the prospect of massive aid from the United States, although Sinn Féin was not asking for it and they were not being bought off. This was best left to Albert Reynolds.

Reynolds also sent over an emissary. When the President phoned after the ceasefire with congratulations, Reynolds told him he wanted Dick Spring to call and see him at Martha's Vineyard. "I said, 'Look, you played a crucial role as a politician, get your credits. I can't get over there but I'll tell you what I will do. I'll send over the

Foreign Minister and Deputy Prime Minister immediately, and you organize your own press conference and everything.' He said, 'Fine, send him over.' "

Spring travelled to Martha's Vineyard two days later to meet President Clinton, who was openly delighted with the ceasefire and its portrayal in the United States as a foreign policy triumph for his administration. The White House laid on a fourteen-seat US Air Force Gulfstream jet to bring Spring to the holiday island from Washington, along with several officials, Ambassador Dermot Gallagher—who had arrived back in the US on the same flight as Joe Cahill—and three Irish journalists.

The reporters were distinguishable from the official party by the fact that we wore ties. The White House had ruled that the officials should come in casual attire. President Clinton, who had just played eighteen holes of golf, was wearing an open-necked shirt and black cowboy boots, with one trouser leg tucked in and one hanging loose, when he greeted Spring on the driveway of his holiday home in bright morning sunshine. They talked for forty-five minutes inside the four-bedroom shingle house with wicker chairs and a stone model of a dog outside, and a glimpse of the blue ocean beyond through a knot of pine trees. It was another knee-to-knee summit in a tiny room into which crushed the two political leaders along with, on the Irish side, Dermot Gallagher, Noel Dorr, Seán Ó hUiginn and Fergus Finlay, and, from the US National Security Council, Sandy Vershbow and Neil Wolin. Afterwards Clinton strolled over to where we waited by the gate.

"We are very, very pleased about developments," he said. "We want to continue to work with the governments of Ireland and Great Britain and we are prepared to take some steps to do whatever we can to help that happen. The United States has tried to be a friend of peace in Ireland and we will continue to do that."

For Seán Ó hUiginn, this confirmed the achievement of an important national goal, that of getting the United States, with its close ties to both countries, to cast its shadow over the British–Irish process. Ó hUiginn was in charge of the Anglo-Irish division in the Department of Foreign Affairs and was a principal architect of the peace process. "At crucial meetings with the British side, he did much of the talking," remarked an Irish diplomat, who described Ó hUiginn as the inspiration of the crucial Framework Document which the two governments constructed on the basis of the Joint Declaration, and as the strategic thinker who set the parameters for Irish policy towards the United States. He worked closely with

Brendan Scannell, was treated as a confidante by Jean Kennedy Smith, and gave critical support to the initiatives of the Irish Americans. He talked regularly by telephone with O'Dowd, sometimes in Irish, and with Tony Lake and other key figures in Washington.

Spring later said that a special committee of the International Fund for Ireland would be set up to identify projects which could benefit from any US-backed economic restructuring package. Clinton had pledged a greater American commitment of new investment and capital into a peacetime Northern Ireland economy. "We would hope to get at this work as quickly as possible," said Spring, following his meeting with Clinton. "Time is of the essence. There's a momentum building as of last Wednesday and we're not going to allow time to elapse." Some Irish officials speculated that an American windfall was in the offing. I was told of a draft administration report which suggested increasing the $19.6 million annual US contribution to the International Fund for Ireland by $120 million over two years. But US officials warned privately it would be a tough fight to secure any increase. There was some griping in the State Department and in the Congress that $40 million of back payments to the International Fund was still in the pipeline because of the time lag between project approval and the provision of funding. In fact, the first real peace dividend came from the private sector. Hilton Hotels announced plans to build a $26.3 million hotel in Belfast.

"We decided that Fall to try and come up with some ideas to reinforce the peace process and try and show some tangible results with this process quickly," said Soderberg. A week after the ceasefire, she set up an interdepartmental committee drawn from the National Security Council, the State Department, the Treasury, the Office of Management and Budget and the Agency for International Development. It tossed ideas around and decided on an investment conference in the United States the following May to encourage American investment for Northern Ireland and the six border counties in the Republic. Similar conferences had been held for South Africa and eastern Europe. The group "tried to drive the inter-agency process as hard as we could to have some tangible benefits by May that we could put on a table," she said. But she discounted the talk of a windfall. "There was a report of a $200-million investment which was widely out of reality. I still to this day do not know where it came from. Once it's out there it's very hard to shoot it down."

A few days after the ceasefire, Vice President Al Gore stopped off at Shannon on his way home from a trip to Cairo. He was on crutches as a result of an achilles tendon injury. Reynolds was there and strongly advised Gore to make contact with the unionists.

"I told him, 'You're the ideal balance because the unionists perceive President Clinton as being totally on the nationalist side—which I don't accept but that's the perception and in politics we have to deal with perceptions.' I said, 'You have connections up there, you're the ideal balance.' He said, 'You think I should get involved?' I said, 'You should. The first thing you should do is ring James Molyneaux.' He asked, 'Will I ring him from here?' I said, 'Don't ring him from here. Ring him from the plane on the way back because if you say you've been ringing from Shannon the same perception's going to come out.' I said, 'You're the man that can be seen as the other link, no matter what you tell the unionists about President Clinton at the moment, to them he's a nationalist, a republican.' The Vice President agreed."

"I was delighted with Al," Reynolds said.

The White House ran into some problems, however, in trying to ensure after the ceasefire, as the British wanted, that unionist politicians went to Washington before Gerry Adams. Tony Lake and the US Ambassador to London, Admiral Crowe, telephoned Molyneaux to press upon him their sensitivity to unionist concerns and ask him to come to Washington, with a good possibility of meeting the President.

There was still some reluctance on the unionist side to play the nationalist game by allowing themselves to be drawn into a Washington-brokered process. At the same time, the Joint Declaration accepted by the three governments embraced the principle of consent and unionists could hardly ignore the fact that the United States was now a player in Northern Ireland's future. Molyneaux said he had booked a lengthy tour of Australia and New Zealand. Ulster Unionist Party MPs David Trimble, Ken Maginnis and William Ross went instead, along with party secretary Jeffrey Donaldson, on 21 September. They were received in the White House by the Vice President who reassured them that the Americans were not trying to impose a political agenda on Northern Ireland.

"They made it absolutely clear that they have no formula for the political way forward, that they want to help in whatever way they can the political process and that it is up to the two governments and the parties in Northern Ireland to determine the political way forward," said Trimble, the lawyer who a year later was to become leader of the party. Maginnis emphasized the unionist demand that the IRA give up its weapons, which he listed as 1,200 high-powered assault rifles, two tons of semtex, a dozen heavy machine-guns, several RPG7 armor-piercing grenades and between seven and twelve SAM7 surface-to-air missiles.

The Americans felt it was also important that credit be given to John Hume before Adams made another celebrity appearance. When the SDLP leader came to Washington that same week he was acclaimed everywhere as the real peacemaker. Clinton singled out Hume for praise at a Democratic Party fundraising dinner in honor of Senate majority leader George Mitchell who was retiring from the Senate. After listing Northern Ireland as one of his foreign policy achievements, Clinton enunciated a theme which he was to repeat for months to come, that America was a country to which other nations in the world turned to for help and example, including South Africa, Middle East countries and Ireland.

"John Hume is here, in the United States, a symbol of peace and hope. Where are you, John?" he said. The Derry man rose to a standing ovation. Mitchell honored Hume in a more practical way, adopting his oft-repeated criticism of Northern Ireland unionists to castigate the Republicans in Congress. "If the word 'no' was removed from the English language," he said to laughter, "they would be speechless."

But the unionists would soon be frequent visitors to Washington, and they would have plenty to say.

18

The Adams Family

"Of course we sang Irish songs, and of course we sang rebel songs, half of our songs are goddam rebel songs for a very good reason."
Fionnuala Flanagan

Much to the embarrassment of National Security Council officials, no one in the administration could actually find the original banning order, when shortly after the cease-fire, the White House decided that it would lift its ban on official contacts with Sinn Féin when Gerry Adams came to Washington. Nancy Soderberg was forced to conclude that it had never existed in written form.

The Sinn Féin leader now applied for a second visa to go to the United States and this time there was no hesitation on the part of the President. Just before midnight on 19 September, while waiting in the Oval Office for news of developments in Haiti where he was sending troops to restore democracy, he signed an order authorizing State Department officials to issue US visas to Adams and two companions from Sinn Féin, Richard McAuley and Aidan McAteer, so they could make a tour of the United States, ending up in the US capital.

British diplomats began a counter-offensive at once to ensure that their access to the center of power was restricted. They suggested forcefully to the administration that the ban on contacts should continue for three months to test the genuineness of the ceasefire. A British diplomat said, "There are two things that matter. That the ceasefire be made to stick, and that we do not lose the unionists. Any new initiative now would have to be measured against these two criteria, and that translates into not rushing ahead with the visa."

British Ambassador Sir Robin Renwick again began lobbying Tony Lake and top officials in the State and Justice departments, pointing out that Adams had not declared that the ceasefire was permanent. John Major sent Clinton a private letter and a copy of a speech he gave in Belfast in which he pointed out that he was still waiting for the IRA to make clear that it had renounced violence permanently. A Downing Street spokesman said in London that whatever the US decided, "It would be unwise to do it at a time which would inflame unionist opinion in Ulster."

The Connolly House Group, which had helped to persuade the IRA of the benefits that would flow from the United States if the violence stopped, began to press the White House to receive Adams when he came to Washington. The unionists had been brought into the White House to meet Al Gore; if Adams was to get parity of esteem, he too should have similar access, they said. Otherwise it would be seen by republicans as an affront.

With both sides gearing up for another fight down to the wire, Adams returned to the United States. He arrived on Saturday 24 September, travelling this time to Boston in the first-class section of the Aer Lingus flight from Dublin. Senator Kennedy, accompanied by his wife Vicky, met him at the terminal building and later they conducted a brief press conference in a dismal open-air bus repair depot on the edge of Logan airport, to which the event was consigned by the airport's director of media relations. Some taxi drivers spent up to half an hour searching for the location.

About one hundred Sinn Féin supporters gathered there with tricolors and a banner saying "England, get out of Ireland." A man held up a placard with the words, "Welcome President Jerry [*sic*] Adams." When I pointed out the mis-spelling, he replied, "It doesn't matter how it's written—he's here."

Adams had been welcomed into the world of constitutional politics in Ireland a few days earlier when Albert Reynolds greeted him at Government Buildings in Dublin and they were photographed clasping hands with John Hume. The pictures of Adams and Kennedy standing together in Boston symbolized his coming in from the cold in the United States. Kennedy—who had had two brothers assassinated and had always refused to meet Adams because of his support for political violence—said that giving respectability to the political representative of a guerrilla group was important to a peace process which appeared to be developing along lines similar to those in South Africa and the Middle East. The handshake with Adams would also not damage Kennedy's re-election prospects in a closely fought Senate race with a Republican rival in five weeks' time. Many blue-collar Irish Americans in Massachusetts had cooled on Kennedy over the years. "By meeting him at Boston, Kennedy was introducing him to Irish America," said Ciarán Staunton, the former Noraid man whose advice to Adams was to prove important in the coming days. "If the Sinn Féin leader was good enough for Kennedy he was good enough for everybody else. Considering Kennedy's role over the years, it sent a signal across America that it was OK to give Adams the keys of the cities." It also meant Irish Americans could come out and celebrate without being tainted with support for violence. A feature of the crowds waiting for Adams would be the numbers of Irish-American judges and police officers applauding his peace drive.

The Senator and the Sinn Féin leader drove off in Kennedy's Chevrolet Silverado van to Boston's Park Plaza Hotel, led by a police car with flashing blue lights, for a meeting with community leaders organized by Kennedy-backer John Cullinane. At the plush hotel, members of Noraid, many of them from the poorer districts of Boston, mingled with local celebrities, such as Harvard law professor Alan Dershowitz. The former president of Noraid in the Massachusetts city of Lynn, Pat Linehan, whose organization had been shunned by many establishment figures, commented, "Now we're at the Park Plaza!"

Among the crowd was Paul Hill, the Belfast man who with three others was wrongfully imprisoned for fifteen years for the 1974 Guildford pub bombing, and his wife Courtney Kennedy, daughter of Robert and Ethel Kennedy. Courtney's marriage to Paul Hill had reinforced the personal involvement of the Kennedy family in Northern Ireland politics. In 1994, when Hill was successfully appealing another conviction for killing a British soldier, a Kennedy delegation led by Courtney's mother, Ethel, and her brother, Congressman Joe Kennedy, travelled to Belfast to lend support. Paul and Courtney Hill now invited Adams to spend his first night in Washington at Ethel Kennedy's suburban home, Hickory Hill.

Later that day Adams travelled on to the industrial town of Springfield, Massachusetts, one hundred miles west of Boston, for his first contact with grassroots Irish America. There was strong support for the IRA in this closely knit community of Kerry immigrants, where people did not ask, "What part of Ireland do you come from?" but "Are you from Dingle or West of Dingle?" Memories were kept alive in Springfield of the time when Irish immigrants fleeing destitution came to Hungry Hill and encountered signs at the Smith and Weston gun factory saying, "No Catholics." Adams went to the John Boyle O'Reilly Club, where some men wearing tee shirts with a drawing of an armalite rifle shouted, "Ooh! Ah! Up the Rah [Republican Army]."

But the message on the banner across the back of the stage read, "SINN FÉIN, A LASTING PEACE." When Richie Lawlor, national vice president of Noraid, rose to introduce the bespectacled, bearded figure in navy blazer and dark trousers, he spoke of "peace, unity, dignity and justice" in Ireland. The IRA was now saying to the British, said Adams, "We want peace and we're declaring for peace," and the role of Irish Americans now was to be "guarantors of this peace process."

But in an interview with the *Boston Herald*, the Sinn Féin leader made what in hindsight was a telling remark: "None of us can say two or three years up the road that if the causes of conflict aren't removed, another IRA leadership won't come along, because this has always happened."

In Detroit, Adams met Rosa Parks, the black woman who had set off the American civil rights movement forty years earlier when she refused to move to the back of a bus in segregated Alabama, a non-violent act which made her a powerful symbol of peaceful resistance.

In Hollywood, he was given a birthday party in a private house, and the Belfast man from the Falls Road found himself being lionized by guests such as Angelica Huston, who played Morticia in *The Addams Family*, Barbara Hershey, who was Mary Magdalene in *The Last Tears of Christ*, Oliver Stone, director of *Natural Born Killers*, Sean Penn, estranged husband of Madonna, and a host of other Hollywood celebrities including Martin Sheen and Gabriel Byrne.

"I was inspired by the peace process," said his host, Fionnuala Flanagan, an acclaimed Irish actress famous for her one-woman show as Molly Bloom. "I never met Gerry Adams until the night he walked into my house in Beverly Hills," she said. "We didn't have any journalists because it was a private party. The *Sunday Times* parked itself at the top of my drive that night. The weather was beautiful, half the party was inside, half was outside, and so there was a lot of people out on the patio and it was a birthday party and we had a cake, and at one point a waiter dropped a tray of glasses and they shattered, and that was written up as "Glasses were smashed and rebel songs were sung" so that, very insidiously you see, the notion was planted, here they go again, the drunken Irish, they just resort to rebel songs. Of course we sang Irish songs, and of course we sang rebel songs, half of our songs are goddam rebel songs for a very good reason, I make no apology for that. Shame is one of the most powerful weapons and they're trying to make us, the Irish, feel ashamed for having dared to step forward, to be ashamed of the fact that we blew it, but we didn't blow it, we didn't blow it, the lack of vision was not ours, the lack of courage was not ours." The publicity from the birthday party harmed her career, she said. "I know of one case where I have not been hired because somebody read in a paper that I had given a party for Gerry Adams. It was, sort of, 'Well, we know her political leanings,' and people are frightened of being associated with someone they perceive as dangerous because she is a republican."

But politicians of all kinds saw no career disadvantages in associating with Adams and the large crowds of voters he was drawing. Back in New York, he was presented with a proclamation hailing him as a "harbinger of peace" by Republican Mayor Rudi Giuliani, who had succeeded Mayor Dinkins. At the ceremony in front of New York City Hall, the New York Police Emerald Society Band played *A Nation Once Again* and four police officers in white shirts and black berets with green cockades stood in a guard of honor with an Irish flag. Giuliani had been the government lawyer who prosecuted Joe Doherty, the IRA man who spent nine years in US prisons fighting vainly for asylum. Standing beside Adams he explained that "as US attorney I carried out my responsibilities faithfully, I agreed with the decision of my government, just as I agree with the decision of my government now" to grant Adams a visa.

The reception he was getting across America dazzled the small Sinn Féin delegation, but when they arrived in Philadelphia for a rally before proceeding on to Washington, they still had no agreement with Clinton officials on how they would be received when they got to the US capital. The Sinn Féin leader was insisting on being invited to the White House, as Hume and the unionists had been, on the basis of parity of esteem, and as part of the peace dividend to demonstrate to his supporters back home.

As the ban on contact by US officials with Sinn Féin had not yet been formally lifted, Adams still had to communicate with the White House through Niall O'Dowd. He asked the *Irish Voice* publisher to make his feelings quite clear to the National Security Council. O'Dowd spoke several times by telephone to Tony Lake and Nancy Soderberg from his Manhattan office and apartment. They were adamant that it was not possible for the Sinn Féin leader to come to the White House. It was too early to accord him such a privilege.

"I was told the White House was off limits, no way, it can't be entertained," O'Dowd said. "And I knew the White House could not be moved. I knew the fix was in."

John Major had obtained a promise from Clinton that Adams would not be allowed into the White House, according to British sources. In Washington, a high-level administration source told me that they had promised the British Prime Minister that Adams would not meet Gore or Lake either. Asked later if the British had been given to understand that the White House would be off limits, Soderberg replied, "Yes and no. I mean we had said at the time that we had no intention of letting him come to the White House and that became, 'We promised the British he wouldn't come to the White House.' But it had never really been an issue."

British diplomats, their trust in Clinton understandably eroded from past experience, kept in constant touch with the National Security Council officials, pointing out that the IRA still had its weaponry intact and that Adams had yet to renounce violence and declare the ceasefire permanent. They were assured that all that was on offer was a meeting with US officials at the State Department. When he raised the matter with President Clinton at a $2,000-a-head fundraising dinner in his Virginia home just outside Washington, Senator Kennedy was given the strong impression that the case was unwinnable.

It seemed that the Adams trip and the American dividend were in jeopardy and that the British were making up lost ground.

On Saturday evening 1 October, the day before he was due to arrive in the US capital, the Sinn Féin leader contacted Niall O'Dowd once more in his New York apartment. It was a different Adams from the one O'Dowd dealt with over the first visa.

"Then he was totally reactive and I was in charge of the process," the *Irish Voice* publisher said. "Now he was in the door, he revealed he could hang tough if he thought there was a five percent chance. He understood something I didn't, how to push the White House. What impressed me was his utter determination, his sense of his community being considered less than equal. He wanted access to the White House and he would not accept a place at the back of the bus."

The image of being put to the back of the bus had stuck in Adams's mind since meeting Rosa Parks in Detroit, with its resonance for Catholics who felt they were forced to accept second-class status in Northern Ireland. Also, Adams was saying privately that the first visa had brought the ceasefire forward by one year and that the process must show that one of the benefits of the American connection was parity of esteem.

"We could see the headlines in the British press—"Adams Snubbed' " said Staunton. "We had to find a way out of that so that the people he represented would not feel snubbed by the US government." The former Noraid official got on the phone to O'Dowd. Vice President Gore had talked to the unionists, he said. Why could Gore not talk to Adams by telephone when he got to Washington? They didn't have to actually meet. Would he put that proposal to the White House?

"The whole idea was that if Gore could have a discussion with unionist leaders, why not with Sinn Féin? That's how I put it to O'Dowd," said Staunton. "They had given their word to the Brits—no White House. But no one was asking them to break their word to the Brits. The issue wasn't the phone call either. It was Vice President Gore talking to Adams. That was the line which would go out on the wires."

On Sunday morning, O'Dowd telephoned Soderberg at her home, and put the suggestion that the Vice President could telephone Adams when he got to the home of Ethel Kennedy where he was spending his first night in Washington.

"It was a beautiful Fall day and I was planning to go out," O'Dowd recalled. "I didn't know what I was in for. Nancy's first reaction was to shoot down the suggestion, to say, 'No way, no how.' Then I knew it was going to be a long day."

Both Soderberg and Lake went to the White House as the morning progressed to try to work out a compromise. They spent much of the time on the telephone to O'Dowd. Several ideas were tossed around, such as Adams coming to the Old Executive Office building within the White House security zone, or a meeting with Clinton adviser George Stephanopoulos and Jack Quinn, Gore's chief of staff, just inside the White House grounds, but they were discarded as gimmicks. The idea of the phone call from Gore was discussed again, and again Soderberg said it wouldn't work.

By late afternoon they were still talking but getting nowhere.

"We argued back and forth but it didn't get any better, and both sides faced the potential embarrassment of a failed Adams trip and a failed White House policy," said O'Dowd. "Nancy and Tony both got on the phone and we spoke on and off right through to 6 o'clock. Tony Lake wanted me to convince Adams he should be happy with the State Department meeting, and I kept saying it would be seen as a disaster at home. He said that someone with the status of the Vice President couldn't be asked to talk to Adams so soon after the ceasefire."

O'Dowd recalled that Lake "had a very laid-back style of negotiating. He would quote—or rather misquote—from *Casablanca*, something about 'This being the end of a beautiful friendship.' And he would try to get your agreement to sign off on his terms by saying something like, 'It's a beautiful afternoon, why don't we wrap this thing up and go home?' "

"This was where I got to know Niall very well," recalled Soderberg. "Every time any of these things would happen we would negotiate through Niall what the terms were going to be." She described their telephone relationship with some amusement. "Actually, it's funny, we'd both spent so many hours on the phone with him over the last couple of years, we all know each other's living and eating habits, Sunday morning coffee, late nights . . ."

The idea of Gore calling Adams came from a "back and forth" between O'Dowd and Lake, Soderberg recalled. She had no way of knowing it originated with Staunton. "They were pushing for a White House meeting and a lot more high-profile reception. They started pushing very hard and they were spinning up the Irish-American community to do more." Senator Kennedy called from his yacht off Cape Cod and had a conversation with Lake which one insider described as "angry." In New York, people were responding to a plea by Paul O'Dwyer to call the White House and demand access for Adams. "I want the phones to ring off the walls," he said, "so that the President of the United States will say, 'What's happening here?' "

Recruiting people across the country to put pressure on the White House was now an established strategy for the Irish-American lobby. O'Dowd and leaders of groups like the Irish American Unity Conference would at moments of crisis alert members all across the country and supply them with the telephone numbers not just of the National Security Council but individual White House officials like Jack Quinn or George Stephanopoulos. Such pressure worked particularly well with members of Congress. "The Achilles' heel of the British in America is that they have no votes," one activist said. "An Irish-American politician can determine there is a mass of voters out there agitated about the Irish issue. There's nothing in it for them to take the English side, apart from getting invitations to British embassy dinners." O'Dowd once got a call from a National Security Council official saying, "Please call them off, we can't cope." He put the word out and it stopped.

Late in the day the White House began to give ground.

"Lake began to take the idea of the phone call from the Vice President more seriously," said O'Dowd. Eventually he went off, evidently to discuss the matter with the Vice President. He came back to say they would settle for a five-minute telephone call, with Gore telling Adams the ban on contacts was ended. "I really had to push for this," Lake told the exhausted publisher. It was also agreed that Soderberg would sit in on the meeting with State Department officials in Washington to give Adams face-to-face contact with a White House official.

"I think ultimately we wanted the meeting to be a positive one, and not one where they were cat-fighting about not having been properly treated," said Soderberg. "Adams was basically trying to up the ante and we finally agreed that we would have the Vice President call him. We had said at the time that we had no intention of letting him come to the White House so that wasn't really an issue. But it gets into this whole parity of esteem, and pride, and it's very important to have things presented in an appropriate fashion."

Soderberg then asked O'Dowd where Adams could be located at that moment, so he could be brought into the discussion. "He's just about now boarding a plane in Philadelphia to go to Washington," said O'Dowd. Soderberg told the White House situation room to find the travelling Adams family.

Lake came on the line again to say to O'Dowd, "Well done."

19

Taking Over Washington

"I'll bring you in the front door, not the back door."
Bob Dole

At that precise moment late on Sunday afternoon, the members of the Sinn Féin group, exhausted after eight days of meetings and receptions, were making their way as quickly as they could to the departure gate at Philadelphia airport to catch a commuter flight to Washington. They were late, the plane was at the furthest gate, and they were half running through the crowds of passengers in the terminal. An airport official stopped them and demanded to speak with Ciarán Staunton. Not knowing what was going on, the Sinn Féin adviser reacted with some initial alarm. Staunton had been a top operative of Noraid, whose members had for twenty-five years been kept under surveillance and sometimes arrested. The official told him that there was a telephone call for him at the boarding desk and instead of being detained, Staunton found himself talking to the White House situation room which patched him through to Niall O'Dowd in Manhattan.

O'Dowd told him his proposal had been accepted and Gore would phone Adams the next morning. Staunton, breathless, asked him to wait while he told Adams. However, the rest of the Sinn Féin party had already boarded the propeller-driven plane and he had to sprint along the tarmac to get his seat, abandoning the call.

The group was so late for the flight that stand-by passengers who had got on were asked to leave. One turned to Sinn Féin member Richard McAuley as he got off. "Are you the IRA?" he asked. "No," replied McAuley, solemnly. "Pity," said the man. "I wanted to say you are doing a great job."

In Washington, a driver was waiting to pick the Sinn Féin party up in a rented car. They had three mobile telephones and they stopped by the Potomac River so that Adams could speak to O'Dowd in New York. One by one the batteries died. They drove on and finished their negotiations at Hickory Hill, a white-brick Georgian house in the prosperous suburb of McClean, Virginia. Adams was told exactly what the Vice President would say and he rehearsed what his responses were likely to be.

Next morning at 8:35, the Vice President telephoned Hickory Hill. Adams picked the telephone up at a desk with Bobby Kennedy's picture on it. Gore told him that Sinn Féin was no longer a banned organization and asked Adams to give his regards to Ethel, though she was away at the time. Shortly afterwards a letter came through the fax machine from Tony Lake, confirming that the ban had been lifted and inviting Adams to begin a "process of engagement" with the White House.

Not everyone on the republican side rejoiced at the way things were going. Michael Flannery, the 92-year-old co-founder of Noraid, who broke with Sinn Féin when they decided to drop their boycott of Irish parliamentary elections in 1986, called the ceasefire a farce. A week after the cessation he fell and was admitted to Flushing Hospital in New York. His old comrade Joe Cahill went secretly to see him there. Flannery said he had no interest in attending his meetings to hear why the IRA had called a ceasefire.

"They have stopped their hostilities without any guarantees whatsoever," said Flannery to a reporter. "I see pictures in the paper of celebrations in Belfast but I have to wonder, what are they celebrating?"

He died on 30 September. It struck many as symbolic that Michael Flannery should give up the ghost as Gerry Adams was drawing Irish Americans into the peace process. The old generation of republicans with bitter memories of the Irish Civil War were fading away. Flannery had fought with Tipperary No. 1 Brigade of the IRA in the Civil War and emigrated to America in 1926. A daily communicant, he told me in an interview in his New York apartment many years earlier that he never knowingly killed anyone in the Civil War, but that he had once put a gun to the head of a Free State soldier. It had misfired. "To this day I regret that it misfired," he said.

Flannery was buried on 3 October in Queens, the same morning that Gerry Adams took the telephone call from Al Gore legalizing US contacts with Sinn Féin. Three shots were fired over the grave from a pistol. There were seven priests on the altar. Among the mourners were former Congressman Mario Biaggi, founder of the Congressional Ad Hoc Committee on Irish Affairs and George Harrison, a co-defendant with Flannery in a high-profile arms trial. Joe O'Neill, Republican Sinn Féin councillor from Bundoran, County Donegal, gave an oration in which he said Flannery "realized fully that compromise with British rule in Ireland must inevitably lead to the abandonment of the active struggle." At a New York function that weekend, Harrison was honored by Bernadette McAliskey, the former Bernadette Devlin, who had come out from Ireland. The civil rights heroine whom Clinton had so admired in 1969 was now a critic of the IRA for ceasing its campaign. "Could we not stop her visa?" a Sinn Féin official asked a colleague, only half-joking.

After his "unbanning," Adams began a round of meetings on Capitol Hill where he was treated as a celebrity.

The two rival Irish lobbies, the Friends of Ireland and the Ad Hoc Committee on Irish Affairs, came together in House Speaker Tom Foley's office to mark what they believed would be a new era of peace, and to celebrate jointly the end of the IRA campaign. Foley, who had expended so much political capital to keep him out of America while the IRA campaign continued, courteously shook Adams by the hand.

"By this time the ceasefire had occurred, so I didn't have a personal animosity towards Gerry Adams, so it's just one of those things where you shake hands," Foley told me later.

"I'll tell you what bothered me more," he went on. "The American press in particular just stumbled over themselves with their cameras to get to him. I was aghast at that. He was interviewed by the most ill-informed and vacuous press. And here was John Hume, whom I thought was a hero for peace, getting pushed into a corner by the American press in favor of a man who was associated with violence. The best credential Adams had was his involvement in talks with John Hume and John's belief that there was a constructive road to a ceasefire. John has got enormous credibility with so many of us here. Adams had to have some constructive opportunity in these discussions, or have brought something to it, or I didn't think Hume would possibly participate."

Among those Speaker Foley invited into his office for the occasion was Peter King. "I was never invited to anything by Foley before," said the Republican Congressman. "Several times I would have my people call Foley's office to say I'd like to be invited to this or that meeting and he never did. Once in the cloakroom someone mentioned my name to him in connection with an education vote, and he said, 'You shouldn't be talking to him, don't you know he's a friend of Gerry Adams?' He even stepped back in a receiving line with Clinton, Hume and Reynolds on Saint Patrick's Day when I came along so he didn't have to greet me." King blamed the British embassy for stirring up trouble for him. A staffer for House minority leader Bob Michael told him a British diplomat had come to Capitol Hill to talk to the Republican leadership about him.

"Foley that day was the perfect gentleman," said King. "After that, Gerry would make fun of me, and say, 'I'm the guy who brought you in from the cold.' "

Adams was also received by Senate majority leader George Mitchell, and Senator Alfonse D'Amato took him to lunch. The wheeler-dealer Senator from New York had some stories to tell about the time he was in Belfast in 1980 with Peter King during the IRA hunger strikes. One night he encountered four men in the Europa Hotel bar who said they were UVF and would get him for talking to Sinn Féin. A terrified D'Amato insisted on King spending the night with him in his bedroom with a dresser pushed up against the door and the light switched off, an episode which had been the source of ribald humor among their friends ever since.

Senate minority leader Bob Dole also met Adams, in his office, along with a small group of legislators. King pointed out the window to the White House. "Next time you come, Senator Dole might be living there," he said. "And I'll bring you in the front door, not the back door," responded Dole, who was even then planning to run for the White House.

After a luncheon address at Washington's National Press Club, where he was advertised in error as a speaker on peace in the Middle East and introduced as the president of "Shine Finn," Adams went to the State Department for his meeting with US officials, accompanied by Staunton, Richard McAuley, Aidan McAteer and Mairead Keane. O'Dowd travelled down from New York to sit in as an adviser.

"I wanted to essentially hand over and say—this is it, you don't have to deal through me any more," O'Dowd said. "I had a great sense of history going in, but I also wanted to be there to interpret what was said, to ensure that what Adams was hearing and what I was hearing was the same thing."

They found a red carpet at the entrance to the building, but it was for another visitor to Washington, Nelson Mandela, the role model for Adams, who that evening wore a Mandela tee shirt in his hotel. As agreed, Nancy Soderberg attended the meeting, along with State Department official John Kornblum, who did most of the talking, and Gore's national security adviser, Leon Furth. Adams alone spoke on the Sinn Féin side. He raised the issue of a multiple-entry visa and the right to raise funds in the United States. He said he intended to return soon to the United States and would request a meeting at the White House. It was too early to make such decisions, he was told.

The comparison of Adams with Mandela made by the Sinn Féin leader's supporters rankled with British Foreign Minister, Douglas Hurd.

"There's a tendency in some places to put him on some kind of level with someone like Nelson Mandela," he told reporters in New York where he was visiting the United Nations, his voice laden with contempt. "We know, because it's measured in free elections, exactly what support Gerry Adams and Sinn Féin have in Northern Ireland. It's ten percent. He's Mr. Ten Percent."

The British were not amused by the treatment of Adams, which observed the letter but not the spirit of the promise to keep the White House out of bounds. The special relationship once again came under strain. One of John Major's ministers, Kenneth Clarke, seeking to insult Labor leader Tony Blair as a practitioner of empty politics, said he suffered from the "Clintonesque thing." The astute political editor of the London *Sunday Times*, Michael Jones, summed up British establishment reaction. He observed that "Clinton's crowd all but caved in." The outcome "prompts the awesome conclusion that we, America's most reliable ally, may have to examine Clinton's undertakings in greater detail before we take them at face value in future. The man has finesse and knows how to use it. Adams is not the principal problem. Clinton, Lake and Soderberg are."

Determined not to let Adams have a free ride in the media, the British government sent former Tory minister Michael Mates to the United States on the British Airways Concorde on which a round trip costs over $8,000. A tired Adams gave a poor performance in a televised BBC debate with Mates which went down badly at home. CNN's *Larry King Live* also flew over Ken Maginnis for the first ever television encounter between Adams and a unionist MP. There was a moment of near-farce in the dressing room. Adams removed his trousers to have a broken zipper fixed and was sitting in his underpants when they heard Maginnis entering the studio. He quickly pulled his pants on again.

The two met in the studio briefly before going on air.

"Welcome to Washington," said Adams.

"Oh! He's trying to take over Washington too," snapped Maginnis, who throughout the joint interview refused to make eye contact or address Adams directly. The program revealed to Larry King's worldwide audience the intensity of the revulsion among unionists for Adams. The MP also refused to shake Adams's hand on screen, saying, "I'm not going to be involved in gimmicks." When Larry King asked him, "Ken, do you trust Gerry?" he retorted, "No, I most certainly don't trust Gerry. I don't know who Gerry is. I don't think he knows who he is. We know him as the leader of the IRA/Sinn Féin. But sometimes he tells us he is not that person. So I wonder who he is. He is someone who fronts for a vicious organization that has killed almost two thousand people during the last twenty-odd years."

"Don't go away!" King told viewers as the debate ended. "When we come back we're going to take your phone calls for Ross Perot."

In the CNN foyer, a few journalists and a British diplomat gathered to greet the contestants. Maginnis told them, "I'm a long way from shaking Gerry Adams's hand. Gerry Adams controls one hundred tons of guns and assault rifles."

Just then Adams came out of the lift. Maginnis sensed him coming but did not turn around. The Sinn Féin man came up behind and put an arm around his shoulder, saying, "Well done, Ken!" The Fermanagh–South Tyrone MP visibly recoiled and hurried off without responding.

From behind the cameras and the arc lights came the voice of Btitain's *Daily Express* reporter Peter Hitchens with a question for the Sinn Féin leader about his alleged IRA past.

"Ach! Hello, Peter," said Adams. "You know, you have made my trip very entertaining, Peter. But let's go forward. The IRA has stopped. Let's stop harking backward. Anyway, well done, Peter!"

"My pleasure," replied the reporter.

20

Guess Who's Coming to Dinner

"Why don't you just say the word 'permanent'?"
Columnist Mary McGrory
"Permanent. Permanent. Permanent. There!"
Gerry Adams

Peter Hitchens had indeed made Adams's trip very interesting. The black-bearded *Daily Express* reporter dogged him every step of the way in his tour of the United States, sending back dispatches with headlines such as, "He calls me Peter but I call his bluff," "St. Gerry cruises into town on a tidal wave of blarney" and "How I shattered Gerry's big day." The last referred to the question he shouted to Adams as he met Rosa Parks in front of the television cameras in Detroit. "Since Mrs. Parks has devoted a lifetime to non-violent protest, and you have spent the last twenty-five years defending murder and terror, how do you have the nerve even to stand in the same room as her?" called out Hitchens, whose subsequent report of the meeting was typical of his style. "Even by the sleazy standards of Adams's behavior, this public relations stunt was cynical," he wrote. "The danger is that the picture of him and Rosa Parks will go round the country increasing his new respectability and turning him into what he wants to be—Ireland's Nelson Mandela."

In a dispatch after the Sinn Féin leader arrived in Washington, Hitchens reported that Adams was "out to dinner in my Washington suburb last night, only about a mile from where I live. I shall be checking under my car this morning in case they left one of their peacemaking devices there."

The location he referred to was familiar to me. Gerry Adams had in fact accepted an invitation to dinner in our home in Bethesda with about a dozen Washington people, all of them curious to see and take the measure of a controversial figure whom none of us had ever met.

One of the guests was Nancy Soderberg. Before accepting an invitation, and because it would be a first-time contact between Adams and a White House official, and as tensions were rising once again between Washington and London over the access issue, she had to go to the Oval Office to seek permission from President Clinton to come to my home at the same time as the Sinn Féin leader.

"I remember thinking how absurd it was to have the President of the United States personally clearing my dinner plans," recalled Soderberg with some amusement. They talked it back and forth, she said, and the President finally said, "Fine."

She wasn't the only guest who had to consult higher authority. Dean Curran, Deputy Assistant Secretary of State, whom I also invited, had to seek and receive clearance from Peter Tarnoff, the Under Secretary of State for Political Affairs, who in turn checked it out with the White House. (I, too, got the OK from my newspaper.)

The event inadvertently became part of the negotiations over Adams, who was seeking access at the highest level in Washington. As the British did not want him to meet anyone in, or indeed from, the White House, they objected to the off-campus encounter in Bethesda when they learned about it from inside the administration. Word of the dinner then leaked out to the British press.

Peter Hitchens, an old friend with whom I had worked when we were both based in Moscow some years before, told me half-apologetically that he and other reporters might have to position themselves outside my house—where he had been a dinner guest himself—to check who was going in.

But in the end he didn't have to, as Soderberg at the last minute agreed to meet Adams at the State Department the following day, so other encounters did not matter that much. "The ultimate hashed-out deal," said the President's adviser, "was that the Vice President would call Adams, and then I could have dinner with him at your house, and then we'd do this meeting at the State Department."

Soderberg arrived slightly late. "It's always funny when you first meet someone whose pictures you've seen so many times," she said. "I remember just saying, 'I've heard a lot about you,' and him saying the same thing, and being surprised at how gentle and professorial he was. He was not hardened and bitter the way I would expect someone of his background to be at all. He was very charming. I thought at the time I'd love to get him in a room and really talk to him. He was a bit "on" with the group. He was giving charming answers as opposed to what he really thought. He said he's been working for peace for fifteen years or so and I remember being rather skeptical about that. Having got to know him now, that was probably an accurate statement."

Adams presented her with a book he had written, inscribed in English and Irish "To Nancy, with thanks and solidarity," which she later kept on a shelf in her White House office.

I placed Adams between Soderberg and Mary McGrory from *The Washington Post,* who was not impressed with Adams that evening. The veteran columnist, now in her seventies, provided an electric moment. She turned to him over the main course and asked, "Was it really necessary to shoot all those fathers in front of their children?"

"No, it wasn't, and I regret that," replied the Belfast man.

"Why don't you just say the word "permanent"?," persisted McGrory, referring to the British insistence that he should declare the IRA ceasefire permanent. Adams, betraying irritation by a quick pinching of his nose and glasses, replied sharply, "Permanent. Permanent. Permanent. There!"

She wrote next week in her column: "He smiles a lot. He is silky, turning surly only when asked about fronting for an organization that shot fathers on their front doorsteps."

Later she told me, "He always maddened me and he did it at that dinner too. His reply was typical handwashing and rather morally ambiguous, don't you think?"

Senator Chris Dodd however was extremely impressed with the Sinn Féin leader, something which would benefit Adams in later months. A former Peace Corps volunteer in the Dominican Republic and a fluent Spanish speaker, the Connecticut Senator had graduated from being a liberal spokesman against human rights abuses, especially in Latin America, to become the rising star of the Democratic Party and shortly afterwards its chairman. His experience with peace projects in central America gave him an extra fascination with what was happening in Northern Ireland. He was friendly with Senator Kennedy—their capacity for late nights was legendary—but was slightly more radical on Irish issues, taking up the cause of IRA man Joe Doherty while Kennedy did not. An Irish American whose ancestors crossed the Atlantic more than a century and a half earlier, Dodd owned a summer cottage in Roundstone in Connemara where he went every year to play golf. He also golfed frequently with the President. "Don't underestimate Chris Dodd," John Hume once told me. "Chris Dodd has been very, very active on Northern Ireland. He's quieter about it than the others."

Dean Curran, a former deputy chief of mission in the US embassy in Dublin, recalled that Adams "told lots of stories and laughed and didn't pick up on openings where he could have used Sinn Féin rhetoric," because, he believed, Adams wanted to communicate that he wasn't the terrorist that people thought he was. The State Department official was quiet throughout most of the dinner, deferring to Soderberg's seniority on the peace process, until the State Department came under some criticism for creating difficulties for Adams. Curran made the point that it was not surprising the State Department took the line it did, as it was protecting a very long and important relationship with Britain which had an impact on a whole range of world issues.

"The most interesting thing for me," he said, "was that Senator Chris Dodd took up this point and emphasized to Adams that he had to take into account larger power relationships in the world."

Dodd displayed a gift for telling funny stories, including, I recall, one about a returned Irish emigrant in a bar in Galway, who said to his companion, "I wish we were back in the Bronx, drinking pints and wishing we were in Galway." Someone said as the party broke up if Adams was given too hard a time, he might wish he was back in Belfast, wishing he could get a visa to come to Washington.

Black humor from Belfast was more the order of the day when Northern Ireland's loyalist politicians came to dinner some time later. After the combined command of the loyalist paramilitary groups in Northern Ireland declared a ceasefire on 13 October, six of the most prominent loyalist spokesmen came to the United States. Like Adams, their visit was sponsored by the National Committee on American Foreign Policy, headed by Bill Flynn. And just as the Sinn Féin man found himself in the care of ex-members and friends of the FBI on his first day on American soil, the loyalists too were met on their arrival by a former FBI special agent, Ed Kenny, a vice president in Flynn's insurance company. Kenny had just resigned from the FBI after twenty-five years in counter-intelligence. Despite his name, he had little connection with Irish America, though his wife Brigid, whose mother came from Leitrim and father from Cavan, had strong feelings on the subject of Ireland. "When I was based in Washington many years ago I worked a little bit with MI6," Kenny said. "Occasionally I would be invited to the British embassy, but my wife always refused to go."

The ex-FBI special agent said Bill Flynn came back from Belfast after the loyalist ceasefire and called him into his office to ask him to look after the visitors from Belfast. "He told me they were coming and were asking for the same courtesies as Sinn Féin, and they would like to meet politicians and academics," he said. "The irony of the situation didn't escape me. Six weeks earlier I probably could have been surveilling these guys."

The loyalist visit was coordinated with the White House, which waived a visa ban on those members of the group with prison records, including Gusty Spence who had served a life sentence for murder. "We have taken into account the fact that they have called a ceasefire in unstinting terms and that they have been invited by a prestigious foreign policy institute and that they are entitled to parity of treatment with Gerry Adams," said Soderberg.

Gusty Spence, David Ervine and Billy Hutchinson of the Progressive Unionist Party, which had ties to the UVF, and Joe English, Gary McMichael and Davy Adams of the Ulster Democratic Party, which was close to the UDA, arrived on 23 October in New York. They made an unexpectedly good impression on the Irish-American activists who encountered them, either in the Irish-owned Fitzpatrick's Hotel in Manhattan with the Irish tricolor flying over the entrance or at Gallagher's Restaurant on 54th Street and Seventh Avenue, where they relaxed with Flynn, O'Dowd, Kenny and others, exchanging banter and making short speeches.

"It was the greatest tribute to Bill Flynn that this happened," said O'Dowd. "We had contacts with loyalists going back some time. The first loyalist community leader we met was Jackie Redpath from the Belfast shipyard. We talked to him in a room in Duke's Hotel in Belfast on our first visit. What he said blew us away. It was the first time I heard an intelligent unionist perspective on the situation, and an articulate account of who they were, where they were coming from, and of their anger at the arrogance of the IRA killing people. My thoughts were that we must engage these people. When they came to New York, the Irish Americans wanted to reach out to them because of the peace process, and partly because they are American and it's a very American thing to reach out to people. But in any event, I see the role of Irish Americans as talking to those that no one else will talk to. The unionists and John Hume and the rest are in the mainstream, our theory was that the extremes needed to be brought to the center."

Ed Kenny thought the loyalists very astute, and despite their polar opposite backgrounds, the ex-FBI agent and the former loyalist guerrillas got on well together. "Fortunately there was pretty good chemistry there, or it could have been a very long week for me," he said, ruefully. "They were genuine and very decent guys, and they enjoyed themselves. There were some sessions at the hotel bar, after which I had to do with one to two hours' sleep a night." David Ervine told him afterwards that they had learned something from him: "They were watching me tipping everyone, barmen, baggage handlers and waiters, and he said this was totally foreign to them, but they were now getting into the American way."

They received little of the publicity which Adams attracted, though *The New York Times* praised the step they had taken towards "resolving the province's intractable civil war." About one hundred members of Flynn's think-tank turned up for a forum on Northern Ireland at New York City University, chaired again by Angier Biddle Duke, the retired US diplomat (who was killed shortly afterwards, aged seventy-nine, in a bizarre accident, struck by a car while roller-blading on a New York street).

David Ervine told them the two sides were like boxers, both claiming victory after fighting to a draw.

"But there are no winners in a twenty-five-year war," he said. "We have had twenty-five years of hell and times have changed. We want the constitutional uncertainty ended. We don't want to get up in the morning and say, 'Am I British or Irish today?' We want to get up and say, 'My God, I'm late for work!'"

Gary McMichael, whose father John McMichael was killed by the IRA, said "everyone in Northern Ireland has been a victim of the conflict and I don't want another family to go through the type of suffering I went through and I don't want my children to grow up in the kind of Northern Ireland I grew up in. I have less reason to sit down with Sinn Féin than many people, but everyone in my country has been touched to some extent by the violence and I recognize we have to sit down and put the past behind us. It's going to be difficult to do so. I will have a lump in my throat when I sit down across the table from Gerry Adams."

In the heady days after the ceasefire when anything seemed possible, these sentiments seemed to presage a real change of climate in Northern Ireland. The loyalists, whose very political existence was based on a bitter conflict with Irish Catholics, travelled next day to Boston for a forum on the future of Northern Ireland at Boston College, a Jesuit institution set up in the nineteenth century for the children of Catholic Irish immigrants. They were welcomed by Thomas O'Neill, son of former House Speaker Tip O'Neill, who said that there had been a lot of criticism and bewilderment at how Irish Americans could welcome loyalist paramilitaries but "we are Americans, we intend to listen." The loyalists spoke of their politicisation in prison, and Spence, who served eighteen years, said he now advocated "a moderacy which is frightening the unionist parties." Back in New York, the group also met Irish President Mary Robinson, making a brief visit to the United States, in the Irish consulate and shook hands, a first for both sides. Ed Kenny got the impression that Mary Robinson's people were more nervous about the occasion than the loyalists. Bill Flynn was there smiling proudly. An Irish official was startled to see that he was wearing a handgun.

Then the group came to Washington, and to dinner at our home in Bethesda on 26 October. This time it was a larger affair, and several British correspondents, including Peter Hitchens, dropped around for a stand-up buffet. I brought him through the guests to meet Gusty Spence and Joe English. They held out their hands in greeting. Hitchens, who had refused to shake hands with Adams when they met on a television program, declined the courtesy and said, "I'm sorry, I have a no-handshake policy on Northern Ireland."

English peered at him through his tinted glasses. "Who is this guy?" he asked me.

"Just a provocateur," I explained, and hustled the *Daily Express* man away.

A couple of times that evening the loyalist came up behind Hitchens, tapped him on the shoulder and said gleefully, his hand outstretched, "Put it there, Peter." But the *Express* man would not give in.

A few months later, when representatives of every political faction on the island of Ireland came to Washington for an investment conference on Ireland, a number of the loyalists returned to our house in Bethesda, this time for a very mixed party with several dozen people, including print and broadcast journalists from Belfast and Dublin, and Irish Ambassador Dermot Gallagher and his wife Maeve. By now the paramilitary types on both sides had come in from the cold, but only Irish diplomats socialized with them. The British held the loyalists at arm's length just as they did Sinn Féin.

Everyone was in high spirits, and we got a taste of some of the macabre humor of the Troubles.

One of the loyalists acted out a story about a young recruit to the UDA who was given a gun by the local UDA commander on his first day and told to shoot a hooded "IRA leader" tied to a chair. But the gun was empty and the intended "victim" was in reality the deputy UDA commander for the district. It was a set-up to test the teenager's resolve. "Go on! Shoot him! Shoot him!" cried the UDA commander. The teenager pulled the trigger. It went "click, click." Before anyone could stop him, the exasperated recruit bludgeoned the hooded man to death with the revolver butt.

Later, Joe English borrowed my daughter's guitar and to the astonishment of many of the guests strummed a republican favorite, *The Fields of Athenry.* Most of the company sang along. When it was over, Billy Hutchinson, who served sixteen years in prison for the murder of two Catholics (and who was now a respected community worker), announced cheerfully, "We've been watching who joined in. Now we've identified who the republicans are."

21

VISA WAR THREE

"They thought we had lost our minds. They made entreaties, 'Don't do it!' and then we'd do it."
Nancy Soderberg

Gerry Adams finally made it to the White House on his next visit to Washington on 6 December 1994, but he arrived without identification and was kept waiting at the gate on Pennsylvania Avenue until an official from Tony Lake's office came to fetch him. "Nobody told us to bring ID," he said. He was invited this time, an administration official said, because "good deeds are rewarded with an open door at the White House," the good deed being the continued IRA ceasefire. He was being rewarded incrementally; first a short visit to New York, then a tour of the country, now a visit to the White House. The British did not press the case against his entering the White House this time: they were more concerned about stopping any moves to allow Adams to raise funds in the United States, where a million dollars could be collected easily by Adams in a short period.

Indeed, when he applied for a new visa on 14 November, Adams's priority was not just access to the White House. He wanted to raise funds for Sinn Féin at a top-dollar dinner at the Plaza Hotel in New York and in Chicago and Philadelphia. The Irish Americans were in a mood to dip into their wallets and finance the peace process. Albert Reynolds had raised tens of thousands of dollars for his Fianna Fáil party at a big dinner in the Waldorf Astoria on 4 November. Sinn Féin as a party was not forbidden to raise money in America, only Adams and other leading figures. The ability to use Adams's drawing power to fill the coffers of Sinn Féin in similar manner was one of the benefits which the Irish-American peace delegation had offered in return for the end of the IRA campaign.

Once Adams asked for a new visa, his supporters began to put pressure on the White House to end the ban on fundraising. As before, the two powerful Democratic Senators, Ted Kennedy and Chris Dodd, led the way. "My view is that we have got to keep the playing field level," said Dodd. "Having now received Gerry Adams and accepted him at his word—and he has fulfilled his obligations—there is no justification to treat him otherwise. It is very important that we demonstrate our continued support for those who have renounced violence and not interrupt this delicate process." They pointed out to the President that Adams was not barred from raising money in Britain.

But the coalition which previously had prevailed for Adams had lost some of its confidence. Albert Reynolds, who had developed a unique relationship of trust with Clinton, was about to step down after a domestic scandal. He would be replaced as Taoiseach by John Bruton, who had yet to meet the President and who was wary of playing a leading role in a pan-nationalist front which could antagonize unionists. With the defeat of the Democrats in the November elections to Congress, Kennedy and Dodd had been relegated to the ranks of the Senate minority, though the new, Republican-dominated, International Relations Committee in the House had come under the control of New York Congressman Ben Gilman, a strong supporter of Irish nationalism, and Peter King had been appointed one of its forty-one members.

This time, too, the British had received a solid commitment that the White House would not allow fundraising. They successfully argued that Sinn Féin was still too closely identified with the IRA and pointed out that the IRA had killed 54-year-old post office worker, Frank Kerr, in a robbery in Newry staged after the ceasefire. The £130,000 was still missing despite the IRA admission that it was a "mistake." This single act undermined the Sinn Féin case more than anything else. The British government now pressed the United States to use its leverage on Adams to make progress on the decommissioning of IRA weapons, which London insisted must start before inter-party talks on the future of Northern Ireland could commence. One British source said, "Given the long history of Noraid fundraising, and perceptions in Britain that it contributed to American guns and detonators finding their way to Northern Ireland, we were inevitably going to have to ask the Americans how sure they were that money raised in this country was not going for terrorist purposes." The State and Justice departments backed the British position. So, too, did Tony Lake and Nancy Soderberg this time. There appeared no prospect that Adams would get his way.

Negotiations to resolve the issue were conducted directly between Adams and Soderberg and involved several telephone exchanges. She was adamant that the White House would not give ground on fundraising. But as a further step towards normalisation, and to prevent the Sinn Féin leader calling off his trip and signalling to the IRA that the Americans were adopting a British agenda, Adams was invited to come to the White House and meet Tony Lake—which was how he came to be at the gates on Pennsylvania Avenue seeking entry.

When Adams stepped inside the door of the White House for the first time and entered Lake's office, he told the President's National Security Adviser that he expected to be allowed to raise funds next time. He said that his party was setting up an organization called Cairde Sinn Féin, or Friends of Sinn Féin, to sponsor, organize and administer the collection of funds. He promised that its accountability would be transparent. Its establishment would send signals which would have far-reaching effects on the peace process.

Adams told me shortly afterwards that when Sinn Féin went to the IRA in August to argue that there was an alternative to the armed struggle, one of the parts of the jigsaw "was the very proactive engagement" by Irish Americans represented by Bill Flynn's group "and their assertion that the US administration was one which was positively disposed towards a peaceful resolution in Ireland." He believed the administration had forced the British to drop their exclusion of Sinn Féin from an investment conference in Belfast; that the ban on broadcasting his voice in the United Kingdom had been lifted because of the feedback from his first trip; that the law excluding him from Britain fell because it was absurd that he could go to Washington and engage White House officials but not go to London. The ban on fundraising had to come next, he said.

Gerry Adams applied for a new US visa on 22 February 1995 to return to Washington in Saint Patrick's week, when many Irish politicians go there for the festivities held around 17 March.

This presented new Republican Speaker Newt Gingrich, who had decided to continue the tradition of the Saint Patrick's Day lunches for the visiting Taoiseach and the President, with a dilemma: should he invite Adams? An invitation to Adams would require Clinton either to decline to attend or to be forced into a handshake he might not want. The White House then announced it intended to have another party to mark Ireland's national day and created the same problem for itself, as Bill and Hillary Clinton traditionally shook hands with every single guest.

British diplomats immediately saw the danger of a handshake with the President, something which would be seen as intolerable by many British people. The embassy did not want Adams invited to either the Speaker's lunch or the White House party and it was implacably opposed to the Sinn Féin leader raising funds around the United States.

A situation had now arisen where Adams could be hit by what one Congressman called a "triple-whammy" if he lost all three, and everyone prepared for another round of negotiations over the status of Adams in the United States.

"Every time this would happen we would get into a give-and-take with him and Congress and his supporters," said Nancy Soderberg ruefully, looking back on the first ten days of March 1995 when the issue landed on her desk again.

Senators Kennedy and Dodd for the second time began lobbying for an end to the fundraising ban. In a letter to the President, Kennedy said, "We have read reports that Mr. Adams's ability to raise funds is linked to the decommissioning of IRA weapons. While everyone wants to see a total demilitarization of Northern Ireland, we believe it would be counterproductive for the United States to impose conditions on Sinn Féin—demanding unilateral actions by the IRA—which not even the British Government has imposed, especially since Mr. Adams is permitted to raise funds in Great Britain and Northern Ireland . . . If we expect Sinn Féin to act like a legitimate political party, we must treat it like one."

In Dublin, Jean Kennedy Smith joined in with messages to the White House and Congress. She made several phone calls to Chris Dodd. "I was convinced the ceasefire would hold forever," she told a friend later. Minister for Foreign Affairs Dick Spring made it clear that the Dublin government was in favor of ending the ban and getting the issue out of the way.

On Capitol Hill, Ben Gilman and the three other co-chairmen of the Ad Hoc Committee on Irish Affairs, Peter King, Tom Manton and Richard Neal, sent a separate letter to Clinton urging the issuance of an unrestricted US visa to Adams.

Concerned that the White House might give in again to Irish-American pressure, Sir Patrick Mayhew went to Washington to put his full weight behind the British case for keeping the ban and for excluding Adams from the White House party. The Northern Ireland Secretary arrived on Monday 6 March for meetings with Al Gore and Warren Christopher, determined to press the British view that there should be substantial progress on decommissioning of weapons by the IRA before Sinn Féin could be admitted to negotiations about the future of Northern Ireland. Mayhew had had his own close encounter with IRA ordnance, having been in Downing Street when mortars exploded outside the window, and his name was on an IRA hit list found in a London apartment. He had an Irish background and among friends he was known as Paddy, but he was not a favorite of Dublin officials, and he was unpopular with some Irish-American members of Congress because of his very British manner, which they considered condescending.

At breakfast with Washington correspondents, Sir Patrick appeared confident that the British view would prevail. He pooh-poohed the idea that when the British and Irish governments differed, the US administration always took the Irish side, pointing out that while Dick Spring had said the previous week that the decommissioning of arms should not be a precondition for talks, US officials expressed agreement with the British view. Secretary of State Warren Christopher, he said, was "aligning himself squarely on how we see the matter." Christopher had said a week earlier that the US urged those who laid down their arms "to begin the process of decommissioning or perhaps more accurately, start disarming."

Mayhew also told the journalists that three conditions had to be fulfilled before Sinn Féin could remove its "self-imposed disqualification" and take their place at the talks table. These were a willingness in principle to disarm progressively, a practical understanding of the modalities of decommissioning and the actual decommissioning of some arms as a tangible confidence-building measure and to signal the start of a process. The last condition was later to become known as "Washington Three." (Mayhew wanted to say "a significant quantity" instead of "some" arms but John Major insisted on the dilution, according to a British press report.) As for Adams's ability to raise funds in London, "he can't raise anything worth looking at in the United Kingdom, whereas here, with this enormous Irish-American proportion of the population, it's a very important matter," said Mayhew. It would be a mistake to allow him to raise funds "in so fertile a field." He also said that Clinton should not meet the Sinn Féin man as "fifty million British people would not like to see Mr. Adams shaking hands with the President of the world's greatest democracy."

It seemed that for the British the "fix" was in again. "I had never seen him more confident," said Peter King after the Northern Secretary had been to Capitol Hill. "He basically dismissed Congress as a bunch of inept bunglers. He didn't give a damn what we thought." Attorney General Janet Reno, representing the FBI, was determined to hold the line against lifting the ban, on the grounds that it would undermine the US stance against international terrorism. Her deputy, Jamie Gorelick, endorsed Mayhew's position at a dinner hosted by Sir Robin Renwick in the British embassy, telling the three dozen guests how she had just reviewed twenty years of files on horrible atrocities committed by the IRA. Sir Patrick advised them that the IRA was still building up its stockpile of arms, training recruits and targeting potential victims.

And the British had an extra reason for confidence: Tony Lake and Nancy Soderberg appeared firmly on their side.

"We were not for fundraising initially," Soderberg confirmed. "We were very wary of it because it is very hard to track where the money goes and that was a big card. I think our initial instinct was to wait." There was also "a lot of pressure from the British" to maintain the ban.

But, as always, it was the President who had the last word.

On Tuesday 7 March as Mayhew was doing the rounds in Washington, President Clinton accepted an invitation to play a round of golf with Chris Dodd at the Army & Navy Country Club in Arlington, Virginia, a twenty-minute drive from Capitol Hill.

The Connecticut Senator described to me what happened near the end of the game—which has now gone into Irish-American folklore.

"At the seventeenth green," he said, "I said to the President, I'm sorry to bring up business, but I think you should give Adams fundraising."

"All the advice I'm getting is not to, but I think I might," Clinton replied.

This was enough for Dodd. After the golf match the Senator, a key figure in Clinton's re-election campaign as chairman of the Democratic Party, was by chance scheduled to attend a strategy meeting in the White House with Al Gore and Jack Quinn, Gore's chief of staff. Mayhew had not impressed the Vice President, and Gore and his top official were unsympathetic to the British case. The Connecticut Senator got the word to his allies to step up the pressure; the White House was leaning their way. Ted Kennedy rang the President and asked him to trust the people whose advice he had taken before. Clinton let him know that things were moving.

Clinton talked the matter over with Tony Lake at their regular session next morning.

The President "wanted to see whether there was a way to get this done," Soderberg said.

She explained how decisions came out of such meetings.

"Normally when the President would be aware of an issue coming up for decision, he would raise it with Tony," she said. "He would say, 'So-and-so mentioned something to me and is waiting to get a decision on this. I want you to take a look at it, see whether or not we can do it.'"

Mayhew's suspicions that things might not be going as well as he expected may have been aroused when he met Lake, Soderberg and another National Security Council official, Kathleen Stephens, in the National Security Adviser's office.

"I think he laid it out," Soderberg recalled. "We just basically listened. We honestly hadn't decided, at the time that we saw him, that we were going to do it. It was only a bit later that we sort of worked it out. What he said at the time was he wanted them [Sinn Féin] to seriously discuss decommissioning. And so we took that and said if we can get them to commit to seriously discuss decommissioning then that will further the process."

Soderberg insisted that the Northern Ireland Secretary did not say he required anything more. "He didn't say he wanted more at that meeting," she said. "At that meeting he said "seriously discuss." He never mentioned Washington Three. So we took that and ran with it and gave Adams the fundraising on that basis. We got a commitment from him to seriously discuss everything. It wasn't until the following August that I even heard what Washington Three was. And he probably that afternoon went out and gave his speech and talked about that."

"There was a complete disconnect between what he told us and that public statement," she said. "I never even heard about the public statement until August."

At this point, Soderberg said, she thought the British were "so disgusted with us that they would say things not knowing we were going to make our own decisions. I think at that point they were just fed up with us. They thought we had lost our minds. They made entreaties, "Don't do it!" and then we'd do it, and I think they were just exasperated with us."

She acknowledged that she was "not entirely" happy they could guarantee where the money was going to "but enough so that we felt that we would know where substantial amounts of money were going."

After the President told his staff to find some way to do it, Soderberg called Niall O'Dowd. The publisher had been pressing hard for the lifting of the ban. He had scoured Irish newspapers circulating in Britain and found a notice of a Sinn Féin fundraising event in London, which he had faxed to Soderberg to make the point that the British themselves did not prevent Adams fundraising.

Another long session of telephone calls followed.

"Niall and I would get on the phone again and go back and forth," recalled Soderberg, laughing, "and this time, I think at that point we felt the ceasefire had been in place for eight or nine months and it was useful for us to continue to reach out to Adams and show the tangible benefits to keeping the ceasefire in place. Every time he came they wanted to ratchet it up one step to strengthen his hand to keep the ceasefire in place. And by March basically the only thing left was the White House [meeting the President at the Saint Patrick's Day reception] and fundraising."

O'Dowd had up to then felt that the fundraising request would be turned down flat once more. "I formed the same opinion I had about access to the White House in October," he said. "There was a done deal somewhere. My read on it was that they weren't going to do it. I had been talking to my contact in Sinn Féin and my honest assessment to him was that things were not changing. The Sinn Féin people were really depressed. There were cracks in the ceasefire all over the place. The American decision could be quite serious."

"Then Nancy called and asked if I thought Adams would make a statement saying he was prepared to seriously discuss decommissioning. I said I don't know. I had been out of the loop a bit. I called Sinn Féin and relayed the language. They were very wary of a trap but my contact called back and said, 'That line is fine with Adams.'"

On the strength of Adams's promise that every issue, including decommissioning, would be on the table in talks with British ministers, the President lifted the ban on fundraising. Early on Wednesday night, Soderberg rang O'Dowd and told him of the decision. Adams would also be invited to the White House, she said, explaining to me later that this was because "it would be an insult and basically negative if we didn't invite him contrary to the whole outreach policy." She said an announcement would be made to the media the following day.

Amazingly, the White House had again made a major decision regarding Northern Ireland without consulting Dublin or London in the final stages or notifying them through normal diplomatic channels of what they were going to do, or had decided.

O'Dowd could hardly believe the news. Thinking back he said, "I suppose what the British never understood was that you could throw ambassadors and ministers into it, but at the end of the day there were no votes in the British position. And this President was always amenable to politicians as against bureaucrats. He is totally at home with politicians and political decisions."

Then O'Dowd made an uncharacteristic error of judgment. He tipped off an Irish official with whom he did not normally confide, and who misunderstood the need for discretion until the White House made an announcement. Lake got a telephone call about the decision from the Irish side, and the story leaked in Dublin. The National Security Adviser was furious. By now White House officials knew what a stink would be raised by the British if they got the news second-hand. He phoned O'Dowd and told him angrily how disappointed he was at the breach of confidence. O'Dowd admitted he had fouled up. He apologized and explained that he had not leaked to the media and told the National Security Adviser what had happened. Lake rang back later and said he appreciated that he had been straight with him.

When the President's National Security Adviser did ring Sir Robin Renwick in the British embassy to break the news, the British Ambassador made it clear he was appalled.

"Lake told us Adams would be coming to the White House and they were permitting fundraising," said a senior British source. He said they had got a piece of paper and that they "think it takes the process forward." The British source explained, "We were very cross. They said arrangements were in place to track the money but there were no such arrangements. Our view is that if one part of the movement gets funding, it relaxes the resources of another part, it gets used by part of the same family."

What really stunned the British was the absence once again of any sign that the US administration—Clinton, Gore, Soderberg, Lake, anyone—ever put serious pressure on Adams to make any concessions. Time after time the administration had ceded to the demands of Adams's promoters on the grounds that to do otherwise would risk unravelling the process.

The feeling they were betrayed hurt the British the most. "A lot of people made promises and the promises turned out to be a pack of lies," the British government source said. "We were embarrassed by the unprofessional way the process was conducted. Lake assured Mayhew that the concerns of the British government would be taken into account and Mayhew interpreted that in a positive way. There had been a feeling we were both working hard to get a certain result and it was important to have leverage with Sinn Féin. We felt the handle had been taken out of our hands."

The normally smooth Sir Robin shocked a couple of British journalists by using a four-letter word to describe the President's National Security Adviser.

They were again furious at Soderberg. "The Brits thought they had Nancy in their pocket at this stage," said one insider. "That's another reason why they were so mad."

There was outrage among John Major's backbenchers. "Just imagine the uproar in the United States if we welcomed to the UK the perpetrators of the Oklahoma bomb, treated them as celebrities, invited them to Buckingham Palace and allowed them to raise money for their demented cause!" Andrew Hunter, chairman of the Tory Backbench Committee on Northern Ireland told me later, referring to the bombing of a federal building in Oklahoma in April 1995. "That's how we felt about the USA administration granting a visa to Gerry Adams," he said. "Sinn Féin and the Provisional IRA are inextricably linked. They are two parts of the Provisional republican movement. Sinn Féin is the IRA's propaganda department."

Officials in the State Department and in Janet Reno's office were also incredulous. They felt that the IRA should be pressed to get rid of its arms, and said so in public statements. Assistant Secretary of State Richard Holbrooke told a Congressional committee a week later that the IRA and loyalist paramilitaries should start getting rid of their arms immediately. Decommissioning must be "mutual, balanced and across the board," he said.

But the White House was finessing policy, not Holbrooke. In every reference to the issue during the rest of the year, Clinton never publicly went beyond asking Sinn Féin to "seriously discuss" decommissioning. The deal with Adams was spelled out in a draft internal White House document headed "talking points" for responding to media queries on the day the decision was made. It declared that "Adams had previously been disallowed to fundraise because of concerns we had about issues related to IRA arms procurement and disarmament. Progress has been made in both these areas. In particular we welcome Sinn Féin's announcement today that it is prepared to engage in discussions on decommissioning and other issues in its talks with the British." A final version omitted the words "arms procurement."

In London, there was barely disguised contempt for Clinton's concessions to Adams. Prime Minister Major sent a letter to the President urging him to step up pressure on the Sinn Féin leader to move on decommissioning. The US Ambassador to London, Admiral William Crowe, acknowledged the fury of British ministers, saying, "We have got a problem on our hands." White House officials expressed irritation at the "overreaction" of the British. The problem was made worse by Clinton's indecision at that time about attending Britain's Victory in Europe Day celebrations. The London *Sunday Times* said the handshake for Adams "represents America's biggest snub to Britain in recent history and the lowest point in a special relationship sustained for half a century by ten presidents." In the eyes of the first American generation with no transatlantic affinity, *The Times* went on, Britain was now relegated to the status of "cultural theme park," an offshore island marginal to America's interests.

The full extent of the breach in the relationship only became clear a week later when it emerged that President Clinton had failed to reach Major, his most senior NATO partner, by telephone for five days. Clinton first sent a letter, hand-delivered to 10 Downing Street by a US embassy official, explaining his reason for lifting the fundraising ban and receiving Adams at the White House. He then tried the telephone. Major was at home in Huntingdon preparing for a tour of the Middle East when the President first tried to call him on Saturday 11 March. He was too busy to talk. He would not be able to speak to Clinton until he got back on Wednesday (and then maybe). The President persisted and next day tried to put a call through to the travelling Prime Minister in Jerusalem. Officials gave all sorts of reasons why he failed. Talks on specific issues needed preparation, there was no secure line, the Prime Minister was in transit, they "didn't connect."

The telephone had become a blunt instrument in Anglo-American diplomacy. It was inconceivable that two senior NATO allies could not set up immediate communications no matter where they were in the world. The state of satellite communications that year allowed editors to chat to reporters on mobile telephones in remote parts of Africa and Central Asia. Former White House spokesman Marlin Fitzwater gave Martin Fletcher of the London *Times* a few telling illustrations: George Bush took a call from the White House when rafting down the Li Jiang river in China. Before the Gulf War, Bush was standing in a "chow" line with Fitzwater in Saudi Arabia when they heard of Margaret Thatcher's resignation. In a matter of seconds, Bush was commiserating with the ex-British Prime Minister by telephone.

White House spokesman Mike McCurry admitted that the two leaders "didn't connect" but dismissed reports of another Suez-type crisis. The British press "exaggerated and hyperventilated on a regular basis," he said. They had written off the special relationship no less than six times in the last year. They would get over it.

22

Guess Who's Coming to Lunch

"I'm catching more shit because of you Irish . . . It's too bad, I don't care."
Bill Clinton

The staff in Speaker Newt Gingrich's office were flabbergasted when they heard that President Clinton had invited Adams to the White House.

The question of how to deal with Adams had been a thorn in the side of the Speaker for some days. A month before he had decided to continue the tradition started a decade earlier by Speaker Thomas "Tip" O'Neill of having a Saint Patrick's Day lunch in the House dining room to which the President, the Taoiseach, any visiting Irish politicians—which in practice meant John Hume for whom the lunches were started in the first place—and Irish-American heavyweights from Congress were invited. They were sentimental affairs. Everyone wore shamrock and green ties and sang *When Irish Eyes Are Smiling.* But there were advantages in keeping it up. "It was like an elite club," recalled Jeff Biggs, ex-Speaker Tom Foley's press secretary. "These were all important guys and they would get business done at these lunches." The Speaker told a colleague: "Let's keep up the tradition. We'll have lots of Guinness."

When Adams said he was coming to town however, Gingrich had to decide whether or not to invite him to his lunch, which by tradition took place on 16 March, the day before Saint Patrick's Day. The Speaker did not want to be caught on the wrong side of an issue he did not care much about. The former history professor with his helmet of white hair was in any case preoccupied with fulfilling the

Contract with America, the conservative manifesto which had helped Republicans take over the House and Senate the previous November.

A couple of weeks before the lunch, Gingrich began to get calls every day from a member of his own party, Peter King, the Republican Congressman for New York's Third District, lobbying him to invite Gerry Adams.

The fifty-year-old King, whose grandmother, Margaret McNamara, was from Limerick City and whose granduncle John fought in the old IRA during the War of Independence, had become one of the most active supporters of Adams and the peace process in the Republican Congress. The New York Congressman was determined that Adams would not be snubbed by the first Republican Speaker in a quarter of a century.

On the other hand, Gingrich was under pressure from the British embassy not to invite Adams. Peter Westmacott had come up to Capitol Hill to tell the Speaker's staff that the British government believed the Sinn Féin leader had a long way to go before he merited such a distinction as a seat at the Speaker's lunch. His best hope was impressing Gingrich's British-born spokesman, Tony Blankley, whose English-sounding accent gave Irish-American lobbyists the impression that he would side with the British on Irish issues, though this was not actually the case.

"The question of inviting Mr. Adams to lunch is, of course, a matter for the Speaker," a British embassy spokesman said, and "the Speaker's office is aware of our view that there is still some way to go before Sinn Féin can be treated on the same basis as other political parties in Northern Ireland." The Speaker also consulted the Irish embassy where an official said, "We raised no objections."

"Frankly," the Speaker told me at his regular press briefing in Congress, "this being the first time we try to do a luncheon like that, I've been very, very cautious. He's obviously a very controversial person and I didn't want to do anything that was inappropriate."

Gingrich, however, had not been returning King's telephone calls and the first the New York Congressman heard about what the Speaker had finally decided to do was on Friday 3 March from James Walsh, the amiable Republican Representative from Syracuse whom Gingrich had appointed chairman of the Friends of Ireland in Congress.

"Jimmy Walsh came up to me and said, 'I've just been talking to Gingrich, he says he's not going to invite Adams,'" King said. "I called Gingrich immediately, and this time he returned my call right away. We had a very heated conversation, I said, 'Newt, this is wrong.' He said, 'The British don't want Adams to come.' I said, 'It's Saint Patrick's Day, it's an Irish feast, the British have no say.' He said, 'Well, that's the way it is.' I said, 'It's not personal but I couldn't show up if Adams is not there.' " King was automatically invited as one of four co-chairmen of the Congressional Ad Hoc Committee on Irish Affairs. "Well, you do what you have to do," Gingrich said.

King told me later how *The Irish Times* then became involved in the dispute.

"You tracked me down the next day and said you heard there would be no invitation for Adams," he said. "I spoke to you on the record. That was a Saturday. Your story appeared on Monday. I got a call from the Speaker's office to say Gingrich was furious. I then got a long letter from Gingrich accusing me of leaking the story to *The Irish Times.* Someone from the British embassy must have faxed your story to Gingrich. He said that only three people in the world knew, and that I had leaked it to you to ruin his reputation. I sent a long letter back saying, 'If I'm going to leak something you're not going to know it, and secondly, what have I to gain by giving it to *The Irish Times*?' Gingrich now acted as if war was declared on him. It was all personal, as if I had intentionally undermined him."

On Thursday 9 March, King, who had very good connections with the handful of people "in the loop" on Irish issues, heard that President Clinton would after all be inviting Adams to the White House. He rang the White House before the formal announcement to express his appreciation for the President's decision. To his surprise Clinton returned his call and talked animatedly for ten minutes about how good he felt about the decision he was about to announce.

Loyal to his party boss, despite their row, the New York Representative called Gingrich's office immediately and left a message on his voice mail saying, "Newt, I certainly don't want you to look bad on this issue, but the President is going to invite Gerry Adams to the White House and it wouldn't look good if you didn't."

King admitted he got a certain zing out of knowing what was going on before other members of Congress. Gingrich's office called back right away. He was less aggressive this time. The Speaker said that obviously Gerry Adams would now be invited to his lunch.

But Newt Gingrich was seething about the way the White House had handled the issue. His aides accused officials there of setting the Speaker up by sending out signals that the White House was going to deny Adams an invitation, so that Gingrich would go out in front and then look bad when he had to change his mind. One even suggested to a White House aide that Peter King, a Republican, was a co-conspirator with the Democratic White House.

"I remember his [the Speaker's] staffer, Gardner Peckham, calling me before they had decided, asking what we thought about it," Nancy Soderberg said. "And we just decided to stay out of it. We didn't want to get into it. We hadn't made up our own minds either."

She agreed that when the President did make up his mind the Speaker "did get hung out to dry a little bit on it." The Speaker's office complained to the White House "because once we decided, it didn't make them look good, and they were under heavy pressure from some others in Congress, but it was basically their issue, not ours."

The question of whether Clinton would shake Adams by the hand at the Speaker's lunch now had to be resolved. It was discussed in the White House. "The way it worked out was that the President would shake his hand as any normal guest, but would not do it in front of the cameras," said Soderberg.

On the day of the lunch, the White House limousine pulled up outside the Capitol just before midday. The President got out and saw Peter King waiting in the spring sunshine for Adams. Clinton walked over to the Congressman, pulled him aside and said in a stage whisper, "I'm catching more shit because of you Irish." Then he shrugged his shoulders, smiled and said, "It's too bad, I don't care." Clinton proceeded into the House dining room with Speaker Gingrich, who was wearing a green carnation, and Taoiseach John Bruton, and they sat at the top table with John Hume. Adams then entered and took his assigned seat at a table nearby, where his luncheon companions were King, Republican Congressman Thomas DeLay of Texas, and deputy assistant to the President for legislative affairs Susan Brophy, who was dressed all in green for the occasion. Brophy was Irish from Massachusetts and was a friend of the Irish diplomat, Brendan Scannell. In her quiet way she had wielded considerable influence on the President's Irish policy. Democratic Senator Daniel Patrick Moynihan was assigned to the same table but went and sat elsewhere.

A small number of reporters, myself and Peter Hitchens among them, were allowed into the dining room to stand behind a rope line for a few minutes taking in the scene, and then we were ushered out to wait in the Hall of Statues until the meal was over. We noticed there were no official cameras to be seen. If there was to be a first-ever handshake between the President of the United States and the President of Sinn Féin, it would go unrecorded.

Inside the dining hall, a farcical little drama played itself out, which I pieced together from some of the guests afterwards. Adams expected to meet Clinton when the press had gone and he avoided catching the President's eye so as to leave the initiative to him. When nothing happened for a while, Susan Brophy left the table, spoke to Gingrich's social co-ordinator and returned to whisper to King that she had been told that Adams could not meet the President.

"Why not?" asked King.

"The Irish embassy doesn't want him to," she said.

King went over to Irish Ambassador Dermot Gallagher at a nearby table.

"Is this true?" he asked.

The Ambassador said "No, that's obviously not the case."

"Are you sure the embassy hasn't vetoed it?" insisted King.

"Well, I'm the embassy and I'm saying we haven't," Gallagher told me he replied.

Susan Brophy relayed this to Tony Blankley, who was sitting near the Speaker. He said it wasn't the Irish embassy which had said a handshake would be inappropriate, it was the Irish Department of Foreign Affairs. King went over to Seán Ó hUiginn, head of the Anglo-Irish division of the Department of Foreign Affairs, who was sitting at a corner table with other Irish officials.

"No, that's not the case," he said.

King approached the Speaker's press secretary again.

"Tony, these guys say they have never said this to you," he said.

Blankley replied, "Well, then I guess there's been a breakdown in communications."

The Congressman told Blankley, "Well, whether there has been or not, the fact is the President's here and Adams is here, this is your lunch, and if they want to shake hands with each other, how can you stop them?"

"That's just the way it's going to be," Blankley said.

The US Ambassador to Ireland, Jean Kennedy Smith, came over to find out what was going on and was overheard to say "It's the craziest thing I ever heard of."

"So we're about fifteen feet away with Clinton sitting there looking over at us," said King, describing the scene. "Adams is sitting there. No one else in the room knows what's going on. People are eating their corned beef. Someone's playing the harp. It's like one of these old-fashioned parties, everyone looks happy. Then I go back and sit down with Gerry Adams, Susan Brophy is there too. Gerry's half kidding, he says, "How about if I just got up and left, walked out the door?" I said, "Jeeze, don't do that."'

A small group, Jean Kennedy Smith, Susan Brophy and Peter King, cornered Blankley again.

"Tony, this is bullshit what you're doing," said King, "and it's going to be a disaster."

"The media from all over the world is here," said Jean Kennedy Smith. "How do you think they are going to react if they find out that the Speaker wouldn't let the President of the United States shake hands with Gerry Adams?"

"Well, how will the media know?" asked Blankley.

Someone replied, "We'll make sure they know."

Finally, the Gingrich aide walked over to the Adams table and said, "OK, here's what we're going to do. John Hume is going to come down. He will bring Gerry Adams up to meet the President." Then he turned to King and said bluntly, "But you can't come."

The appropriate moment arrived when a division bell sounded and several members hurried off to vote. As some diners got up and stretched their legs, Hume came over and escorted Adams to the top table. Clinton put his left arm around Hume's shoulder, and only then, anchored to the champion of constitutional Irish nationalism, did the President of the United States reach out and shake the Sinn Féin leader's hand.

It was, in the end, as carefully choreographed as the historic hand-pumping session between Yassir Arafat and Yitzhak Rabin on the White House lawn eighteen months earlier.

Most of the seventy-six diners, some of whom were still nibbling at their lunch of raspberry vinaigrette, boiled corned beef and cabbage and Irish soda bread, didn't notice what was happening until Congressman Tom Manton, another co-chairman of the Ad Hoc Committee, started to clap. Several joined in. Speaker Gingrich got up and spoke to Adams too. Clinton looked down at King and gave him a thumbs up, then whispered something to Gingrich who came over and told the New York Congressman the President wanted him at the top table, "and I guess that's appropriate," he added curtly. The President, Adams and Gingrich had a brief conversation. Clinton spoke about his diplomatic skirmishes with the British. Adams replied, "Now you know, Mr. President. You've found out in the last two weeks what I've had to live with for forty-seven years."

President Clinton at one point said, "We're going to make this thing work! We're going to make this thing work!" and waved his fist in the air, a gesture which was reported later in a newspaper as a victory salute for the Provisionals and their slogan "Tiocfaidh ár lá," "Our day will come."

King told Clinton how his mother admired him for his Irish policy. He told the President, "I just want you to know I was talking to my mother this morning and she said, 'Tell the President I've decided who I'm voting for for President, but I've not decided who I'm voting for for Congress.' "

The guests who had left filed back in and the speeches began, for which we were readmitted. John Bruton got a standing ovation when he said he hoped to see a future gathering which would also include the unionist leaders, Ian Paisley and James Molyneaux. The Speaker gave him a jar of peanuts from his native Georgia. Clinton said something about it being a long road with no turning. As the entertainment got under way, with tenor Mark Forrest singing "Danny Boy," the President retold King's story to his fellow-diners: "Imagine this guy," he said, "his own mother won't vote for him, but she'll vote for me."

The gratitude of the Irish Americans was expressed in a full-page advertisement in *The New York Times* next day, drafted by Bill Flynn and Niall O'Dowd. It featured a smiling girl in a peaceful Belfast street with the words: "President Clinton, thank you very much."

John Bruton, who in opposition in 1994 had spoken against the Adams visa, told Clinton when they faced the media the next day after a meeting in the White House, "I was wrong, Mr. President and you were right."

But there were confused signals coming from the Irish side. Minister for Foreign Affairs Dick Spring had expressed the conviction that the IRA could not be expected to decommission before talks, but Bruton made several remarks in the United States that week which put him closer to the British side. Before meeting Clinton, he said that the US administration was trying to lever some movement on the decommissioning of arms in its contacts with Sinn Féin, and he expected "major steps" would be taken on the issue the following week. Standing beside Clinton in the White House, he said that Adams had tremendous influence on the IRA and he should use it to get movement on the arms issue. Somebody had to make the first move, he said, and a reduction in IRA arms would lead to a reduction in loyalist arms and British army levels.

British diplomats were pleased to see this apparent endorsement of what they had been saying all along. Many Irish-American activists were not.

At the White House party next evening, billed as a "Celebration of Ireland," Clinton shook Adams by the hand again in the little room through which all three hundred guests filed, two by two, to be greeted by the First Couples of the United States and Ireland. Again, no press photographers were allowed. When Bruce Morrison came by, Clinton said to him, "Well, Bruce, I delivered for you."

The party had a cross-border dimension, symbolized by a buffet dish described as "Dublin Bay prawns with Black Bush whiskey." But like the first Saint Patrick's Day party, it turned into a celebration of Irish America, unified as never before. Some guests had tears in their eyes as the Irish tenor Frank Patterson led the crowd in *God Bless America.*

Looking on dry-eyed were Gary McMichael, leader of the Ulster Democratic Party, and colleagues Joe English and Billy Blair. In the interests of balance, the loyalist leaders had been invited at less than a week's notice. They sat thirty feet from Adams during the formal entertainment. It was the first time McMichael and Adams were in the same room, but they did not meet or shake hands. Many guests lionized Adams and queued for his autograph, including the actor Paul Newman, but there was also a warm welcome for the three loyalists, and several people came up to them to say, "Glad to see you here, we admire your courage."

"Adams was being treated like a statesman and getting an open stage in the US," said McMichael, explaining why they had come. "The decision to attend was not taken lightly. But we felt that for too long loyalist views had not been heard openly, and had gone merely by default. Sinn Féin does not represent the people of Northern Ireland. The IRA propaganda machine must be challenged." He added that unionists were deeply offended that the British government had allowed a foreign government a role in part of the United Kingdom, but the United States was the most important country in the world and whether or not loyalists liked it, Washington took more than a passing interest in the events in Northern Ireland.

A beaming Bill Flynn, who had befriended both camps in Belfast, stood out among the informally dressed guests, as he had mistakenly arrived in a tuxedo. Taking him for a waiter, someone tried to hand a dirty plate to the Mutual of America head. Flynn declined. The guest stalked off, complaining loudly.

The presence of Adams and McMichael gave an edge to the occasion and caused much "rubber-necking" among the guests, who included the major players in the visa dramas: Tony Lake, Nancy Soderberg, Tom Foley, Ted Kennedy, Chris Dodd, Niall O'Dowd and many others. There, too, was Jean Kennedy Smith who had just been awarded the title of Irish American of the Year by O'Dowd's *Irish America* magazine in New York, where her crystal trophy had been accidentally knocked over and smashed in front of a large crowd just seconds before it was to be presented. After the Clintons and their guests of honor, John and Finola Bruton, retired, a sing-song started in the East Room. John Hume rendered, yet again, the song which he and Phil Coulter had made the anthem of the nationalist side at Washington functions, *The Town I Love So Well.* Gerry Adams got up and stood beside him, half a head taller. They each held big hand-microphones like crooners, and sang in harmony. What a double act, the "Pan-nationalist Duo," said an Irish civil servant out of the side of his mouth, observing this picture of nationalist unity in the heart of the White House which few could have imagined they would see in their lifetime.

A more sober party took place the same evening in the British embassy residence across town. It was to mark the departure of diplomat Jeremy Greenstock from Washington. The State Department was represented by Peter Tarnoff, head of the European desk. The presence of Adams at the White House party and the latest defeat for British diplomacy had cast a pall of gloom over the embassy, and there was a strong feeling that Clinton had gone too far in welcoming the political representative of the IRA.

In his farewell speech, Greenstock, an expert on Bosnia, said with heavy irony that he had to admit to a deep sense of failure. He had not succeeded in getting (Serbian leader) Slobodan Milosevic to the White House for the Saint Patrick's Day reception.

23

The Big Tent

"Threads are being woven, one stitch at a time, into the shimmering cloak of peace."
Al Gore

At a gun show in Spokane near the Pacific coast, the trestle tables groaned under the weight of enough weaponry to equip the IRA twice over. Winchesters, Brownings, Makarovs and armalites, new and second-hand, were laid out in rows for buyers in Stetson hats and leather fringes. The talk was of guns, and of House Speaker Tom Foley. It was October 1994, and the mid-term elections to the United States Congress were under way. A Republican tide was washing over America, and the Democrats were on the defensive. Foley had won fifteen straight elections in Spokane in Washington State, but in his latest two-year term he had supported President Clinton's crime bill, which included a ban on nineteen kinds of assault weapons, and he had lost the backing of the National Rifle Association and the conservative voters of his district. A grey-haired woman walking by with an AK-47 on her shoulder said to me, "I voted for Tom Foley every time, but he betrayed us. Now we're out to get him."

They succeeded. For the first time in 134 years, a Speaker of the House was tossed out of Congress. Foley was forced into political retirement, though he opted to remain on in the US capital to practise as a lawyer and serve on prestigious committees.

The Republicans took over both the House of Representatives and the Senate, and the Speaker's chair was taken by Newt Gingrich, a new-age conservative from Atlanta with little or no interest in Irish affairs. In the Senate, Ted Kennedy and Chris Dodd, the most important backers of the Irish peace process, went into opposition.

Perhaps sensing the way things were going in American politics, George Mitchell, the Democratic Senate majority leader, had decided not to seek another term as Senator for Maine. He was offered a vacancy on the Supreme Court by the President, which he declined, and was said to be in line for the job of Baseball Commissioner, which carried near-celebrity status in America. But Clinton had another idea in mind. On 1 December, his last day in the Senate, the British and Irish ambassadors and a few dignitaries and reporters were invited into the Oval Office where President Clinton announced that he was going to appoint a special economic envoy to Northern Ireland and that Senator Mitchell was his choice.

It is "an issue of central importance to me and to our country," said Clinton, as Tony Lake, Nancy Soderberg, Commerce Secretary Ron Brown and Deputy Secretary of State Strobe Talbott applauded politely. They were on the verge of a new and peaceful era in Northern Ireland and the historic ceasefire by the IRA and the loyalist paramilitary groups had held for three months (his script said "parliamentary groups" which is how Clinton read it, but no one seemed to notice). "A just and lasting settlement that respects the rights and traditions of the two communities in Northern Ireland is, after so many years of bloodshed, finally within reach," he said.

The appointment of the 61-year-old lawyer as Special Adviser to the President and Secretary of State for Economic Initiatives in Ireland allowed Clinton to fulfil partially another presidential campaign promise. Mitchell would not be a peace envoy—not yet—but he was a more substantial economic envoy than the promoters of the idea could ever have hoped for. This was what John Hume had asked the President to do. Mitchell was one of the most highly rated political professionals in the United States and a close personal ally of the President, and his appointment meant that the White House was serious about staying involved in Northern Ireland.

The White House, under the guidance of Nancy Soderberg's inter-agency committee, had by then compiled a package of economic incentives designed to build peace in Northern Ireland by reviving the economy after twenty-five years of conflict. A document on the prospects for peace, issued on 2 November, urged that the chance of a generation must be seized. Northern Ireland's heavily subsidized economy badly needed investment. The unemployment rate was 13 percent, and many more people were losing jobs because of the dismantling of the security structure. In the circumstances, the President recommended that a conference on trade and investment in Northern Ireland and the six border counties in the Republic be held in the United States the following year. The President also promised to seek Congressional approval, though he didn't get it, for an increase from $20 million to $30 million for two years in the annual subvention to the International Fund for Ireland. He ordered increased co-operation in the fields of science and technology and business and political training, and more exchanges by the United States Information Agency and other business and political initiatives.

The US economic outreach was not entirely altruistic. Clinton acknowledged that Americans could build on the strong business, trade, political and cultural links it enjoyed with both parts of the island. Ireland was an English-speaking gateway to Europe, with fine golf courses and people who liked Americans. The US was already the biggest source of investment in both parts of the island. Forty American companies were operating in Northern Ireland and four hundred in the Republic. There were strategic advantages too. It was in America's interests that the Republic of Ireland, politically neutral and already a carrier for American investment, should be dependent on the United States for a significant proportion of jobs and industrial output. In the Republic, 47,000 jobs, one-fifth of the total manufacturing workforce, already depended on US investment. The policy tied the western periphery of Europe closer to the United States and enhanced an opening to the European Union.

The goodwill towards Ireland had already ensured that a measure proposed in Congress to limit tax concessions to US firms based abroad, which could have had serious long-term consequences for the Irish economy, was watered down for the Irish Republic. It was part of an economic package aimed at reducing the US deficit by $500 billion. When it seemed that the relevant section would go through unaltered, Irish Ambassador Dermot Gallagher made personal representations to the President. Taoiseach Albert Reynolds and President Mary Robinson also raised the issue with Clinton on visits to Washington. Few other countries could gain such ready access to the top in the United States to lobby on one issue.

Clinton also instructed Commerce Secretary Ron Brown to lead a delegation to an investment conference in Belfast announced by John Major for 13–14 December 1994. It was the first ever official visit to Belfast by a member of a US cabinet. The British event was put together with suspicious haste after it became known the President was planning an investment conference in America. If there was a connection, an administration official said, "it serves to underline the extent to which Washington is now driving the agenda." He suspected "that this was a move by the British to seize back the initiative and to return the focus to a strictly Northern Ireland context." American protests at British attempts to exclude Sinn Féin from the Belfast conference and threats of a boycott by Irish-American executives obliged the Northern Ireland Office to change the rules at the last minute and admit Sinn Féin councillors.

Irish-American lobbyists were overjoyed with the choice of George Mitchell. He had backed the Adams visa, though the Maine Senator had generally kept a low profile on Northern Ireland. He associated with the Friends of Ireland, and in December 1992 co-signed a solemn appeal to "all those who have relied on bullets and bombs in the past—lay down your arms." He had never gone out of the way to antagonize the British, and British Ambassador Sir Robin Renwick said as he left the White House after hearing of Mitchell's appointment, "I admire him a lot, he is a very good choice."

Many people regarded Mitchell as an Irish American, but his family did not see him that way. He was one of five children from an Irish father, George Mitchell and Lebanese mother, Mintaha Saad Mitchell. His father's father was an Irish immigrant, Michael Joseph Kilroy, who had put him up for adoption. At the age of three his father was chosen for adoption by a Lebanese family from a line-up of boys from a Boston orphanage, and brought to live in a poor Lebanese district in Waterville in Maine. There he grew up and married a Lebanese girl. Ireland was never a topic of discussion in their house and hardly anyone knew of Mitchell's father's Irish connection. Even the name Mitchell was misleading. It was taken by his parents to replace a similar-sounding Arab surname. His father worked as a janitor at Colby College. He was raised as a Maronite Catholic and learned Arabic from his parents. As a child, the future Senator was so sickly that for two years his parents drove fifteen miles once a week to fetch goat's milk to build him up. They put the goat's milk in an ordinary bottle so he never knew he was getting special attention. After working his way through law school, Mitchell became an aide to Senator Edmund Muskie and served for a brief spell in army counter-intelligence. In the Senate, his main achievement was the passage of a clean air bill, which took ten years.

"What I hope to do," Mitchell told me in his new office on the seventh—the most prestigious—floor of the State Department, "is to point out to Americans and American companies that it is not only in the national interest of the United States but it is in their economic interests to invest in Northern Ireland and the border counties, and I think there will be an economic benefit to all of Ireland as a result of this."

The President's investment conference on Ireland took place in May 1995 in Washington's Sheraton Hotel, ironically at the same time as a weapons and surveillance equipment exhibition for government and private agencies at which bomb disposal robots, night vision equipment and bullet-proof vests were on display.

Though the scale was vastly different, this White House event represented the high point of the most significant economic engagement by the United States in any western Europe country since Truman's Marshall Plan in the 1940s which helped set postwar Europe on its feet. It attracted many of the leading Irish-American business executives from the boardrooms of America. They were the products of the most successful generation of Irish Americans, many of whom got their start in the world of commerce when the postwar GI bill gave millions of ex-servicemen a chance to enter university they would not otherwise have had. Chuck Feeney was one. Don Keough was another. Because of the GI bill, Keough was able to go to Creighton University and make his way in the business world to become president of Coca Cola. Niall O'Dowd, whose publication *Irish America* drew up a Business 100 every year, described the conference as "a coming of age for corporate Irish America, the equivalent in business terms of John F. Kennedy becoming the first Irish-Catholic President."

Forums to discuss one of the world's most intractable problems had become a by-product of the Northern Irish Troubles. One of the first was held at Amherst University in Massachusetts in August 1975, bringing together political and paramilitary participants from both sides of the border, two of whom, Seamus Costello of the Irish Republican Socialist Party and Sammy Smyth of the Ulster Defence Association, later died violent deaths. Since the mid-1970s annual "off-the-record" conferences on Northern Ireland were staged by the British Irish Association at Oxford or Cambridge University. Much the same people turned up each year and greeted each other as old friends. It had one major drawback: Sinn Féin was never invited. This institutionalized the isolation of a section of the Catholic population, though the organizers were hostages to a basic political reality; if Sinn Féin turned up, British and Irish government ministers and unionists would stay away.

But the Clinton conference was too big an occasion to allow that to happen, and it was about promoting investment, not a political dialogue. It was hosted by the United States President and attended by the Vice President and Secretary of State. It was organized by Commerce Secretary Ron Brown and his Assistant Secretary Chuck Meissner. Its purpose was to address the economic problems of a peacetime Northern Ireland. An invitation to such a forum was almost impossible to refuse, though unionist leaders Ian Paisley and Jim Molyneaux sent their deputies rather than attend an event to which Gerry Adams was invited. Clinton's economic conference brought together representatives of every strand of political opinion on the island of Ireland. Such a gathering had never taken place in Irish history. There was an "only in America" feel about it.

"It was fascinating," said Nancy Soderberg, who mingled with the delegates, "just to be a fly on the wall and watch the various groupings back and forth. It really made you understand for the first time the power of America. All these leaders who won't talk to each other, much less be under the same roof, could come here."

Its dynamic provided another example of how American involvement broke down barriers and prodded the process along. Sir Patrick Mayhew, who had refused up to then to meet Adams or shake his hand, could hardly spend his time hiding behind the potted plants at the conference hotel in Washington to avoid him, and the Northern Ireland Secretary made arrangements for a first-ever meeting with the Sinn Féin leader on the eve of the three-day event. This took place at 7:13 p.m. on Wednesday 24 May behind the solid wooden doors of suite 6066 of the Sheraton Hotel. As Mayhew arrived and pushed through a mob of reporters and camera crews, an American photographer asked, rather plaintively, if he would allow one shot of the encounter. "No," the minister replied. "Just one," she wailed. "Not even one," he said. Just ten weeks earlier Mayhew had said that fifty million British people would not like to see the President of the world's greatest democracy shaking hands with Adams. He did not want them to see him do it either.

Michael Conlon of north Belfast arrived first from the Sinn Féin delegation, and found himself in the midst of a bunch of British officials, who laughed when he complained he felt like a hostage. He told me later that he struck up a conversation with Sir Robin Renwick about fly-fishing; Conlon favored Donegal but Sir Robin recommended Alaska. Adams arrived with his colleagues, all in suits and impeccably courteous to everyone. During the conference the Sinn Féin group refrained from drinking or staying up late. Adams spent thirty-two minutes inside in conversation with Mayhew. The atmosphere was cordial but tempers flared in the corridor as seventy media people jostled for position, ignoring warnings from hotel security men that they were creating a fire hazard.

At the official dinner that evening, several other firsts were recorded among the thousand diners. Paisley's deputy, Peter Robinson, who had never supped before with republican politicians, sat at a table with the leader of the Progressive Democrats, Mary Harney. One table away was Gerry Adams. At the next sat the British Ambassador. Nearby were the loyalists David Ervine, Joe English and Gary McMichael. Beside them, smiling munificently, was Mayhew, who had never before spoken with the loyalist leaders either.

Surveying the scene from the stage, Vice President Gore told the diners that "threads are being woven, one stitch at a time, into the shimmering cloak of peace."

The only verbal contact between Gerry Adams and David Ervine, representing two of the main warring groups in the North, came as they passed in a corridor later. "How have you been?" asked Adams. "Fine," replied Ervine. Veteran loyalist Glen Barr, who attended many conferences on conflict resolution since Amherst, showed how far apart the two sides still were. Asked if he would shake Adams's hand, he retorted: "If Gerry Adams is shaking my hand, he'd better look at what's in the other one."

There was nevertheless an extraordinarily cheerful atmosphere in the hotel bars, and unlikely groups from Britain, Northern Ireland and the Irish Republic joined in sing-songs and cocktail chatter. One British junior minister responded to a round of Irish ballads in the Sheraton bar with Gilbert and Sullivan. Belfast City Council held a reception in the Sheraton's Virginia Suite at which almost everyone turned up, including David Ervine, Billy Hutchinson, John Alderdice, Gerry Adams, Unionist MPs Willie Ross and Jim Nicholson, Senator George Mitchell, Northern Ireland junior minister, Malcolm Moss and British Labor Party spokesperson on Northern Ireland, Mo Mowlam.

But many delegates from the unionist community clearly felt ill at ease among the Irish Americans. The conference had an all-Ireland dimension, being concerned with the six counties of Northern Ireland and the six border counties of Donegal, Sligo, Leitrim, Cavan, Monaghan and Louth in the Republic. This meant that the hundreds of potential American investors were being asked to look at two different jurisdictions. They would see that the Republic had a ten percent corporate tax rate for manufacturing and computer-related operations compared with over 30 percent in Northern Ireland, though the North offered better capital grants. The disparity was already clear with ten times as many American companies in the South. The British government, however, resisted pressure from Dublin before the conference to put Northern Ireland on a par with the Republic. This would bring ferocious complaints from Wales and Scotland, which competed for foreign investment. It would also imply a dilution of the Union of Northern Ireland with Great Britain.

The goal of Irish America, supported by the White House, was to get negotiations under way on the future constitutional arrangements for Northern Ireland. To Irish nationalists, the peace process meant movement at last and the conference was part of that. Many unionists saw it as inevitably leading to a weakening of the Union. To them, the peace process was a political power play. But they could not ignore the American role or the investment potential arising from the peace process, and some knew that to gain high political office in Northern Ireland again they would have to enter real negotiations.

A number were prepared to engage the enemy more readily than others.

The Ulster Unionist Mayor of Ballymena, Robert Coulter, told me at a White House reception, "Three days ago I would have preached that we should have established some sort of relationship with the Ulster Scots here. Now I don't think so, as there is a hand of friendship here from Irish Americans and we should be in there letting our voice be heard in a friendly manner. They are the ones who have influence here."

During his address to the conference, the first major speech ever given by an American President on Ireland, Clinton did his best to reassure unionists that he was even-handed. Speaking against a surreal pink and black map of Ireland with the six Northern Ireland counties and the six in the Republic outlined as one unit, he pointedly praised Ulster Scots, "some of them my ancestors," as well as Irish Catholics, for their contribution to building America. "That meant a lot to us," said John Laird, a businessman and former unionist politician from Belfast.

Economics of a different kind were on the mind of Sinn Féin during this particular period. They had a chance to reap the economic dividend of peace, now that the ban on fundraising had been lifted. One such chance was a big function held in the Essex House Hotel in Manhattan. Gerry Adams came fresh from his "triple-whammy" victory in Washington. Presiding over the $200-a-head lunch, actress Fionnuala Flanagan said Lord Essex would be turning over in his grave "like a flapjack" if he knew that the four hundred people filling the hotel dining room were the "descendants of the very savages Essex was sent to Ireland to get rid of." Donald Trump, owner of the next-door Plaza Hotel and New York's most colorful entrepreneur, turned up to lend support, as did Bianca Jagger, ex-wife of the rock singer Mick Jagger, Ambassador Raymond Flynn who was on home leave from the Vatican, screen writers Michael Moore and Terry George, political activists Mario Biaggi and Paul O'Dwyer, and former Mayor David Dinkins, who was given a standing ovation. Two years earlier, if anyone had attempted to predict how far they had come, "they would have been dismissed as being a dreamer," said Adams, looking around the gathering.

Adams was fortunate to get the restriction on fundraising lifted when he did. In April, three days after the Oklahoma bomb, the veteran IRA man, Joe Cahill, returned to the US to attend a Noraid dinner in Boston. This time the State Department successfully lobbied the White House to ensure that he was not allowed to raise money. As America mourned its dead, British officials took some grim satisfaction in pointing out that this was the type of thing the IRA had been doing to them. "After Oklahoma, things tightened up on visas for members of groups supporting paramilitary organizations," a senior State Department official said. But Adams had secured a visa with no restrictions, and when he returned on 9 May for a full-scale, nationwide tour timed to end at the investment conference, he set Sinn Féin well on the road, on his very first day, to its target of a million dollars by the end of the year. Four hundred guests turned up for dinner in the New York Plaza at $1,000 a plate. By 30 June, Friends of Sinn Féin had taken in $897,328 in contributions, according to returns made by their president, Larry Downes, a lawyer in the New York firm of Gilroy, Downes, Horowitz & Goldstein. This was exactly twice the largest annual amount Noraid ever reported, and that was in 1972, when Irish America was outraged over internment and Bloody Sunday. The prisoners' aid organization had since been discredited by gunrunning charges against its members and was a declining force. By the end of June, Friends of Sinn Féin had also run up expenses of $351,162, mostly in hotel, catering and telephone bills. The Sinn Féin support organization was registered with the Department of Justice, as required under Section 2 of the Foreign Agents Registration Act, and it undertook that all money received went to "supporting the activities and purposes of Sinn Féin as a democratic political party engaged in Ireland and in many countries throughout the world in promoting the Irish peace process by social welfare, education and lobbying activities." The returns, which itemized every donation of $50 or more, revealed that Bill Flynn gave Sinn Féin $1,000, as did Local 59 of the Bricklayers Union in the Bronx, and the friends of Sheriff McFaul in Westlake, Ohio.

By September, approximately half the money collected had been sent to Ireland, where Adams said he wanted to upgrade Sinn Féin's computer system. Some of the rest went to finance an office Sinn Féin had established in Washington, staffed by 41-year-old Mairead Keane of Dublin, the party's former director of education. The returns also showed that one wire transfer alone of $65,000 from Chuck Feeney was diverted to Washington to pay office bills. Of all the main figures from corporate Irish America, he alone had contributed substantial sums from his own resources to increase the republican movement's access to the political process. One Sinn Féin official said, "He was in many ways the person who made it possible." Estimates of his commitment to Sinn Féin ranged as high as a million dollars, enough to keep open the office in Washington for a period of four to five years.

Gerry Adams had formally opened the office in March. It was located in a modern building near Du Pont circle, a popular restaurant and gay center just ten blocks from the White House. At a reception in a nearby hotel to mark the occasion, at which regular and decaffeinated Colombian coffee and English Teatime tea were provided for the media, a far cry from Sinn Féin press conferences of old, Adams described the Sinn Féin office as "a diplomatic mission."

"Will it have a military attaché?" cried Peter Hitchens from the back of the room, in what came to be regarded as his finest moment in a year of Adams-baiting. The Sinn Féin leader retorted dryly that it might be a good time for Hitchens to decommission himself.

The White House encouraged the opening of the office. "Our whole approach on this was that the more interaction and engagement with them the more moderate they would become," said Nancy Soderberg.

The Sinn Féin initiative prompted the unionists, who had little fundraising potential in the United States, to accept an offer from a Northern Ireland businessman of the use of his offices at a commercial building at Dulles airport, fifteen miles outside Washington, with a full-time staff member, Scottish-born Ann Smith, at their disposal. Tony Cully-Foster, the Derry-born president of an international business consultancy firm, had both Protestant and Catholic family ties but felt that in the interests of fairness the unionists should not be put at a disadvantage in the United States. One restriction was put on Smith—she could not talk to Mairead Keane when they attended the same functions. The no-handshake policy was still in effect for unionists and those who represented them.

For the American and Irish business executives and company heads at the investment conference, business handshakes were at the heart of a process of deal-making which the organizers hoped would lead to a boom in US investment. Everybody could see unparalleled opportunities opening up for "match-making" said Sir Patrick Mayhew, as one encounter session got under way. He startled some of the clergy present by concluding a pep talk on future business alliances with a line borrowed from Shakespeare, "Let nature take its course . . . let copulation thrive!"

The President's investment conference ended, literally, with a bang. A tremendous thunderstorm hit Washington as a farewell party got under way in a marquee on the White House lawns, where the band hired for the occasion was appropriately called Celtic Thunder. Unionists and nationalists, British and Irish, American and Irish American, crowded round trestle tables laden with delicacies in a friendly and relaxed manner, though Jean Kennedy Smith was shaken by the ferocity of a unionist supporter who berated her rudely for her performance in Ireland. "A little red-faced man" had shouted at her, she complained to a friend.

As Clinton stood up to speak, thunder crashed, lightning flashed, and the heavens opened, as befitted a momentous occasion.

"We are all here in a very large tent in more ways than one," said Clinton, but a roar from the skies drowned out the applause. The rest of his speech went unheard as the microphone system broke down and the lights dimmed ominously.

24

Getting a Bounce

"There was a bargain when Gerry Adams was given a visa and a handshake . . . that the IRA would begin to hand over weapons."
Sir John Kerr

At the last minute, White House speech-writers altered the text of the keynote address President Clinton gave to the investment conference in Washington. An early draft contained a reference to the President's intention of visiting Northern Ireland in August 1995. But it was dropped because US and British officials could not agree on the dates.

Both the American and British governments had problems with their timetables. In the United States, a budget battle between the Republican Congress and the Democratic White House was threatening to shut down Washington at the time the President wanted to travel across the Atlantic. He could not be out of the country if Uncle Sam could not write cheques. Other proposed dates clashed with Hillary Clinton's schedule. John Major's party had a leadership crisis and a party conference to be dealt with.

Nancy Soderberg blamed domestic problems more than any tensions between Clinton and Major. "I think they were genuinely trying to work it out," she said. "Between their timing and our timing it was awkward. Having the President of the United States land in your town does sort of put everything on hold for a while."

It wasn't until 5 July that the three governments agreed that the President would visit London, Belfast and Dublin between 28 November and 2 December. One of the goals, the White House said, offering an olive branch to the British, would be the "strengthening of the transatlantic partnership." Clinton also arranged to play a round of golf at Ballybunion in County Kerry before flying back to the United States from Shannon airport.

The prospect of golfing at the spectacular Ballybunion course exercised Clinton to an extraordinary degree. An ardent golfer with a handicap of thirteen, he would slip away from the White House for a game whenever he could. Dick Spring had invited him to play at Ballybunion during their meeting at Martha's Vineyard, at which the President spent some time debating golfing techniques with Irish deputy government press officer, John Foley, a better golfer with a handicap of eight. During the summer the President's legislative aide, Susan Brophy, visited Kerry and brought back a Ballybunion golf cap which Clinton treated as a treasured talisman. Somehow it got mislaid, causing a full-scale crisis in the White House. As the Ballybunion shop had no more caps of the same type, Brophy had to ask a friend for whom she had brought the same gift to hand it over for the President. Clinton talked constantly about playing in Kerry. A White House official sitting beside the President at a meeting one day glanced into his briefcase and saw that it contained the handbook of the Ballybunion course.

Meanwhile the President and the British Prime Minister had made up after their latest row. They met a month after the fundraising decision, and over a White House lunch of roast monkfish and grilled mushrooms more or less repaired the breach in the alliance. Their relationship was close enough, John Major said, "to enable the President and me to have the occasional disagreement if we want without any harm coming of it." By this stage, according to a source who sat in on some meetings with Clinton, "the passport files and all that stuff was off the screen and the President had developed a genuine respect for Major and figured he was trying to do the right thing and understood why Major might need to make a gesture by not taking a phone call."

But the peace process was by now in trouble. In the middle of one of Ireland's hottest summers of the century, shortly after the dates for the President's visit were agreed, Sinn Féin broke off exploratory talks with the British government. They were getting nowhere over the decommissioning issue as London was still insisting on Washington Three, the condition which required that there be actual decommissioning of some arms before Sinn Féin could participate in inter-party talks.

The British had some support for their demands in the US administration, though not in the White House. The State Department decided independently to advise Adams that it was up to him to move. A document was drawn up, listing "talking points" to be raised with Sinn Féin, and sent to the US ambassadors in both Dublin and London after being cleared by the National Security Council. It contained three main recommendations: (1) that contacts with the British government should continue; (2) that Sinn Féin should consider measures to build trust with other parties; and (3) that Sinn Féin should seriously engage with Britain in establishing a process to be used for disarming.

Though the last looked very like Washington Three, Jean Kennedy Smith chose to see no change in administration policy in the document and simply faxed a copy to the Sinn Féin office in Belfast. But Admiral Crowe read more into the State Department communication. The former chief of the joint chiefs of staff interpreted it as a more formal *démarche,* a diplomatic device conveying a strong desire for action. The American Ambassador flew to Belfast and at a tense meeting with Adams insisted that it was time to deliver and that Sinn Féin should persuade the IRA to make a start in decommissioning its arms. Adams retorted that this was not US policy. He complained to Washington and received an assurance from the National Security Council that he was technically correct.

The incident shook Adams but Crowe was made to look as if he had exceeded his brief. The rebuff for the Ambassador angered State Department officials, one of whom said, "That's typical of Lake and his people. They give instructions to diplomats for the record and then they go and undermine them." One insider in Washington said that the incident underlined that Crowe was "not a definitive carrier of the message or a central player." But the fact that the document went further than the public request to Adams to "seriously discuss" decommissioning meant that the administration was now speaking, as one London source put it, "with forked tongues."

The Connolly House Group returned to Belfast in late summer. "We couldn't believe that the British were going to allow the decommissioning question to destroy the process," said Bruce Morrison, who criticized Taoiseach John Bruton for giving it a second wind by his remarks on Saint Patrick's Day. "We knew the security people were saying it wasn't the issue." Morrison, Bill Flynn, Chuck Feeney, Joe Jamison and Niall O'Dowd met the Northern Ireland Minister for Political Development, Michael Ancram, who told them that the unionists wouldn't sit down with Sinn Féin before the issue was settled and they couldn't have empty chairs at the conference table. "The situation was festering and the President's visit was still a long way off," said Morrison later, and "we thought it was better to have empty chairs than death and destruction." They also visited John Hume at his holiday home in Donegal. To bring home their concern to the administration, they placed a full-page advertisement in *The New York Times* saying, "Mr. Major, you must act now. Convene all-inclusive talks or be judged on your failure to act." The $25,000 cost of the advertisement was paid by Chuck Feeney.

Morrison was now himself a member of the US administration having been appointed on 1 June chairman of the Federal Housing Finance Board in Washington, an agency with over one hundred officials. This caused some tensions between the former Congressman and Soderberg, who insisted that the only two people authorized to speak for the administration on Northern Ireland were herself and Tony Lake. The matter came to a head when Morrison commented on television about the need for the British to move, at a time when she and Lake were in delicate negotiations with the British and Irish. She rang him to emphasize sharply that as a member of the administration he could not make comments which would compromise the White House.

The fact that a presidential visit was planned created a new dynamic in the British–Irish political process, however. "This is a trip I have wanted to make for a long time," Clinton said in response to questions I submitted to him at the end of July. "I will have the opportunity to talk face-to-face with people from different traditions and hear their views on how to achieve a lasting settlement to a conflict that has cost over three thousand lives." He said he wanted to bring a message of support for "their courageous stand in favor of peace."

But he also wanted results before Air Force One touched down in Belfast. "When an American President travels abroad, he needs to get a bounce out of his trip," said a White House official. "You can bet the President will want to celebrate something when he goes to Belfast. Can you imagine what it would be like for him if the whole thing is breaking down while he is in town?"

"I would be pleased if talks were under way by the time I visit Northern Ireland," the President went on. "While decisions on prisoner issues are internal matters for each government, I would welcome any measure aimed at helping the process of healing and reconciliation in Northern Ireland, including movement on prisoners."

Both remarks were aimed at London, and signalled to the Irish side that the United States was still intent on nudging things forward. The comment on prisoners was particularly pointed. Since the IRA ceasefire eleven months previously, Dublin had freed thirty-two of seventy-eight republican prisoners but London had not released any of one thousand republican and loyalist prisoners; it had however set free Private Lee Clegg, the only member of the security forces in prison convicted of murder. Clinton repeated that "bombs and guns must go," and again urged both Sinn Féin and the loyalists to engage in a "serious discussion" of decommissioning.

The task of engineering an end to the stalemate fell once again to Tony Lake and Nancy Soderberg, who had begun a new round of discussions with both governments and the parties during the investment conference. Their immediate concern was how to get around the roadblock of decommissioning. Washington Three had met the immovable object of Sinn Féin's "no surrender" of weapons.

The two presidential advisers had come to the conclusion over the summer that the only way round the decommissioning roadblock was the "twin-track approach," with the politicians talking about a settlement while an international commission examined the problem of illegal arsenals. The idea had originated with Dick Spring and his officials in the Department of Foreign Affairs. George Mitchell, the President's economic envoy to Ireland, told both governments privately he would be willing to act as chairman of the commission if invited.

The British and Irish governments appeared to be about to agree on the twin-track proposal when at the last minute a summit between John Major and John Bruton, planned for 6 September, was called off by Dublin. Sinn Féin would not agree to work with the commission, because the British were saying that, whatever the commission recommended, there still had to be actual decommissioning before all-party talks. It was a major setback for John Bruton, who had confidently forecast in Washington during Saint Patrick's week that Sinn Féin would move on the issue in a short period of time.

During this period, London insisted, as Bruton had in Washington, that the US administration was in fact using its leverage with Sinn Féin on the arms question, and that Gerry Adams had promised the White House progress on handing over arms in return for fundraising and access to the President. But there was no evidence of White House pressure on Sinn Féin, and both

Gerry Adams and the White House kept denying it every time such a claim was made.

In July, for example, the director of the British Information Services in New York, Peter Innes, said in a letter to *The New York Times* that "the British Government is not isolated in asking for some IRA decommissioning" and that "the President and the Vice President of the United States gave the IRA the same message." Soderberg, speaking as a "senior administration official," said next day this was not the case, and that the President had not specifically asked for "some IRA decommissioning" but for "serious discussion" of decommissioning of IRA weapons.

Even the British Prime Minister insisted on contradicting this. In September, Major gave an interview to American reporter Morgan Strong for the November edition of the magazine *Modern Maturity*. He told him: "The US administration has, in particular, underlined that political negotiations cannot start before there has been substantial progress on the decommissioning of paramilitary weapons." Strong queried this with the White House. The reaction was swift. Mary Ann Peters, a director in the European affairs department of the National Security Council, told him, "The administration has not taken a position either way in regard to decommissioning as a precondition to the peace talks. This has been made clear in several speeches President Clinton has given on the subject. The British will be so informed immediately."

Within minutes Strong received a telephone call from Peter Westmacott in the British embassy, who had just got off the phone with Peters. Westmacott said to Strong, "Please amend the Prime Minister's penultimate sentence to read, 'The US administration has in particular underlined that paramilitaries on both sides must get rid of their bombs and guns for good.'" Strong reported that when this revision was read to Peters she said it still did not accurately reflect the US position, which "has been strictly neutral."

Around the same time, the new British Ambassador in Washington, Sir John Kerr, a 53-year-old Scotsman whom John Major had dubbed his "Machiavelli" for a nimble performance as British representative to the European Union, told British and Irish correspondents essentially the same thing as the Prime Minister. At a briefing in the British embassy he said that there was a conviction in the White House "that there was a bargain when Gerry Adams was given a visa and a handshake . . . the bargain was that the IRA would begin to hand over weapons." Again, when this was put to the White House, Soderberg restated the position that it encouraged those engaged in ceasefires to "seriously discuss" decommissioning. By now it appeared that either the British had misinterpreted what they were being told by the White House or they had been oversold in private as to what the White House understood by "seriously discuss."

Gerry Adams returned to Washington in mid-September for further discussions with Tony Lake. He gave the National Security Adviser, a keen baseball fan, a video of a hurling game showing how the Irish settled their sporting contests. "When I see Adams I try to convince him of the merits of baseball as a metaphor for politics," Lake said later. "He sent me a video of hurling, which looks like a game with no rules." Lake also compared the peace process to a bicycle—it toppled over if it went too slowly—and Adams adopted this metaphor to tell reporters that Major saw the process "as a bicycle which must be kept upright but moving at the lowest possible speed."

After a two-hour discussion which Al Gore joined for a while, Lake and Adams agreed to meet again before Adams returned home. But the second session was cancelled at short notice by the Sinn Féin leader. He claimed later that there had been a "British-inspired spin" that the meeting was called so that US officials could put pressure on him, which, he said, was "nonsense." For Sinn Féin any hint that the White House was insisting on movement on arms was worrying. It would signal to the IRA that the President was now leaning towards a British agenda, and that the much-vaunted international dimension was being turned against them. The truth about the "spin" was more mundane. An official had given me what is called in Washington a "heads-up" about the second meeting. I in turn tipped off a visiting colleague, Ken Reid of Ulster Television, so he could have his camera crew ready. He naturally alerted his office in Belfast which put out a news item saying Adams had been summoned back to the White House. This was fed back to the Sinn Féin delegation in Washington, which immediately denied there was to be a second meeting in the White House. Nor was there. Lake and Adams did get together again, privately, however, before the Belfast man returned home.

Michael Ancram, the British minister responsible for political development in Northern Ireland, had been in Washington just before Adams and had given Lake and Gore a first-hand briefing on London's position. The British had now adopted new tactics in their approach to Washington. Ancram, with his engaging manner and non-confrontational style, was a much more effective emissary in

America than Mayhew. On more than one occasion when Adams said he was going to the US capital, Ancram arrived just beforehand to brief the administration and the Washington-based media. The new Ambassador also stepped up the propaganda war. When an editorial, an opinion article or a letter critical of Britain appeared in a newspaper anywhere in the United States, the canny, cigarette-smoking Scotsman instructed his diplomats to respond immediately. Dermot Brangan, the Irish diplomat who liaised with US editorial writers, found out about the new tactics when he called into the office of a west coast newspaper and was told that in the preceding few weeks the editors had had three separate visitors, Sir John Kerr, the local British consul and Peter Westmacott, all taking issue with their interpretation of the peace process. The British diplomats also clipped any editorials in *The Irish Times* which were critical of the Irish side and faxed them around to American leader writers.

Minister for Foreign Affairs Dick Spring went to Washington again shortly afterwards to apprise Clinton of Ireland's attempts to salvage the twin-track process. In a strong show of support, both the President and Vice President joined him in Lake's office. Both Bruton and Spring were now saying that Washington Three should be dropped by the British so that talks could begin. Spring told the White House that they sought to avoid as far as possible "symbolic overtones of surrender." He also spelled out the Irish position in a speech to the United Nations General Assembly in New York. The British precondition, he said, ignored the psychology and motivation of those on both sides in Northern Ireland who had resorted to violence. A British diplomat, Stephen Gomersall, took the unusual step of putting a critical response on the record to the General Assembly, recalling that in December 1993 Spring called in the Irish parliament for a handing up of arms.

As the time for the presidential visit came ever closer, the White House grew increasingly anxious about the division between the two governments. Nancy Soderberg, who kept telling reporters that the gap could be bridged—as if willing the thing to work—travelled to Ireland to engage in some shuttle diplomacy among British and Irish officials and party leaders, including the new Ulster Unionist Party leader David Trimble. One of her main purposes was to talk Sinn Féin into endorsing the twin-track proposal while seeking reassurances for the IRA's political wing from the British and Irish governments that it could work.

Later, Soderberg told me that Sinn Féin's refusal to accept the twin-track delayed the talks process by two months. "Basically we were getting very nervous that the process wasn't moving fast enough and we wanted to get a sense directly from the parties whether we could move things forward, particularly in light of the President's visit," she said. The peace process was on hold. "The twin-track was originally rejected by Sinn Féin and we felt we had a role in trying to get them back on track, and in talking directly to the British and Irish and the parties about what it meant and didn't mean. I think our role there was helpful in reassuring them. We had a lot of discussions with Adams that Fall, explaining what it was and what it wasn't. And I think that helped move things forward, but their rejection of it cost a couple of months in the process. They could have got a target date by the end of the year but since they took two or three months to sign on to it, it got pushed back to February."

Less than two weeks later, both Lake and Soderberg travelled to London to try again to help break the impasse. It was rare for Tony Lake to leave his office, but Northern Ireland and Bosnia had become major issues of concern between the US and UK. They conducted a round of talks with British officials and politicians, and with John Hume and David Trimble. As is his style, Lake appeared to listen more than talk, all the time teasing out the possibilities of getting everyone out of the box in which they were trapped.

Describing his role in those talks, Lake told me that occasionally in a very quiet way the US would offer an idea "but not as an American proposition, not insisting on it, but simply trying to advance the process, being very careful not to make it into an American negotiation." If they had done that, it would have injected the US into the internal politics on all sides, which they did not want, and the parties would have looked to Washington for solutions rather than having to work it out among themselves. When the parties bumped up against very real differences, or said they were not sure if the others wanted something, "one of our roles was to say, we've just been talking to them, they do want it, try again, work it through, keep it going." The US sensed some months previously, as it did in Bosnia, that the parties in Northern Ireland wanted to find a way forward, he said. It was like a harvest where seeds were planted and watered and crops grew for harvesting. "We've hit harvest periods in Bosnia and Northern Ireland at approximately the same time," and if there was going to be another harvest down the road in Northern Ireland "we need to get working on it right away." But it was important for the US not to say where things should come out, "because we honestly don't know." The best outcome was the one that the parties agreed to, and "it's up to them to do it and we'll support them."

Lake and Soderberg left London still expressing a dogged optimism that the two governments and the parties could bridge the gap under the pressure of an imminent presidential visit. Their encounter with David Trimble had been a sobering one. He was a different type of unionist from the gentlemanly Jim Molyneaux. The MP for Bann left the Americans in no doubt that in the future there would be a more aggressive unionist lobbying effort. White House officials had privately expressed dismay when he won his party's leadership contest, preferring the more moderate-sounding John Taylor. But Trimble had come across as clever and calculating, and he succeeded in one thing. His proposal that elections should be held in Northern Ireland before talks had taken hold with the Americans. It would get them off the decommissioning hook, they believed, and keep the bicycle in motion.

On 30 October, shortly after his election as party leader, Trimble arrived in the United States to be greeted by a quarter-page advertisement in *The New York Times* inserted by a lobby group, the Irish American Unity Conference. It was headed "A welcome to David Trimble, the David Duke of Ireland." In drawing attention to his membership of the Orange Order, "a sectarian organization that preaches Protestant supremacy and is anti-Catholic" it compared him with David Duke, a former leader of the Ku Klux Klan. Duke told me from his New Orleans office, "I think this is a cheap shot on both of us." Niall O'Dowd criticized the advertisement in an *Irish Voice* editorial, pointing out that the Ancient Order of Hibernians, the biggest Irish-American organization, was exclusively Catholic. This didn't stop the unionist leader launching a fierce verbal assault on O'Dowd when they met in New York. The publisher challenged Trimble's assertion that punishment beatings meant there was no IRA ceasefire. The unionist leader retorted hotly that he was "a craven apologist for the IRA, incapable of independent thought."

Trimble went to the White House for a further discussion with Lake. President Clinton dropped in for the first ever meeting between an American President and a unionist leader. Trimble again pressed hard his election argument. That day the unionist delegation found Washington a small world. On the way into Lake's office, Trimble encountered Mairead Keane of Sinn Féin waiting in a corridor. On the way out he met John Hume going in with fellow socialist MPs from Europe. They chatted cordially but in meetings with members of Congress, Trimble and Ken Maginnis excoriated the Derry man. At an American Ireland Fund reception in his honor, Trimble found himself standing, uncomfortably, a few feet from Sinn Féin's Vice President Pat Doherty.

Two weeks before Clinton was due to travel to Belfast, Gerry Adams returned to Washington and this time Gore joined the National Security staff for a meeting with him in Lake's office. It was an exhaustive discussion. Adams said that the situation had seriously deteriorated. Lake assured him that if a formula was agreed, the administration would help work it out. And he was encouraged not to react negatively if the two governments announced a new arrangement on the way ahead within the next few weeks.

At this stage, it looked as if the peace process might have run its course. Leaving La Tomate restaurant on Connecticut Avenue in Washington on the last evening of his visit, Adams remarked ruefully to his dinner companions, "We should have brought a camera. This might be the last time we are here." The Sinn Féin leader left for a $250-a-head cocktail party in Long Island before returning home.

25

My Mama Told Me, There'll Be Days Like This

"This day . . . will long be with us as one of the most remarkable days of our lives."
Bill Clinton

At the end of September 1995, an advance team of a dozen White House staff flew to London to work out the details of President Clinton's trip to Northern Ireland—and ran straight into a wall of resistance from the British side.

Everything the Americans wanted to do, the British said could not be done.

"We were stunned," said a White House aide who attended the negotiations. "Their resistance was breathtaking in terms of what they didn't want to do. They threw up all these security objections."

The chasm between the two sides became evident immediately after the American officials arrived with their schedules, maps and timetables at the Foreign Office and began discussions with a team of officials drawn from Prime Minister Major's office, the Foreign Office, the Northern Ireland Office and the security branches. The US visitors expected problems with security. What they did not expect was the cold reaction of the British civil servants.

The White House officials said the President wanted to meet the people on the streets and to stay overnight in the center of Belfast to demonstrate his confidence in the peace process. He also wished to visit Derry. He might make an excursion to the village of Ballycassidy in Fermanagh, if it was established that relatives of his mother, Virginia Cassidy, lived there. To each proposition the British officials said, "No." Instead they suggested the President travel to Belfast in the morning and leave in the evening. Walking on the Belfast streets, they insisted, was too dangerous, so he should make carefully screened public appearances only. Overnighting in Belfast posed enormous security and logistic problems. There were not enough bedrooms to accommodate the seven hundred support staff and media. And if he did insist on staying overnight, it should be behind the safe security fences around Hillsborough Castle outside Belfast, the one-time residence of governors of Northern Ireland. They did not want Clinton to visit Derry, Northern Ireland's predominantly Catholic second city, also for security reasons. Nor did they want the President to meet Gerry Adams.

"They talked about Northern Ireland as if it was a third world country," said one of the White House team. "They said the weather conditions were bad, the roads were impassable, or there were no roads. Well, come on, if the roads were bad, who's in charge up there? Their attitude was—those people, they're impossible—and they were making no distinction between Catholic and Protestant when they said that."

"So we knew it was political," the aide said. "The resistance didn't come from the Northern Ireland police, it was the Brits. They just wanted the President in and out. It was like the visa fights all over again. Don't give them anything."

One aide made private inquiries about security and was told that the RUC had coped with several royal visits in the previous ten years without problems.

Paige Reefe, the White House director of advance scheduling, fought the British on every point, the White House source said. "He would say the President wants to do this. They would say that is impossible. He would say we really understand your concerns but the President wants to do this. In the end we got everything, except the trip to Fermanagh but we hadn't been able to find any relatives. We thought they would relax a bit after the meeting but they never did the whole time."

Some of the advance team members travelled on to Belfast. One suggested to a Belfast council official that the President could speak in Donegall Place outside City Hall. "Oh, no," came the reply. "There'll be a Christmas tree in the way." The Clinton aides looked at each other. "We'll take care of that," they said, thinking immediately of the symbolism of the President switching on the lights for a Christmas of peace. "We'll supply the tree." Belfast was twinned with Nashville in Tennessee and a fifty-foot Nashville conifer was soon on its way in a US Air Force Galaxy aircraft to

Belfast. The children's television heroes, the Mighty Power Rangers, had been hired to switch on the tree lights at a fee of £7,000 ($11,000), but they agreed to do the street illuminations instead on a different date.

There remained only the delicate problem of the President's desire to meet the party leaders. The City Hall was rejected as a venue because of its association with unionism. Queen's University was chosen as neutral territory. Behind the scenes British diplomats urged the White House not to honor Adams by meeting him separately elsewhere. Supporters of Adams argued furiously that he should not be excluded from the gathering of political, church and community leaders which the President would address at Mackies factory, a symbol of religious balance and commercial success on the Belfast peace line which had once been an exclusively Protestant works bordering a Catholic area. One of the principal purposes of the peace process, as far as republicans were concerned, was to gain parity of esteem for Sinn Féin. A member of the advance team said, however, that the management at Mackies were warning that many Protestants in the engineering factory, where the workforce was split seventy to thirty between Protestants and Catholics, would walk out if Adams appeared.

The problem had not been solved when Air Force One took off from Andrews Air Force Base in Maryland on the evening of Tuesday 28 November, bound for London. But another one had.

The British and Irish prime ministers, nudged along by the Americans and with the President about to arrive within hours, announced at a dramatic 10 p.m. summit in 10 Downing Street that they had found a way to agree on the twin-track process. Tony Lake heard the news from Irish Ambassador Dermot Gallagher, who rang from a car phone in Washington just as the National Security Adviser was leaving the White House to change for the journey. A joint communiqué said an international body would be established with George Mitchell in the chair "to provide an independent assessment of the decommissioning issue," and that the two governments aimed to start all-party negotiations by the end of February.

There was a burst of applause on Air Force One as Clinton presented Lake with a bottle of the best American champagne for "midwifing" the breakthrough. But the ever-cautious Lake put the champagne on ice. It was far from a settlement. Sinn Féin had not signed on, though it could hardly cast aside a deal which President Clinton endorsed, especially in the next couple of days.

The champagne "was a very well-deserved tribute to someone who did a lot of extraordinary work on behalf of the agreement," said White House press secretary Mike McCurry, who credited the United States with playing an important facilitating role. Another senior official on Air Force One boasted that the Americans had in fact helped write the communiqué. "You'll notice in the draft communiqué it has a reference to an elected assembly; that's a direct result of the conversations with David Trimble," the official said, referring to a section which said parties would discuss "whether and how an elected body could play a part." He added, "There's some other language in there that moves toward the nationalist side."

In London, John Major told reporters that the Americans had nothing to do with the agreement. The next day, standing beside Clinton in Downing Street, he conceded that the President's imminent arrival had "concentrated the mind." British officials were pleased about the deal with Dublin. It differed little from the arrangement which had fallen through in September because of Sinn Féin disagreement. In their view, Dublin had blinked and the American card had been played to their advantage. They also believed that Lake and Soderberg were prepared to encourage all parties to take part in elections in Northern Ireland, despite nationalist opposition. For the first time, the alliance was back in good shape. Major and Clinton had come together again on Bosnia, and 13,000 British servicemen and 25,000 American troops were about to deploy there to enforce the US-brokered Dayton Accord which brought the war in Bosnia to an end. "The allied relationship is restored with a vengeance," said a senior Major aide. But Dayton would also mean no golf in Ballybunion. The President had decided at the last minute to skip Kerry to go to Germany to meet American troops preparing for the Balkans.

Clinton warmly endorsed "the unique and enduring relationship" between the two countries when he addressed the joint Houses of Parliament the next day among the gilded statues and paintings of Westminster's Royal Gallery. He recalled two world wars in which they had fought together, and announced that to honor the alliance he would name a new US guided–missile destroyer, the most powerful ever, after Winston Churchill. There was prolonged applause from the Lords and Commoners, among them Margaret Thatcher. "On a score of one to ten, the relationship jumped from four to six just then," said an American diplomat. The White House, added Clinton, still bore the scorch marks of the time when British forces laid siege to the US capital. "Now, whenever we have the most minor disagreement, I walk out on the Truman balcony and I look at those burn marks, just to remind myself that I dare not let this relationship get out of hand again."

But behind the scenes, the American and the British officials did not warm to each other. The United States might be the only country in the world that had no complex about the British and that could bend it to its will, but it could not dictate personal relationships. There were only a handful of places provided for the official party at a dinner given for Clinton by John Major in Downing Street. Space in the old terrace house was severely limited but some perceived a slight. "I didn't see you last night," the President said to one of his top officials next day. "No," came the reply, "we had to go and get a meal ourselves."

Next day, Clinton became the first serving American President to visit Northern Ireland. Three thousand police and one hundred secret service men were deployed to ensure his security. Five-ton glass screens were in place around the presidential podiums and police sniper units took up position on rooftops with instructions never to look at the President through their rifle sights. Three Black Hawk helicopters guarded Aldergrove airport where Air Force One touched down on a grey morning. Travelling in a bomb- and bullet-proof Cadillac limousine, Clinton swept into Belfast along the closed-off M2 motorway and onto the loyalist Shankill Road. He got out at Violet's Fruit Shop, next door to Frizell's fish shop where ten people died in an IRA bomb attack in 1993, and strolled in and bought chrysanthemums, four apples and a net of clementine oranges. It was a gesture to Protestants who saw him only in terms of the Adams visa, and the visit took off from that moment.

The President's stop looked spontaneous but it had been carefully planned. Every move and speech had been scrutinized for balance. If the President referred to Derry, he would say it was in the County of Londonderry, thereby using the Catholic and Protestant versions of the name. If he mentioned the harp and the fiddle, typical Catholic Irish instruments, he spoke also of the fife and the Lambeg drum, favored by the Ulster Protestants. A team of officials worked on every detail of his twenty-four-hour visit for weeks, helped by Professor Brady Williamson of the University of Wisconsin who did advance work on "tricky" trips. In London, the schedulers had the assistance of Mort Engelberg, producer of the movie, *Smokey the Bear*, who said he found the British "devilishly polite" when asked to co-operate with his ideas on presidential choreography. A United Airlines pilot called Jamie Lindsey, who doubled occasionally as a presidential advance man, also helped out in Belfast. One of the things he did was to pick two letters from school children to welcome the President in Mackies factory. One was by a nine-year-old Catholic schoolgirl, Catherine Hamill. She read it in Clinton's presence to a crowd of 1,500 in the engineering works, providing one of the most poignant moments in twenty-five years of violence.

"My first daddy died in the Troubles," she said, standing on a wooden box with a Protestant schoolboy, David Sterrit, beside her, and speaking in an innocent, sing-song Belfast accent. "It was the saddest day of my life. I still think of him. Now it is nice and peaceful. I like having peace and quiet for a change instead of having people shooting and killing. My Christmas wish is that peace and love will last in Ireland for ever." Her father Patrick had been shot by loyalists when she was only a few months old.

Suddenly, the Troubles were not abstract any more for Tony Lake, Nancy Soderberg, George Mitchell, Tom Manton, Richard Neal, Jim Walsh, Joe Kennedy, Peter King, Chris Dodd, Don Keough, Bruce Morrison, Niall O'Dowd and the dozens of other American officials, writers, legislators and business executives listening in silence.

The most powerful message the President brought to Belfast came in the middle of his speech in Mackies. In a phrase redolent of the IRA slogan, "Our day will come," he said people "must say to those who still would use violence for political objectives—you are the past, your day is over."

There was a barely heard note of discord when Clinton said those who renounced violence "are entitled to be full participants in the democratic process." "Never!" cried a follower of Ian Paisley. Paisley's annual party conference just a few days before had been a festival of Clinton-bashing. His spokesman, Sammy Wilson, referring to reports of bark weevil in the Christmas tree, had said, to sustained applause, they should be more concerned about "the draft-dodging, IRA-loving pest that's coming with it."

Having visited the Shankill Road, the President drove onto the Falls, its Catholic counterpart, and stopped at McErlean's home bakery at 105 Falls Road as a Catholic crowd surged forward cheering wildly. They could hardly ever have imagined that an American President would walk on their graffiti-marked streets which had seen so much chaos and bloodshed. It was near the junction of the Falls and Springfield roads which was known as "hijack corner" because vehicles were regularly taken and burned at this spot during unrest.

Gerry Adams, as if by chance, emerged from McErlean's to greet the President with the words, "Céad míle fáilte," "a hundred thousand welcomes." Photographers were blind-sided by a white van which blocked their view while police kept them back, but Sinn Féin press officer Richard McAuley managed to get a still photograph of Adams and the President shaking hands and smiling which appeared in several newspapers next day. Clinton told the Sinn Féin leader he had been reading *The Street*, his book of short stories about the Falls, until 5 a.m., and now saw where he got his inspiration from. This time the planning had been more chaotic. Up to late the previous evening, the British had maintained their opposition to a public handshake. Adams was curiously deflated after Clinton left. He had done well. He had got parity of esteem, but it had been a wearying fight again.

In East Belfast, the palm which had just embraced Gerry Adams's was pressed against that of Peter Robinson, Paisley's deputy, who welcomed Clinton cordially, saying it was "a great compliment to our area that the leader of the world's most powerful nation is prepared to take time out and listen to our views on employment, business and economic life." His list pointedly did not include politics. Whatever about his political agenda, a President of the United States had come to East Belfast. Protestants "were generally pleased," said a veteran Belfast journalist. "I suppose they're so unused to having any attention paid to them at all, that they were surprised and pleased when it is."

Derry became an American city for the day. Its ancient walls and streets were swathed in American flags, and the Stars and Stripes fluttered from official buildings. At a reception in the Guildhall, Phil Coulter once more entertained the President with *The Town I Love So Well*—this time Clinton was able to mouth the words—and when the President stepped into Guildhall Square and mounted a wooden stage with John Hume, a huge roar went up from a flag-waving crowd which had been waiting three hours in the cold. Sir Patrick Mayhew stood beside the President looking distinctly uneasy and was ignored by the largely Catholic crowd. "It's extraordinary, it's truly overwhelming," said Nancy Soderberg. Martin McGuinness of Sinn Féin stood watching under the Christmas tree, standing not far from the loyalist politician, Glen Barr. The only person in what looked like a paramilitary outfit turned out to be Maureen Dowd, a columnist of *The New York Times* who was travelling with the White House press and was wearing a black beret and sunglasses.

Back in Belfast to turn on the lights of the Christmas tree, Clinton seemed awestruck at the size of the vast, good-humored crowd of Catholics and Protestants waiting for him outside the City Hall. As far as he could see, people crowded into Royal Avenue and Donegall Place. They were entertained by Belfast's Van Morrison in black Homburg and dark shades, who performed Belfast's song of hope, ending with the words, "Oh, my mama told me, there'll be days like this."

The fundamentalist Lord Mayor of Belfast, the Rev. Eric Smyth, once a civilian searcher who checked buses for bombs, began preaching "Behold the Virgin shall be with Child . . .," but from the throng someone shouted, "Save it for Sunday, Eric! We want Bill!"

The President of the United States, who in twenty-four hours had defined himself as part Irish, part Ulster Scots and part British, said, "This day . . . will long be with us as one of the most remarkable days of our lives." He recalled how American troops had been stationed in Belfast during the Second World War and President Eisenhower had been named a burgess of the city, and he read from letters he had received from local children. He ended on a humorous note. "I got a letter from thirteen-year-old Ryan from Belfast," he said. "Now Ryan, if you're out in the crowd tonight, here's the answer to your question. No, as far as I know, an alien spaceship did not crash in Roswell, New Mexico, in 1947. And Ryan, if the United States Air Force did discover alien bodies, they didn't tell me about it either, and I want to know." At a briefing for White House press later, a reporter asked White House spokesman Mike McCurry, "Mike, this will probably end the briefing. Did the President actually inquire of the Air Force in gathering the information for the answer he provided thirteen-year-old Ryan from Belfast if they were holding extraterrestrials?" "You're right, Mark, that ended the briefing," replied McCurry.

That evening, Clinton spent twenty minutes separately with each of Northern Ireland's political leaders, including Adams. At a reception at Queen's University, Ian Paisley faced him in pin-stripe suit, his hands clasped on his lap, and afterwards handed Clinton a large blue brochure on his policies. He complained to reporters, "He wasn't well-briefed on what is really happening." The President gave David Trimble a ride in his limousine for his twenty minutes in the Europa, the most bombed hotel in western Europe, where the White House had taken several floors and where Clinton stayed the night, despite the British objections. It was a recognition that

Trimble led the largest party and a gesture to balance the extra time spent with John Hume.

One of the reasons the visit succeeded, Tony Lake told me afterwards, was "the exquisite choreography that made the third act of any Mozart opera seem easy, and that was to make sure that all of the parties got equal or deserving treatment in the time they got with the President."

At 1:30 a.m. in the White House press room in the Europa, Mike McCurry came in waving a special edition of the *Belfast Telegraph* with its splash headline, paraphrasing the President at the City Hall, "This Day Was the Most Remarkable Day of Our Lives." He punched the air.

The crowds in Dublin the next day matched those in Belfast and Derry. Traffic halted in the city center for Clinton's appearance on a platform erected outside the Bank of Ireland building at College Green. Jean Kennedy Smith literally rubbed her hands with glee. From the American embassy, Clinton telephoned Ted Kennedy in Washington and told him, "Now I know how President Kennedy felt." The boy from Arkansas who shook John F. Kennedy's hand at the White House in 1963 was reliving his hero's role. His gestures, his pose, his high-flown rhetoric, were reminiscent of JFK, as was his declaration, "I am now a Freeman of Dublin" echoing Kennedy's "Ich bin ein Berliner" thirty-two years previously.

"My God, what pictures," rhapsodized Mandy Grunwald, media director of Clinton's 1992 election campaign. "You can't buy this stuff. You can't invent it. It's the real thing. Ireland. Peace. Unfortunately, these people don't live in America. Maybe their relatives do."

Clinton had not attracted such enthusiastic crowds since the heady days after the Democratic Party convention in New York in 1992, when he went on a cross-country bus tour and received such adulation that *The Washington Post* called him "Heart-throb of the Heartland." Now he had become the catalyst of the national mood for peace in Ireland. The Irish Americans whose advice he took on Northern Ireland were euphoric. Chris Dodd, not normally given to hyperbole, said, "I'm just glad to be alive to see this day." As chairman of the Democratic Party, he was already planning the promotional video clips for the next presidential election. "The sight of those crowds, many of them young people who had not gone through a year of their lives without a threat of violence, really rocked him," the Connecticut Senator said of Clinton. "This is hard to underestimate in terms of confidence building, of telling him he's on the right track."

"We're in Day Two of the 1996 campaign," said a member of the administration peering across the crowd from the press platform. "We have to rent these people for the convention." A Clinton aide said, "The Catholic vote could decide the election next year and I somehow think we're going to do OK with the Irish-American Catholics." In the press room in Dublin Castle, Mike McCurry predicted that it would make people feel better about their President, because he had an effective foreign policy. Even the world-weary White House correspondents were impressed. Helen Thomas of UPI, who covered the White House since the Kennedy administration, said no President had two such good days at home or abroad.

The only controversy on this leg of the trip was whether Clinton drank Guinness or Murphy's stout in Cassidy's pub in Camden Street, which he visited in deference to his mother's name. Both breweries claimed that the President sipped their product.

The President portrayed himself as a peacemaker in post-Cold War Europe. The administration had triumphed at Dayton, Ohio, only weeks before, when American negotiators had cajoled the presidents of Bosnia, Serbia and Croatia to sign a peace accord. In his two speeches in Dublin, Clinton used the word "peace" a total of thirty-five times. "The people want peace and they will have it," he declared. It was a seductive logic. "There's no going back now," I told Colonel Jim Fetig of the National Security Council, as we drank a pint in a crowded Temple Bar pub that evening. We all really believed it.

That night, every member of the official White House party, plus the accompanying Congress members and Friends of Bill, were guests at a dinner hosted by Taoiseach John Bruton in Dublin Castle. This time some on the Irish side felt slighted; some junior government ministers were "bumped" to make room for all the Americans. Jean Kennedy Smith accompanied the President in his limousine to the airport early the next morning. The ten-minute drive was her only private time with him. She had several important things to say. But to her chagrin, Chris Dodd climbed into the limousine beside Clinton and for most of the journey the two men talked enthusiastically about golf.

Reflecting on the visit afterwards, Tony Lake said that the President's visit had "fundamentally altered the equation" in Northern Ireland and given the peace process momentum by putting the burden of proof on those who did not want to compromise.

"Before, political leaders probably felt that they had to make the case to their own constituencies for why they had to compromise," he told me. "Now I think the burden of proof is on those who don't want to compromise for the sake of keeping the peace, and that really is a fundamental difference—and that fundamental change came at the moments when the crowds gathered in Belfast and Derry." In Northern Ireland, the two governments and the politicians now had a political interest in overcoming their differences because of the popular pressure for peace from Protestants and Catholics, he said.

He also believed the television pictures from the visit would combat isolationist tendencies back home. People could see that the United States was the one country in the world that could get things done and that people all round the world wanted the Americans involved. There was a struggle for the soul of American foreign policy, he said. The American people had to be convinced of the benefits of engagement and that it touched a lot of people's lives and that they loved it. This would help encourage Americans "to support not just our efforts in Northern Ireland but our efforts in Bosnia and the Middle East."

In Germany, Clinton told American soldiers waiting to be deployed in Bosnia, "The power of the United States goes far beyond military might. What you saw in Ireland, for example, had not a whit to do with military might, it was all about values."

It was the high point of Bill Clinton's odyssey into Irish politics, and of his role as world peacemaker. Tony Lake popped open his bottle of best American champagne when he returned to the United States.

Postscript

"I don't know if in my life I'll ever have a couple of days like that again," Bill Clinton said, after he returned from Northern Ireland. The President decorated his private quarters in the White House with knick-knacks and posters from Ireland. He displayed in his office a framed copy of the words of Seamus Heaney, in the poet's own handwriting, about "the moment when hope and history rhyme." He hung on the wall a framed *Irish Times* article about his Irish connections, headlined, "Bill O'Clinton." He received the Belfast children, Catherine Hamill and David Sterrit, and their families in the Oval Office. Clinton reveled in the boost to his prestige as an international mediator. Mary McGrory wrote in her *Washington Post* column: "If President Clinton had listened to the likes of me, he would never have had his Irish triumph. I was one of those who thought he was mad to let in Gerry Adams, the IRA propagandist. But he paid no attention to us, Adams was the key, and last week Clinton brought genuine joy to Belfast, one of the planet's most cheerless sites." The President even agreed to travel to New York in March 1996 to accept personally the title of "Irish-American of the Year" from O'Dowd's *Irish America* magazine. Senator Edward Kennedy and Jean Kennedy Smith attended the function in the Plaza Hotel, at which Clinton joked that Nancy Soderberg "wanted to put an 'O' and an apostrophe in front of her last name."

Other players in the drama of the previous two years received recognition of a different kind. Former House Speaker Tom Foley, still expressing no regrets for opposing the first Adams visa, was made a Knight Commander of the Order of the British Empire for his services to Britain, receiving his honorary award at a ceremony in the British embassy, where the Irish-American legislator was afterwards greeted affectionately as "Sir Thomas" by the attendant when he arrived for dinner, though only British Commonwealth citizens could use the title. The dissenting diplomats in the US embassy in Dublin, John Treacy and Jim Callahan, were reassigned, and received $2,500 each in May 1996 for their "integrity" and "courage," in the annual awards for dissent given by their trade union, the American Foreign Service Association. Bill Flynn was made grand marshall of the 1996 Saint Patrick's Day parade in New York, the highest honor available to any Irish-American, and dedicated the parade to peace.

But peace proved elusive. The euphoria generated by that magic day in Belfast and Derry lasted only ten weeks. It was shattered at 1 p.m. US Eastern Standard Time on 9 February, 6 o'clock in the evening in Dublin, when the IRA announced "with great reluctance" the end of its ceasefire. An hour later, a massive bomb exploded at Canary Wharf in London, killing two people. Republican activists had become restless over the failure of the British government to set a date for multi-party talks, despite a year and a half of peace. The ceasefire was brought to an end, the IRA said, because the British Prime Minister did not rise to the "historic challenge" to "create a just and lasting settlement," and along with the unionists "squandered this unprecedented opportunity to resolve the conflict."

The President was told the bad news by Tony Lake while relaxing in his family quarters. The National Security Adviser and Nancy Soderberg had heard of the IRA statement in the course of a conference call to London in which they had been discussing the stalemate in the peace process with British officials. Almost immediately afterwards, Soderberg received a telephone call from Gerry Adams in Belfast. He said that he was trying to establish what was going on, and reassured them he was still committed to the peace process. He called again, just before the explosion, to say he was hearing very disturbing news.

Later, Nancy Soderberg held another conference call, this time with White House correspondents who had been on the trip. She had felt sick about the bombing, she told us. "This is truly horrible."

"The terrorists who perpetrated the attack cannot be allowed to derail the efforts to bring peace to Northern Ireland," said Clinton, as he saw the enormous investment of time and effort by his administration suddenly put at grave risk.

The Irish-Americans who believed that they had brought about the conditions for a negotiated settlement were stunned at the return to violence. They had relished their role as peacemakers. They had held their heads high for the first time in a generation. Often criticized as "sneaking regarders" of the IRA and rarely able to mount an effective lobby like the Jewish community did in Washington, the Irish-Americans had come to be seen as peacemakers and had established their highest ever contacts with an American president.

Senator Kennedy, having given his benediction to Adams when he came to the United States after the ceasefire, was particularly angry at the turn of events. He announced that he would not meet the Sinn Féin leader again until the ceasefire was restored. Senator Chris Dodd, who had gone far out on a limb for Adams over visas and fundraising, and who had anticipated using video clips of Irish crowds cheering Clinton the peacemaker to promote the President's re-election prospects, was equally upset.

The feeling that they had been betrayed by the IRA was felt strongly by the amateur Irish-American peacemakers. O'Dowd wrote in the *Irish Voice* that the message from Irish America had to be loud and clear. "There is immense support for the peace process and violence can play no part," he said. Irish-Americans found themselves on the defensive again. Having dug deep into their pockets to finance Sinn Féin in the United States, the most generous of the benefactors of Gerry Adams could now be accused of a naivety about the nature of the violent people they were dealing with.

The sense of betrayal was sharpened by the conviction of many Irish-Americans that they had helped create for the republican movement the most propitious circumstances possible for the IRA to cease its campaign and allow Sinn Féin, along with the SDLP and the Irish government, to take its chances at the negotiating table.

Fundamental changes had occurred in the previous two years. Sinn Féin leaders had gained access to the United States and Adams was welcomed to the White House, as O'Dowd had promised in his secret document before the ceasefire. President Clinton had come to Belfast and shaken Adams by the hand on the Falls Road. Senator George Mitchell's commission, set up at the dramatic late-evening summit before President Clinton arrived, removed the "Washington Three" precondition for multi-party talks to get under way. A date for the talks—10 June—was set not long after the Canary Wharf bombing. In elections for negotiating teams, Sinn Féin got 15.7 percent support, its biggest share of the popular vote ever. Mitchell and his Canadian and Finnish colleagues, John de Chastelain and Harri Holkeri, came to Belfast to preside over the talks, representing the internationalization of the effort and putting an influential American politician at the heart of the peace process in Northern Ireland. President Clinton went so far as to promise at a press conference in March that the United States would guarantee the integrity of any settlement.

With supreme irony, when David Trimble and Sir John Kerr became the first unionist leader and the first British ambassador to attend the now-annual Saint Patrick's Day party in the White House, on 15 March 1996, Gerry Adams was excluded, because of the IRA's return to violence.

All of the Americans, from the President down, now had to face the same question as that posed by Senator Daniel Patrick Moynihan to Senator Kennedy at the time of the Heathrow bombings—have we been had?

Despite his continued refusal to condemn the use of force, the stature of Gerry Adams as a peacemaker, assiduously built up in the United States from the time of his first US visa, survived in Washington. Accustomed to setbacks in other peace processes throughout the world, White House officials brought a global perspective to the first tentative steps to end centuries of conflict. Lake and Soderberg did not sever their links with any of the parties as the situation deteriorated. They came indeed to trust Adams as an ex-revolutionary now dedicated to leading his movement away from armed struggle. They did not believe they had been duped, though during the summer madness of 1996 they were forced to the conclusion that they had underestimated the depths of the sectarian bitterness in Northern Ireland.

One incident illustrated how trust survived the most testing moments. On 28 June, Gerry Adams and Tony Lake spoke on the telephone. Just an hour later, three IRA mortars were launched from the back of a flat-bed truck at the British Army barracks in Osnabrück, Germany, breaking a little-known four-year-old IRA ceasefire in Germany which had been negotiated by a priest-intermediary with the German authorities. Next day, the Sinn Féin leader felt confident enough to ring Lake to assure him, once again, that he had no prior knowledge of the attack and that he was as ever devoted to bringing about peace. The National Security Adviser took it in his stride. White House officials accepted what they were told in private, that Adams had 85 percent of republicans behind him but that he needed the movement fully united to bring it voluntarily to the point where it would give up a tradition of armed struggle dating back to Fenian times while the national question remained unresolved.

But the bloody events of July in Northern Ireland brought near-despair to the White House. The President received a memo from Nancy Soderberg advising him of a serious situation developing in Portadown, and turned on CNN news in his residential quarters to watch the Orange Order stand-off in the County Armagh town. To his deep dismay, rioting erupted in Belfast and Derry, where he had—we all had—interpreted the acclaim of the crowds which turned out to greet him less than eight months earlier as an expression of an overwhelming desire for peace.

All the careful diplomacy appeared to lie in ruins as passions boiled over, first on the loyalist side over the refusal by the RUC to let Orangemen walk down the Garvaghy Road in Portadown, then on the nationalist side when the policy was reversed and peaceful Catholic demonstrators were batoned off the road to let the triumphalist bands through. Clinton was able to see hijacked cars blazing on the very spot in Belfast where he had climbed out of his limousine to greet the Sinn Féin leader.

As Northern Ireland succumbed to an orgy of violence, the ground-breaking work that US Commerce Secretary Ron Brown and his top official Charles "Chuck" Meissner had done to attract investment to Northern Ireland was put at risk. They were not around to see it, having both been killed in an air crash at the end of April as they tried to promote investment opportunities in the Balkans. Business and tourism had revived in Northern Ireland, partly due to President Clinton's investment conference in May 1995 which Brown and Meissner organized. In July 1996, the sight of buildings and vehicles burning as mobs roamed the streets of Northern Ireland returned to the world's television screens. It was a devastating blow for Clinton's efforts to encourage peace with a major economic dividend in the form of new investment from the United States and other parts of the world. It clearly would be a very long time before the atmosphere of hope and wonderment at the prospect of a more peaceful and prosperous future which marked the Washington investment conference could ever be recreated.

An incident in mid-July brought home the extent of the damage for Northern Ireland. A team from the Japanese firm of Hitachi arrived in Dublin en route to Belfast to sign a contract which could have brought hundreds of new jobs. They could not get to the northern capital because of the disturbances. The Industrial Development Authority in the Republic took them in hand instead and showed them the investment opportunities south of the border.

Administration officials were privately scathing about the role of the unionists in the descent into anarchy. "I think these guys look ridiculous. Why don't they get over it and grow up?" said one adviser to Clinton, referring to the Orangemen mustered by David Trimble who marched down Garvaghy Road. "They just look silly," another Washington insider snapped, while watching television pictures from Portadown, "These people need adult supervision." But Nancy Soderberg would not be shaken from her dogged optimism. "We're very disturbed and disheartened by what is happening and it's depressing to see the anger of twenty-five years ago back on the streets," she told me after the first week of mayhem in Northern Ireland, "but we are not giving up. Our role is to try and push things forward. We shall continue to do so." The impact of the President's visit, she said, was to encourage those who sought peace, and to "appeal to the better angels in human nature."

During the 1996 presidential campaign, Clinton did not have to appeal to the better nature of Irish-Americans for votes. He had delivered on his "Irish promises" and gone much further in getting the United States involved in the ancient Irish conflict than anyone could have imagined in that crowded room in the New York Sheraton in April 1992 when he first pledged a visa for Gerry Adams and a special envoy. Nor did the Republicans make Clinton's daring diplomacy on Ireland a serious campaign issue, though on 14 August, James Baker described the President's foreign policy, in a speech at the Republican National Convention in San Diego, as "Gullible's Travels," adding "We have also seen a representative of the IRA hosted in the White House just prior to its resumption of terrorist bombings in London." The result, said the former Secretary of State, "has been the worst relationship with our closest ally, Britain, since the Boston tea party." Republican candidate Bob Dole echoed these sentiments on the campaign trail, criticizing Clinton during a speech in Johnson City, Tennessee, on 3 October as someone "who invited a terrorist to the White House." But that was as far as he went. Dole's heart wasn't in it. Many Republicans, himself included, had warmly welcomed Gerry Adams to Washington a year earlier. Indeed, during a campaign rally in the New Hampshire primary election in January, Dole had told me he fully supported Clinton on Northern Ireland. George Mitchell, who took a break from chairing the talks in Northern Ireland to return to the United States and play devil's advocate for the President as he prepared for election debates with Bob Dole, pointed out to Irish journalists that Northern Ireland was "not a major factor in the American presidential campaign." He said he believed many people in the US and in Britain and Ireland "have a mistaken view in that they think somehow this [White House involvement] is all oriented towards the election. In fact it hardly ever comes up."

The American President who brought Gerry Adams to the White House had by now convinced the unionists that he was fair-minded. Just after Clinton's re-election, David Trimble commented that Clinton was less generous to the "Provos" than John Major, and conceded that one should "not assume that the White House is always automatically on the nationalist side." Unionist voters in Northern Ireland, however, remained deeply suspicious of American involvement. In a poll published in *The Irish Times* on 9 September, some 64 percent of Protestants said they believed American interest in the affairs of Northern Ireland was likely to hinder rather than help attempts to secure a settlement. By contrast, 75 percent of Catholics thought American involvement would help bring about a settlement.

In Northern Ireland an uneasy situation of "no-war no-peace" followed the events at Drumcree. The IRA ceasefire was not renewed, but neither in the months up to the American presidential election was a full-scale IRA campaign, though there were several discoveries of large bombs primed and ready for use in border areas, and some isolated acts of violence. The most deadly came on 7 October when two IRA car bombs were detonated inside British Army headquarters in Lisburn, County Antrim, killing an English soldier—the first since August 1994—apparently in retaliation for the shooting by British police of an unarmed IRA man in a raid on a house in London shortly before. Three weeks later the IRA and leading supporters held an informal review of strategy at a meeting in an Irish town which coincided with the Notre Dame–US Navy football game in Dublin on 3 November. Some Irish republican activists from the United States joined the thousands of Americans visiting Dublin for the game and weighed in with their opinions.

The covert contacts and veiled conduct of public affairs of this period did little to inspire confidence in ordinary people who longed for peace. As Christmas 1996 approached, the threat of a new period of violence hung over Northern Ireland again, and when children's entertainer, Zoe Ball, switched on the Christmas lights outside Belfast City Hall, the euphoria of a year earlier when Clinton had performed the same task before a cheering multitude had become a distant memory.

The Irish-American "emissaries of Gulliver" responded in different ways to the impasse in Northern Ireland and the IRA's refusal to renew its ceasefire before John Major gave commitments on the genuineness of the talks process. Bill Flynn went to Ireland in mid-October, wearing his hat as Chairman of the National Committee on American Foreign Policy, and told journalists that in the US there was "massive disaffection with tactics being used by the republican movement since the end of the ceasefire" and "not just a lack of support but real disgust" at the IRA actions.

O'Dowd remained in touch with the White House and Senator Kennedy's office and the Sinn Féin leadership, and continued to trade information back and forth. Soderberg and Lake occasionally asked him for his assessment of the situation in the Irish republican movement. But his unique role as intermediary more or less ended when direct contact was established between the White House and all the parties. The "Connolly House Group" otherwise retained its role as an informal bridge between Ireland and Irish America. Bruce Morrison, Niall O'Dowd, Chuck Feeney and Joe Jamison visited both parts of Ireland in September to talk to all the parties. Feeney, who contributed so much of his personal resources to the effort, refused to be disheartened. As a friend put it, "Chuck's there until the last dog dies and there's no hope of renewed peace."

The end of a chapter in the White House involvement in Northern Ireland came on 5 December, when Clinton moved Tony Lake from his post as National Security Adviser to head the CIA, replacing him with his deputy, Sandy Berger. Though he had been privy to the process from the time of the first visa war, Berger now faced a daunting task in building a similar relationship with the two governments and all the parties as Lake had enjoyed. Right to the end of his time as National Security Adviser, Lake was working the phones to Belfast, London and Dublin, talking two or three times to Adams in a particular tense 48 hours in November. When Lake left, a vast institutional memory of what had gone before went with him. His departure meant that the role of his close colleague, Nancy Soderberg, on the Irish issue would also never be the same again.

But Irish-Americans who attended a meeting with the Democratic Party National Committee after Clinton's re-election were struck by the fact that Vice President Al Gore—an almost-certain candidate for the Democratic nomination in four years—sent his political director, who told them, "We've got to talk about the year 2000." Clearly, the issue was not going to go away.

Some critics maintained that the peace process was in fact a power play in which the Irish-Americans and some Irish politicians and officials succeeded in duping a President into putting misplaced trust in Irish republicans. But if this was so it had the effect of diminishing support for republican violence among Irish-Americans, a point frequently overlooked in Britain. From the time of the granting of the first Adams visa to the bomb at Canary Wharf, tolerance for the activities of those engaged in the armed struggle ebbed steadily, at least until nationalist outrage over Drumcree spilled across the Atlantic.

Historians may look back at the 1994 IRA and loyalist ceasefires, in which the American played such a significant role, and see only a lost opportunity. During the US election campaign and in the transition period afterwards, as many of the key administration figures involved brushed up their CVs for new posts, the Americans "took their eye off the ball," as O'Dowd put it. But at the start of Clinton's second term in office, the official line from the White House was that the commitment was worthwhile and would continue. For the peace process to succeed there had to be a "genuine cessation of violence," said Clinton in his first press conference after his re-election, adding that he would do whatever he could to be of assistance, and "I very much hope that in the next four years we can make some contribution to the ultimate resolution of the problem."

Though Washington's leverage with London diminished after Clinton's visit to Northern Ireland, the US administration remained influential as an honest broker and as the arbiter of Sinn Féin's right to enter the US and raise funds. They also retained a quality lacking in so many quarters across the Atlantic—optimism—at least officially. Even as the inter-party talks in Northern Ireland bogged down without Sinn Féin, George Mitchell commented on 31 October, "I believe it is worth continuing our efforts because I believe there will be a positive result. The overwhelming majority of people in Northern Ireland want a peaceful resolution. They do not want to go back to the bitterness of the past. But the decisions will be made by the participants themselves, not by the Americans, not by the President, not by me. We can help, we can support, we can encourage. That's what we are trying to do.'

John Hume told his party conference in Cookstown, Northern Ireland, on 11 November, that "the 18-months ceasefire transformed the mood of the people of Ireland, North and South, strengthened the will for peace, and created massive international goodwill, particularly in Europe and the United States, which can be translated into real economic benefits for all sections of our people."

Nancy Soderberg insisted that the American effort had not been wasted. "Hundreds of people are alive today because of our efforts," she told me.

If that is indeed the case, it was due to a unique set of circumstances in the Irish peace process coinciding with a once-in-a-century placement of the right people at the right time in the United States: President Clinton in the White House; Nancy Soderberg in the National Security Council; Senators Kennedy and Dodd in Congress; Trina Vargo in Senator Kennedy's office; Niall O'Dowd and his "Connolly House Group" in New York; Jean Kennedy Smith and many others.

"It's all still to play for," O'Dowd said after the presidential election. "Clinton is in office for four more years and there will be new elections in Britain and Ireland which will alter the landscape. It's a matter of trying to hold things together in the meantime. Once you start down the road of peace, however, it's hard to get off it."

His words were echoed by Frank Durkan, a New York attorney and former Noraid lawyer, who succeeded Bruce Morrison as Chairman of Americans for a New Irish Agenda. "We're into politics now," he said. "We believe that nobody else should have to die for Ireland. It may take ten years, but look what we've done so far."

Added O'Dowd, "We've no other option but to go on with politics, to keep trying."

Bibliography

Congressional Quarterly, *Politics in America 1992*, Congressional Quarterly Press, 1992

Cronin, Sean, *Washington's Irish Policy 1916–1986*, Dublin, Anvil Books, 1987

Duignan, Sean, *One Spin on the Merry-Go-Round*, Dublin, Blackwater Press, 1996

Goldman, Peter, Thomas De Frane, Mark Miller, Andrew Mure and Tom Mathews, *Quest for the Presidency 1992*, Texas, A & M University Press, 1994

Holland, Jack, *The American Connection*, Dublin, Poolbeg, 1989

Kelly, Virginia, *Leading with My Heart*, New York, Simon & Schuster, 1994

Leamer, Laurence, *The Kennedy Women*, Villard Books, 1994

Mallie, Eamonn and David McKittrick, *The Fight for Peace*, London, Heinemann, 1996

Maraniss, David, *First in His Class*, New York, Simon & Schuster, 1995

Wilson, Andrew, *Irish America and the Ulster Conflict*, Belfast, Blackstaff, 1995

Belfast Telegraph
Boston Globe
Boston Herald
Daily Express
Daily Telegraph
Guardian
Independent
Irish America
Irish Echo
The Irish Times
Irish Voice
Modern Maturity
New York Daily News
The New York Times
Sun
Sunday Times
Vanity Fair
The Washington Post

Index